STAGE OF THEATER BUILT BY RICHELIEU IN PARIS (1639) AND OCCUPIED BY MOLIÈRE (1661–1673)

(Page 60)

A STUDY OF THE DRAMA

BY

BRANDER MATTHEWS

PROFESSOR OF DRAMATIC LITERATURE IN COLUMBIA
UNIVERSITY, MEMBER OF THE AMERICAN
ACADEMY OF ARTS AND LETTERS

BOSTON NEW YORK AND CHICAGO
HOUGHTON MIFFLIN COMPANY
The Riverside Press Cambridge

PN
1661
M3

THIS ANALYSIS OF AN ART
IN WHICH HIS COUNTRYMEN HAVE LONG
EXCELLED IS GRATEFULLY INSCRIBED TO
JULES JUSSERAND
AMBASSADOR OF THE FRENCH REPUBLIC
AND HISTORIAN OF ENGLISH LITERATURE

PREFATORY NOTE

THIS book is a study of the technic of the drama. It is intended, not for those who want to write plays, but for those who wish to learn how plays are written now, and how they have been written in the past. It is the result of a belief that the fundamental principles of the drama are the same throughout the ages, and that they can be discovered as well in the plays of Sophocles as in the plays of Shakspere, as well in the plays of Molière as in the plays of Ibsen. And therefore the author has not confined his attention to the English drama alone; he has preferred to consider the whole history of the theater, ancient and medieval and modern, in the belief that this is the only method which will result in a real understanding of the dramatic practices of any particular period and of any particular people. He has held fast also to the conviction that all the masterpieces of the dramatic art were originally written to be performed by actors, in a theater, and before an audience of the dramatist's own contemporaries; and he has therefore kept in mind always the theatrical circumstances which conditioned the work of the dramatist. In other words, this study is devoted mainly to an examination of the structural framework which the great dramatists of various epochs have given to their plays; and it discusses only incidentally the psychology, the philosophy, and the poetry which we now admire in these pieces. Although the author had no intention of neglecting the content of the masterpieces of the drama, he has centered his attention rather on the form wherein this content is presented, since it is only by so doing that he can set before the student certain of the secrets of the art of the stage.

In the preparation of this volume, in which he has endeavored to consider the differing aspects of the playwright's craft, the author has availed himself freely of the various papers which he has published during the past few years in the *North American Review* and the *Forum*, the *Atlantic* and the *Century*, *Scribner's* and *Putnam's;* but, of course, this material has been unhesitatingly rehandled to adjust it to the ampler scheme of this more comprehensive treatment of the subject.

The author takes pleasure in recording here his indebtedness to the friends who have kindly lent him their aid as this book was passing through the press, — Professors Ashley H. Thorndike and William W. Lawrence of Columbia University, and Professor Charles Sears Baldwin of Yale University.

B. M.

COLUMBIA UNIVERSITY
IN THE CITY OF NEW YORK
February 21, 1910.

CONTENTS

I. THE STUDY OF THE DRAMA 1

II. THE INFLUENCE OF THE ACTOR . . . 24

III. THE INFLUENCE OF THE THEATER . . 44

IV. THE INFLUENCE OF THE AUDIENCE . . 68

V. THE LAW OF THE DRAMA 92

VI. A CHAPTER OF DEFINITIONS . . . 109

VII. TRADITIONS AND CONVENTIONS . . . 132

VIII. DRAMATIC CHARACTERIZATION . . . 152

IX. THE LOGIC OF CONSTRUCTION . . . 175

X. THE ANALYSIS OF A PLAY 211

XI. THE ELIZABETHAN DRAMATISTS . . . 232

XII. THE POETIC DRAMA AND THE DRAMATIC
POEM 249

XIII. THE THREE UNITIES 272

APPENDIX

A: SUGGESTIONS FOR STUDY 299

B: BIBLIOGRAPHICAL SUGGESTIONS . . . 302

INDEX 309

ILLUSTRATIONS

Stage of Theater built by Richelieu in Paris (1639) and
occupied by Molière (1661–1673) . . . . *Frontispiece*

[1] Plan of the Theater of Dionysus at Athens 48

Plan of the Roman Theater at Orange 50

Plan of the Fortune Theater, London 60

Plan of the Richelieu-Molière Theater, Paris . . . 60

Plan of the Drury Lane Theater, London 60

Plan of the Empire Theater, New York 60

Remains of the Theater of Dionysus at Athens . . . 74

Restoration of the Stage of the Roman Theater at
Orange 140
    [After a drawing by Paul Steck, from the model in the Library of the Opéra, Paris.]

Stage-sets of the Italian Comedy-of-Masks in Seventeenth
Century, as used by Molière in many of his Plays . 172

[1] [The plans were drawn by Albert D. Millar, Esq., on exactly the same scale, thus indicating the striking difference in size.]

Interior of Drury Lane Theater, London (1808) . . . 192

[From an aquatint by Thomas Rowlandson. This theater was substantially identical with the earlier house on the same site, for which Sheridan wrote the "School for Scandal" (1777).]

Interior of the Fortune Theater, London (1599) . . 238

[From the restoration by Walter H. Godfrey, Esq., after the builder's contract. Reproduced (by permission) from an article by William Archer, Esq., in the *Quarterly Review*.]

Restoration of the Stage on which a Passion-Play was acted at Valenciennes (1547) 292

[From the model belonging to Columbia University, New York.]

Plan of the Passion-Play Stage at Valenciennes . . . 292

A STUDY OF THE DRAMA

CHAPTER I

THE STUDY OF THE DRAMA

A history of the stage is no trivial thing to those who wish to study human nature in all shapes and positions. It is of all things the most instructive, to see not only the reflection of manners and characters at several periods, but the modes of making their reflection, and the manner of adapting it at those periods to the taste and disposition of mankind. The stage indeed may be considered as the republic of active literature, and its history as the history of that state. The great events of political history, when not combined with the same helps towards the study of the manners and characters of men, must be a study of an inferior nature. — EDMUND BURKE, *Letter to Edmund Malone.*

He therefore who is acquainted with the works which have pleased different ages and different countries, and has formed his opinion upon them, has more materials, and more means of knowing what is analogous to the mind of man, than he who is conversant only with the works of his own age or country. What has pleased, and continues to please, is likely to please again; hence are derived the rules of art, and on this immediate foundation they must ever stand. — SIR JOSHUA REYNOLDS, *Discourses on Painting.*

I

WHEN we approach the study of the drama, we must begin by reminding ourselves that this art does not lie wholly within the limit of literature, a fact which makes investigation into its principles at once more interesting and more difficult. The novel, the short-story, the epic, the lyric, the essay, can all of them be weighed and measured by purely literary tests; the drama can-

not. And here it has a certain resemblance to history
on the one hand, and to oratory on the other. There are
not a few historians highly esteemed by their fellows
whose work, however scientific it may be, lacks art,
and is deficient in those twin qualities of literature
which we term structure and style. There are public
speakers, able to move multitudes by their impassioned appeals, whose perfervid addresses when put
into chill print seem empty and inflated. So there are
playwrights of the past as well as of the present, many
of whose pieces, although they may have pleased the
vast majority of playgoers when they were performed
in the theater, are now none the less quite unworthy
of serious criticism when the attempt is made to analyze them from the standpoint of literature alone. The
success achieved by these pieces on the stage itself is
proof that they possessed theatrical effectiveness, —
which is the first requisite of a good play. But even
though they had this indispensable quality, they were
not lifted up into literature by any mastery of structure,
by any charm of style, by any grace of poetry, by any
sincerity of treatment, or by any subtlety of psychology.
Pieces of this kind are abundant in every period when
the theater has been flourishing; but they are the mere
journalism of the stage. They are for their own day
only, not for all time.

We may even go further and point out that a pantomime proves to us that there is at least one kind of play
which can exist and achieve its purpose satisfactorily
without the use of words, and thus without the aid
of the most obvious element of literature. In a pantomime, we see a story told in action, by gestures only;
and a few years ago an adroit and inventive French

playwright composed a play without words, the "Prodigal Son," in which he showed that it was possible to make a pantomime very interesting to the spectators in the theater and to endow it with all the needed elements of the drama, especially pathos and humor. And the ingenious narratives in action devised of late for the moving-picture machines are equal evidence of the adequacy of pantomime to tell a dramatic story, either serious or comic, so clearly that every beholder can apprehend it at once.

We may note also that while the drama does not lie wholly within the limits of literature, it is at liberty to call to its aid others of the arts, not only the art of the actor, — with which the art of the playwright must ever be most intimately associated, — but even the arts of the musician, of the painter, and of the sculptor. It can force each of these into its service whenever it wishes, and it can borrow from them any device it may need. Not without good reason did Wagner assert that the music-drama was "the art-work of the future," since the theater is the one place where the arts may all unite, each contributing its share to the harmony of the whole.

Thus it is impossible to consider the drama profitably apart from the theater in which it was born and in which it reveals itself in its completest perfection. All the masterpieces of the dramatic art were planned and elaborated on purpose to be performed by actors, in a theater, and before an audience of the poet's contemporaries. The great dramas of the mighty masters, without a single exception, were intended to be played rather than to be read; they were prepared primarily for the stage, and only secondarily — if at all — for the study. Neither Shakspere nor Molière was eager to publish his immortal plays in his own lifetime, seemingly careless, each of them, in regard to any other judgment than that which had been passed in the theater itself. Lope de Vega and Calderon took the same attitude. They had contrived their plots in accordance with the conditions of the theaters of their own time, the only conditions with which they were familiar; they had fitted the chief parts to the best of their fellow-actors; and they may very well have distrusted any criticism not the result of the actual performance under the special conditions with which they themselves were content. Indeed, Molière, in the preface to his "Précieuses Ridicules," was emphatic in declaring his own willingness to abide by the test of the theater alone and to refrain from any appeal to the test of the library. Again in another preface, that to his "Amour Médecin," Molière asserted that everybody knows "comedies are written only to be acted."

II

When we take up the study of any art, we find that there are two ways of approach. We may trace the growth of the art, or we may inquire into its processes. In the one case we consider its history, and in the other we examine its practice. Either of these methods is certain to lead us into pleasant paths of inquiry.

If we determine to investigate the slow development of the drama through the ages, we shall find ourselves in time better fitted to answer questions which are often very puzzling to those who do not recognize the necessity of going back into the past if they wish to understand the present. Why did the Greeks put a chorus into their tragedies? In Shakspere's plays, why do the scenes change so frequently? These are queries which many a commentator has striven vainly to answer, — simply for lack of historical knowledge. Research into the origin of the Attic theater reveals to us that the Greeks did not put a chorus into their tragedies and that on the contrary they put a tragedy into their chorus, — since it was out of the chorus that their drama was evolved. Inquiry into the growth of the Elizabethan theater shows us that the scenes in Shakspere's plays do not change frequently, — or at least that the scenery does not, since in Shakspere's stage there was apparently no scenery to change.

On the other hand, we shall not err if we decide to devote ourselves not so much to the development of the drama as to its technic. The basis of a genuine appreciation of any art is an understanding of its principles. Any attempt to discuss architecture as separate from construction is certain to be sterile, for the beauty of architecture is often in the exquisite adaptation of the means to the end, — a beauty not to be appreciated by those who are indifferent toward the technic of the art of building. So also some acquaintance with the various methods of putting pigments on canvas is a condition precedent to any firm grasp of the principles of pictorial art. And the technic of the drama is less simple than either of these, since the architect builds in stone and steel, and the painter draws with colors, whereas the work of the dramatist must be devised for interpretation by the actor. The dramatic art is really twofold, since it is the result of a necessary union of the efforts of the playwright and of the player. Neither of them is able to accomplish his purpose without the aid of the other. To achieve a dramatic masterpiece, the dramaturgic skill of the author must utilize to the utmost the histrionic skill of the actor.

As we seize the importance of these lines of approach, the historical and the practical, we see that a sound knowledge of the drama is not possible unless we seek to attain both a perspective of its development and an insight into its technic. Just as the study of music is most stimulating when it includes an inquiry into the value of each of the several instruments, and also into their gradual combination into the most marvelous instrument of them all, the modern orchestra, so the study of the drama is most likely to be profitable when it leads us to consider the successive modifications in the shape and size of the theaters wherein plays were acted; the varying circumstances of performance to which the playwrights had to conform; the conventions of the art, some of them shifting from century to century or from country to country, and some of them immutable in the very nature of the drama. Especially stimulating is it for us to recognize the real unity of history, the continuity of the art of the drama, which enables us so often to explain the past by the present and the present by the past.

If we combine the study of technic with an inquiry into the history of the dramatic art, we shall find ourselves in a condition to make many suggestive comparisons. We shall be in a position to see, for instance, that the comedies of Menander were probably in their outward form very like the comedies of Molière, and that the former varied from the latter in content partly because of the difference between the two dramatists themselves, and partly because of the unlikeness of the social conditions in which they were each of them placed. We shall find pleasure in contrasting the comedy-of-manners as it was composed at the end of the eighteenth century in France by Beaumarchais and in England by Sheridan, arch-wits both of them and masters of inventive ingenuity.

We can also make the striking comparison between two dramatists of genius separated by a gulf of twenty centuries, Sophocles and Ibsen, discovering in the "Œdipus the King" of the one the same massive simplicity that strikes us in the "Ghosts" of the other, the Greek showing how fate is inevitable and the Scandinavian seeking to prove that heredity is inexorable. Sophocles, it is true, "saw life steadily and saw it whole," while Ibsen seems to some of us to have rather a morbid liking for the abnormal; but none the less is there a startling similarity in their constructive ability and in their surpassing technical mastery. We can instruct ourselves by tracing the potent influence exerted now and again by the drama of one nation upon that of another, inquiring how Spanish pieces affected Corneille in his tragedies, how Italian plays supplied an early model to Molière for his comedies, how French comedy was the exciting cause of English comedy under the Restoration, how the English drama served to stimulate Lessing in his reform of the German drama, how the social plays of Ibsen have powerfully modified the aims and ideals of latter-day dramatists in France and in Spain, in Germany and in England. And in preparing ourselves to make these international comparisons we can scarcely fail to gain a more intimate knowledge of the dramatic art.

III

But we need always to bear in mind that Sheridan and Beaumarchais, Shakspere and Molière, Sophocles and Ibsen, however much they may differ from one another, are alike in this at least, — that they all represent an advanced development of the drama as a department of literature and that they were preceded and made possible by countless unknown experimenters. The masterpieces of these accomplished craftsmen are the final achievements of a long effort sustained through the dim centuries. They are the culmination of an artistic evolution, the beginnings of which must be looked for far back in the history of mankind. They are the final expression in cultivated and self-conscious communities of the primary play-impulse of primitive man. The literary drama, the play in which the finer attributes of structure and style are added to essential theatrical effectiveness, is the direct outgrowth of a wholly unliterary drama, which emerges into view very early in the annals of civilization. At first, when man still lingers in the lower levels of savagery and barbarism, the dramatic instinct expresses itself boldly enough, but crudely and coarsely. It is only after long centuries of striving that a more shapely drama at last emerges in view, even if far back in man's progress upward we are able to discover that desire to personate and to get out of himself, which is the foundation of the art of the theater. Very early also can we perceive the allied pleasure of being a passive spectator of this active personation.

Until recently, it was the general belief that the drama arrived comparatively late in the history of any literature. This belief is voiced eloquently in Victor Hugo's preface to "Cromwell," in which he asserts that the chronological sequence is first of all the lyric, then the epic, and finally the drama. There is a sense in which this is true; that is to say, the literary drama, the play which is also poetic or philosophic, comes into being only after the lyric and the epic have given flexibility and elevation to the language and after they have also invented the stories which the literary dramatist can re-handle. But the researches of the anthropologists have made it indisputable that there is a dramatic element in the very earliest lyrics themselves, and that a rude drama is perhaps earlier even than these earliest lyrics.

Letourneau insists that the drama in its rudimentary form

"goes back to the very origin of literary esthetics, for choral and mimic dances constitute nearly all the literature of primitive peoples, and a rudiment of scenic art has been found, even in Tasmania, among an extremely inferior race. In reality, scenic poetry preceded all other kinds, and most frequently constituted their mold. By the simultaneous employment of mimicry, song, speech, and instrumental music, the opera-ballet of the early ages was the form of esthetics most fitted strongly to impress spectators and actors, and at the same time to satisfy a very lively psychical want, that of projecting mental images outward, of reproducing with all the relief of reality what exists in the brain only in the state of recollection or desire. The civilized theater is only the natural development of this opera-ballet, and it preserves an equal attraction and an equal power, even after losing the lyrical form, which dated from its origin."

And Hirn takes the same point of view.

"A literary drama, which fulfils all the claims of a work of art," so he declares, "is possible only on a highly advanced level of culture, and it has consequently by most authors on esthetics been considered as the latest of all art-forms. When dealing, however, with the productions of primitive tribes, we have to adopt a lower esthetic standard. Although we do not meet with any tragedies, nor even with any real comedies, at this stage of evolution, we can at least point to the fact that simple farces, pantomimes and pantomimic dances are to be found among tribes who have so far been unable to create any kind of epic, and whose lyrical poetry is restricted to a few rhythmical phrases with no intrinsic meaning. And if we use the word in its widest sense, so as to include every representation by action, drama can be spoken of as the very earliest of all the imitative arts. It was certainly in use long before the invention of writing, either by pictures or letters; perhaps it is even older than language itself. As an outward sign of thought, action is more immediate than words."

Grosse is quite as emphatic.

"The drama is regarded by most historians of literature and esthetics as the latest form of poetry; yet we can say, with a certain degree of right, that it is the earliest. The peculiar feature of the drama is the representation of an event simultaneously by speech and mimicry. In this sense nearly every primitive tale is a drama, for the teller is not simply relating history, but he enlivens his words with appropriate intonations and gestures. . . . Children and primitive peoples are unable to make any narration without accompanying it with the appropriate demeanor and play of gesture. Pure relation requires a command of language and of one's own body which is rarely found among civilized men and hardly ever among savages. Pure epic is therefore probably the latest among the three chief kinds of poetry."

Grosse further maintains that "common usage means by a drama, not the relation of an event enlivened by mimicry, but its direct mimic and verbal representation by several persons"; and he asserts that "we can prove the existence of the drama even in this narrow sense in the lowest stages of culture." He then points out that these primitive plays are partly mimetic, merely imitative representations of hunting or fighting, but that they are ever tending to rise to the depiction of "an action in constant development." He admits that "words play so subordinate a part in the dramatic performances of hunting peoples that they rather resemble our pantomimes than our dramas," — but a pantomime may be just as truly dramatic as a play in which there is spoken dialogue.

IV

In the quotations from Professor Grosse, there is one specially significant passage, — that in which he classes together "children and primitive peoples." If we wish to understand the feelings and the actions of primitive peoples, we can get great help from a study of the ways of children. It seems now to be generally admitted that in our infancy and childhood we live over again, more or less completely, the slow evolution of humanity from savagery to civilization. We find in children the same tendency to mimicry, the same desire to personate which we discover in primitive peoples. Professor William James, after noting that "a successful piece of mimicry gives to both bystanders and mimic a peculiar kind of esthetic pleasure," and that "the dramatic impulse, the tendency to pretend one is some one else, contains this pleasure of mimicry as one of its elements," then remarks that "in young children this instinct often knows no bounds." He cites one of his own children who, at the age of three, delighted in playing that he was "a hyena or a horse-car, or whatever the feigned object might be." A hyena or a horse-car! — that is to say, it did not matter to the child whether the object he impersonated was animate or inanimate. This childish attitude is excellently illustrated in the familiar anecdote of the three little boys who explained that they were "playing automobile." The eldest was the chauffeur, the next was the machine itself, — while Baby ran in the rear, representing the lingering odor of the gasoline.

A more elaborate illustration of this youthful fondness for assuming another personality can be found in the chapter of the "Adventures of Tom Sawyer," wherein we see Tom about to begin the distasteful task of whitewashing his aunt's fence. Just then his friend Ben Rogers hove in sight eating an apple and

" giving a long, melodious whoop, at intervals, followed by a deep-toned ding-dong-dong, ding-dong-dong, for he was personating a steamboat. As he drew near, he slackened speed, took the middle of the street, leaned far over to starboard and rounded to ponderously and with laborious pomp and circumstance — for he was personating the *Big Missouri*, and considered himself to be drawing nine feet of water. He was boat and captain and engine-bells combined, so he had to imagine himself standing on his own hurricane-deck giving the orders and executing them:

"'Stop her, sir! Ting-a-ling-ling!' The headway ran almost out and he drew up slowly toward the sidewalk.

"'Ship up to back! Ting-a-ling-ling!' His hands straightened and stiffened down to his sides.

"'Set her back on the stabboard! Ting-a-ling-ling! Chow! ch-chow-wow! Chow!' His right hand, meantime, describing stately circles, — for it was representing a forty-foot wheel.

"'Let her go back to the labboard! Ting-a-ling-ling! Chow-ch-chow-chow!' The left hand began to describe circles.

"'Stop the stabboard! Ting-a-ling-ling! Stop the labboard! Come ahead on the stabboard! Stop her! Let your outside

turn over slow! Ting-a-ling-ling! Chow-ow-ow! Get out
that head-line! *Lively* now! Come out with your spring-
line — what 're you about there! Take a turn round that
stump with the bight of it! Stand by that stage, now — let
her go! Done with the engines, sir! Ting-a-ling-ling! Sh't!
s'h't! sh't!' (trying the gage-cocks)."

A friendly correspondent in Arizona once sent me
an account of a play his two children had performed.
They were found in the ruins of an old house; and in
a sad voice the boy explained that they were "offering
up little Isaac." A broken toy was Isaac. A brick under a bush was the ram. They told how they had built
a fire under Isaac, admitting at once that the fire was
only make-believe. And when they were asked, "Who
was Abraham?" the little girl promptly answered,
"We was." The girl was four years old and the boy
was only three. It is easy to seize the likeness between
the scene thus acted by these children and the rudimentary dramas which are performed by savages.
Underlying both is the desire to personate, the impulse
to take part in an action, and the abundant willingness to make believe.

v

The real difference between the little play of these
children and the rudimentary drama of savages lies in
the fact that the children are acting as individuals,
whereas the savages are playing in large groups. In the
rudimentary drama of savages there is likely to be a
communal element. At certain seasons of the year,
especially at springtime and at harvest, at midsummer
and at midwinter, the whole community takes part in
the performance, — or if not the whole community, a

representative group which expresses the sentiment of all. In the primitive stages of poetry, so Professor Gummere tells us, there is seen

"a throng of people without skill to read or write, without ability to project themselves into the future, or to compare themselves with the past, or even to range their experience with the experience of other communities, gathered in festal mood, and by loud song, perfect rhythm and energetic dance, expressing their feelings over an event of quite local origin, present appeal and common interest. Here, in point of evolution, is the human basis of poetry, the foundation courses of the pyramid; in point of poetic process here is the social as opposed to the individual element."

Sometimes the individual element is evolved after a while out of the social element, or is superadded to it; and then we may have a rapid development of the drama. This is the way that the Greeks slowly achieved their glorious drama. Out of the humblest origins, it was elevated to a lofty pinnacle. As Sir Richard Jebb has told us, the Greek drama

" sprang from the species of lyric poem called the dithyramb . . . originally a convivial song definitely associated with the god Dionysus . . . a song to the wine-god had presumably a wild, impassioned character, and was accompanied with gesticulation. . . . When Arion formed his dithyrambic chorus of satyrs, he was assigning the song of Dionysus to specially appropriate performers . . . and he was also making the performance something more lively, more characteristic than an ordinary choral song. Thespis, in producing a dithyrambic chorus, came forward as a reciter of verses, addressing his chorus of satyrs and doubtless personating a satyr himself. . . . But even then the entertainment fell short of being dramatic. The reciter of verses who addressed the dithyrambic chorus could indeed relate action. But action could not yet be represented as taking place be-

fore the eyes of the spectators. . . . Instead of the single reciter, Æschylus introduced two persons, both, like the single
reciter, detached from the chorus. These two persons could
hold a dialogue and could represent action. By this change
Æschylus altered the whole character of the lyric tragedy,
and created a drama. The dialogue between the actors now
became the dominant feature of the entertainment; the part
of the lyric chorus, though still very important, had now
only a diminished importance."

Sophocles employed a third actor, and each of these
three performers could appear in several characters.
It was possible then to show a story in action and to
present before the spectators that conflict of human
wills which has ever been the mainspring of the drama.

These are the successive stages of the evolution of
the noble Greek drama out of a rude communal song.
And not unlike are the successive stages of the evolution of the drama of the several modern languages out
of very simple mimetic interpolations into the ritual
of the medieval church as prescribed for Christmas
and Easter. At Christmas, a single chorister was set
apart to announce the glad tidings, and a group of
choristers was assigned to represent the shepherds
who were guided by a star to the manger. At Easter,
three priests spoke the words set down for the three
Marys, at the tomb, and another appeared "in the
likeness of a gardener." In time, the Christmas cycle
of dialogues and hymns and narrative was combined
with the Easter cycle, and the passion-play came into
being. Its several episodes had each of them been devised to illustrate the service of a special day of the
church year; and they had each of them been first
performed in Latin in the church by ecclesiastics or
choristers. Then, after the mystery was full grown,

it was felt to be too great a burden; and it was thrust out of the church, confided to laymen and translated into the several vernaculars. The laymen who took it over meant to continue all the traditions of the performance within the church, yet sooner or later they were led to apply the same methods to secular stories. Thus it was that in each of the modern languages the drama had a common origin in a religious exercise, and that in each of them it developed in accord with racial characteristics, so that in time there came to be a wide differentiation between the plays performed in the several tongues, although they were all outflowerings from the same Latin stock.

As we study these evolutions of dramatic form, we see that what was at first more or less communal becomes more or less individual, and what was at first more or less spontaneous becomes more or less traditional. In time, custom crystallizes; and then out of the established custom there is a new departure, another step forward. There comes into existence an accepted way of telling a story in action, a formula satisfactory to actors and spectators alike; and this formula tends constantly to become more effective theatrically as the casual performers more and more take on the aspect of professionals, conscious that they are exercising an art. The plays they present may still be rough and crude; their art may be rather elementary as yet; but it is alive and it contains the possibility of progress. At this moment, the drama is still unliterary; there is little skill of structure, little polish of style, little insight into human nature. But the dramatic formula is slowly getting into shape, and making itself ready for the hand of the literary artist whenever he shall happen along.

As the earlier unliterary efforts have not been preserved, no one can now specify with any certainty the
exact moment when the Greek drama began to lift itself into literature. Only literature is permanent; and
the unliterary drama is never cherished and guarded.
A few of the plays of Æschylus have been handed down
to us, probably the best of them, since only the best
would be multiplied in many manuscripts; and we can
see that they are literature beyond all question. But
the dialogues of Thespis with his chorus have all per-
ished; and we shall never know whether or not they
really attained to literature. In the Middle Ages, it was
not till long after Latin had given place to the several
vernaculars that we begin to find gleams of literary
merit; and the most of the mysteries and moralities,
which have been abundantly preserved, are deadly dull,
whether they are in French or English, in Italian or
in German. The mystery had been succeeded in England by the chronicle-play, and this had long pleased
the public before any man of indisputable literary gift
undertook to compose it. And in France, it was not
until Corneille succeeded Hardy that the drama rose
to the lofty level of poetry.

Corneille did at first very much what Hardy had
done, but he did it better, being more richly endowed
with the native playmaking instinct. So Marlowe did
very much what his predecessors had done, using the
same rough framework, but putting into the mouths
of his characters the mighty lines of which he alone
was then capable. At any period of the development
of the drama, in the days of Corneille as in the days of
Marlowe, in our own time as well, the same framework,
the same external form, the same method of handling

the material, characterize both the literary play and
the unliterary play. They are always very much alike
in outward appearance; it is in the inner soul that
they differ. Kyd's "Spanish Tragedy" belongs to the
strange type of piece now known as the tragedy-of-
blood, and so does Shakspere's "Hamlet." Victor
Hugo's "Ruy Blas" is essentially a melodrama distinguishable only by its lyrical affluence from the contemporary pieces of Ducange and Pixérécourt, on which
it was modeled. To-day, the social dramas of Ibsen
and Hervieu, the comedies of Barrie and Shaw, are
composed in accord with the same formula which serves
for the hack playwrights who write uninspired pieces
to order. The difference between the play which is literature and the play which is not literature, which is in
fact only a form of journalism, sufficient unto the day
and no more, — this difference is not external but internal. It is to be felt far more easily than it is to be
defined. And the play which we gladly hail as literature
succeeds in the theater, pleases its many audiences,
delights a succession of spectators, year after year,
and century after century, because of its possession
of qualities not in themselves literary, because it has
the intangible but essential something which makes
a story interesting to the multitude when it is set forth
in action on the stage.

The unliterary plays of any period are likely to be
neglected by the historian of dramatic literature because they are now more or less unreadable, although
in their own day they were preëminently actable. These
unliterary plays are likely also to be inaccessible, even
if they have been preserved, which is rarely the case.
Of the thousands of plays produced in Greece, we have

only a few selected masterpieces of Æschylus, Sophocles, and Euripides. Of the thousands of plays produced in England while Shakspere was yet alive, only
a few hundreds have come down to us to-day. In so
far as the writings of the less literary of the Elizabethan
playwrights have been transmitted to us, they are in-
valuable for the light they cast on the theatrical conditions of the time and for the insight they give us into
the circumstances of actual performance, the circumstances which governed Shakspere as much as they
governed Heywood; but in themselves these pieces
are not really important.

Charles Lamb ventured to call Heywood a "prose
Shakspere," but it is only now and again in a few passages of "A Woman Killed with Kindness," and occasionally in another play or two, that Heywood rises to
the level of literature. Heywood was the most adroit
and prolific playwright of his time; but for the most
part his work is journeyman and journalistic; it was
actable then, but it is well-nigh unreadable now. Yet
Heywood's plays were written for the same audiences
as Shakspere's, and they conform to the same theatrical conditions. And in the nineteenth century in France,
Scribe was the master of the theater, a wizard of dramaturgy, a technician of marvelous dexterity. But he
is a man of the theater only; he is not a man of letters, and very few of his countless pieces have any pre-
tension to literature. Yet when Dumas *fils* and Augier
followed in Scribe's footsteps and borrowed Scribe's
formula, enlarging it to contain their vision of life,
they were able to lift their plays into literature. They
were men of the theater who were also men of letters,
and their plays are readable as well as actable.

When we undertake to consider whether a play deserves to be considered as literature or not, we need to clear our minds of a current misconception as to the constituents of literary merit, so-called. True literary merit is not a matter of fine writing, of pretty phrases, of style only. The real literary merit of a play does not reside so much in its mere wording as in its solid structure, in the logic of the plot, in the sincerity of its character-drawing. Fine writing has never yet made a good play; and the good play is a good play independently of all its phrases, however glowing and gorgeous these may be. This Aristotle saw quite as clearly as Lessing and Sarcey; and he was emphatic in insisting on the primary importance of plot, of the story which is interesting in itself, and which is interestingly articulated. We may be sure that the great Greek critic would have approved of the shrewd remark of a modern Frenchman, to the effect that the skeleton of a good play is always a pantomime. That is to say, the story must be so strong and so clear that it can stand by itself, whether well or ill written, whether the audience can or cannot appreciate its added poetry or philosophy. We may see many things in "Hamlet," we may acclaim it as the absolute masterpiece of the poetic drama; but it would move the majority of the spectators if it should be acted before the inmates of a deaf-and-dumb asylum, unable to seize the beauties which delight us, but quite capable of being carried away by the sheer power of the splendidly theatric plot.

This is what has always been felt by the literary as well as by the unliterary playwrights. Scribe used to say that "when my subject is good, when my scenario is very clear, very complete, I might have the play written by my servant; he would be sustained by the situation; — and the play would succeed." From Scribe, who was only an ingenious mechanician of the drama, this may not surprise us; but his saying would not be greatly objected to by any true dramatist, poet, or prose-man, for it is only an overstatement of the truth. Menander, the master of Greek comedy, was once asked about his new play, so Plutarch tells us, and he answered: "It is composed and ready; I have only the verses to write." Racine's son reports an almost identical remark of his father's in answer to a similar inquiry. And there is no dispute possible as to the elevated position attained by Racine and by Menander when they are judged by purely literary standards.

In other words, the literary quality is something that may be added to a drama, but which is not essential to its value as a play in the theater itself. And while we cannot have a great play unless it is lifted into literature by skill of structure, by veracity of character, by felicity of dialogue, it does not attract the public by its possession of these qualities alone. Joseph Jefferson, speaking out of his long experience on the stage, declared that "you may have all the good literature you wish in a play, — if it does not interfere with the play's action." He added that "the absence of fine writing in a play will not injure it if the story and construction are right. Literary merit will enhance the chances of success if it be subservient to the action." And so declaring his opinion, Jefferson was only echoing what Aristotle had said two thousand years earlier.

This is a hard saying for the merely literary critic,

whether it comes from the mouth of the Greek philosopher or from that of the American comedian; and yet it needs to be taken to heart by all who seek to penetrate to a real knowledge of the drama. The merely literary critic is competent only to perceive the less important of the merely literary qualities of a drama. He can appreciate the external poetry with which the action of the play may be clothed; but this action itself is not easy for him to estimate at its true value. He studies the play in the library, where the quality of style is most obvious, and not in the theater, where story and structure are more important. The merely literary critic tends to neglect, and perhaps even to despise, the purely theatrical qualities which must always sustain a vital play; and he does not care to consider the contemporary unliterary pieces which would often help him to a better understanding of these purely theatrical qualities, revealed at once where the piece is acted on the stage.

There is one thing that every student of the drama should try to train himself to accomplish. In reading any play, ancient or modern, in English or in a foreign tongue, he should endeavor always to transport himself from the library into the theater and to visualize an actual performance. He should strive to translate the cold printed page of the book into the warm action of living performers on the stage. He should call up a mental image of the scene where the story is laid; and he should evoke moving pictures of the several characters, not merely with his eye reading the dialogue, but with his ear hearing it as actors would speak it. He should do his best to put himself in the place of the spectators for whose enjoyment the play was originally composed; and he should make what Jebb aptly termed an "effort of imaginative sympathy," that he may as far as possible realize the conditions of actual performance. Stevenson recorded that his friend, Fleeming Jenkin, had acquired this art of visualizing a drama from the printed page, and he asserted that this was "a knack, the fruit of much knowledge and some imagination, comparable to that of reading score." To do this is not easy; indeed, to achieve it completely is not possible; but the effort, however feeble it may be, is worth while. And it will be its own reward, for only by its aid can we teach ourselves and train ourselves to disentangle the essential theatrical effectiveness of the masterpieces of the great dramatic poets.

CHAPTER II

THE INFLUENCE OF THE ACTOR

For ill can Poetry express
    Full many a tone of thought sublime,
And Painting, mute and motionless,
    Steals but a glance of time.
But by the mighty actor brought
    Illusions perfect triumphs come, —
Verse ceases to be airy thought,
    And Sculpture to be dumb.

      THOMAS CAMPBELL, *To John Philip Kemble.*

I

IN the nineteenth century, there were British and American poets of high distinction who were attracted to the dramatic form, and who sought to express themselves in it, but without considering the conditions of the stage of their own time, which seemed to them a period of decadence. They disregarded the spectator in the theater itself and sought to interest solely the reader in the library. They liked to think of themselves as dramatists and to claim praise for dramatic achievement, but without facing the ordeal by fire before the footlights. Looking upon the drama as an easy form, they took no trouble to spy out its secrets or to master its technic. And perhaps deep down in their hearts, there was a vague contempt for the acted drama, because it had to appeal to the mere mob, to the vulgar throng. We can listen to their sentiments as these

are voiced by the Poet in the *Prologue on the Stage* of
Goethe's "Faust": —

> "Speak not to me of yonder motley masses,
>   Whom but to see puts out the fire of Song!
> Hide from my view the surging crowd that passes,
>   And in its whirlpool forces us along!
> No, lead me where some heavenly silence glasses
>   The purer joys that round the Poet throng."

This attitude may not be unbecoming in the lyric
poet, who has but to express his own emotions; but
it is impossible in a true dramatic poet, who feels that
what he has wrought is not complete until he has seen
it bodied forth by actors on the stage before the motley
masses and before the surging crowd. The true dramatic poet would never hesitate to adopt Molière's statement of his own practice: "I accept easily enough the
decisions of the multitude, and I hold it as difficult to
assail a work which the public approves as to defend
one which it condemns." But however much the lyric
poet may detach himself from the surging crowd and
despise the motley masses, even he must not forget
his readers absolutely; it is only at his peril that he
can neglect the duty of being readable. Taine declared
that Browning had been guilty of this fault in "The
Ring and the Book," wherein the poet "never thinks
of the reader, and lets his characters talk as though
no one were to read their speeches."

What may be only a minor fault in the lyric poet
becomes a gross blunder in the dramatic poet, who can
never claim the right of solitary self-expression, which
the lyrist may assert. The drama has for its basis an
appeal to the whole public, and not to any coterie of
dilettants. Since we write poems to be performed,

"our first duty ought to be to please the court and the people and to attract a great throng to their performances "; so said Corneille, declaring frankly the doctrine of every genuine dramatic poet. "We must, if we can, abide by the rules, so as not to displease the learned, and to receive universal applause; but, above all else, let us win the voice of the people." The great dramatists of every period when the drama was flourishing would have echoed this firm declaration of Corneille's. By their own splendid experience, they had learnt how greatly the artist may profit by a resolute struggle with limitations and with obstacles; and they could scarcely refrain from contempt for the timorous poets who have shrunk from this profitable effort. And as the result of a choice of the easier path, these craven bards have failed to reach the goal toward which they fondly believed themselves to be aiming. The closet-dramas are all unactable; most of them are unreadable; and many of them are unspeakable. Although important poets have condescended to the composition of plays not intended to be played, their importance is not due to their closet-dramas; and perhaps their fame would be almost as high if they had refrained from these poems in dialogue.

The dramatic poets — Sophocles, Shakspere, Molière — have always been willing to take thought of the players by whom their plays were to be presented, and of the playgoers whom they hoped to attract in motley masses. Consciously, to some extent, and unconsciously more often, they shaped the stories they were telling to the circumstances of the actual performance customary on the contemporary stage. Whether they knew it or not, their great tragedies and their great comedies, as we have them now, are what they are, partly because of the influence of the several actors for whom they devised their chief characters, partly because the theater to which they were accustomed was of a certain size and had certain peculiarities of structure, and partly because the spectators they wished to move had certain prejudices and certain preconceptions natural to their race and to their era. This is why it is useful to consider the influence which the actor, the theater, and the audience can severally exert upon the dramatist, — influences necessarily felt by every dramatic poet, great or small, in every period in the long evolution of the drama.

II

Of these three influences, the most immediate is that of the actors, with whom the playwright has ever to work in cordial sympathy, and without whose assistance his play cannot be represented as he has conceived it. The critic nowadays who looks upon the drama as lying wholly within the circle of literature, and who fails to perceive its vital connection with the actual theater, is often moved to make it a matter of reproach to certain contemporary playwrights that they are wont to write plays to fit a special actor or a special actress. In thus finding fault, the critic reveals not only his misunderstanding of the needful relation between the dramatist and the performers who are to personate his characters, but also an inability to appreciate the way in which the mind of the artist is often set in motion by accidents that may seem casual and trifling.

In every art, there is often a startling disproportion

between the exciting cause and the ultimate result.
We might almost liken the artist to the oyster which
is moved by a grain of sand to produce a pearl of great
price. More than one of the most triumphant artistic
feats of the Italian Renascence is what it is because
the painter had to make the best of a certain particular
wall-space over an altar or because the sculptor had
to get his statue out of a given block of marble of unusual shape and size. The painter and the sculptor
accepted the limitations of the wall-space and of the
marble-block, and found their profit in so doing; they
made a stepping-stone out of that which would have
been only a stumbling-block to the less ingenious and
the less imaginative.

So the artist in playmaking sees his opportunity
and finds his profit in the special accomplishments
of the actors of his own time. Of course, the dramatist
ought not to subject himself to the actors, nor ought
he to limit what he conceives to the capacity of the
special performers he may have in view. But he must
always take account of them and keep them in mind,
because the art of the drama is a twofold art, and because the playwright and the players must work in
unison, ever aiding each other because they always
depend on each other. The dramatist is quite as help-
less without the actors as the actors are without the
dramatist. Without them, the playwright has only the
barren appeal to posterity, which is certain never to
reach its ears. Without him, the performers can be
seen only in old plays, of which the public is sure to
tire, sooner or later.

This ideal harmony of these partners in art has not
always been obtained, since both parties to the alliance

are likely to be endowed with the occasional irritability
and with the swift susceptibility of the artistic temperament. But the best results have been achieved by both
when they have labored together loyally. It is without
surprise, therefore, that we find it recorded that Sophocles, the foremost of Greek tragic dramatists, the supreme artist of a most artistic race, was believed to
have composed his chief characters for some one particular actor, although we do not now know the name
of this special performer, whose histrionic gifts stimu-
lated the dramaturgic energy of the austere poet. In
more than one of the surviving plays of Sophocles,
we can easily discover what would nowadays be called
a "star-part," a single character who has always the
center of the action and in whose fate the interest of
the story culminates.

It is a matter of inference, rather than of actual record,
that Shakspere kept in mind the histrionic capacity
of the several leading performers of the company of
which he was himself a member, and for which all his
plays were composed. Apparently, the greatest of dramatic poets was not himself an actor of abundant
native endowment, however keen might be his insight
into the principles of the histrionic art. So far as we
know, he confined his efforts to parts for which intelligence, dignity, and delivery were sufficient equip-
ment, — the Ghost in "Hamlet," old Adam in "As
You Like It," and the elder Knowell in "Every Man
in his Humor." In other words, the greatest of dramatic poets was probably as an actor of only respect-
able rank; and he seems to have yielded the chief characters even in his own plays to the more gifted of his
fellow-players. It was not for his own acting that he

wrote "Hamlet," but for Burbage's; and Burbage created the most of the star-parts in Shakspere's pieces.

A close scrutiny of Shakspere's text will enable us to make more than one inference about the actors with whom he was associated and for whom he wrote his comedies and his tragedies. It has been pointed out how the gauntness of Holofernes is evidence that there was a lean actor in the company, — the same performer probably who was later to play the envious Cassius. There were no actresses in the Shaksperian theaters, as there had been none in the mysteries and moralities which had preceded the Elizabethan drama and which had made it possible. All the women's parts were performed by boy-actors, difficult as this fact may be to reconcile with the variety and subtlety of the female characters in Shakspere's dramas and with their essential womanliness and abundant femininity. It has been said that even if there are few heroes in Shakspere's plays, there are many heroines; and yet all these heroines sprang into life for the acting of one or another of the smooth-faced boys who were then employed by the associated actor-managers. Only a little while before Shakspere composed the gloomy group of comedies, so-called, of which "Measure for Measure" and "All's Well that Ends Well" are the most significant, he had produced a swift succession of gay and joyous romantic-comedies, "As You Like It" and "Twelfth Night," the "Merchant of Venice" and "Much Ado about Nothing." Perhaps we may ascribe the existence of the delightful heroines of these witty and pathetic pieces, Rosalind and Viola, Portia and Beatrice, to Shakspere's appreciation of the unusual ability of some clean-shaven lad to personate these charming maidens, sparkling yet tender, willing to be wooed and yet coy.

In our modern theaters, when these parts are entrusted to actresses, there is an obvious lack of plausibility in the performance as soon as the girls try to pass themselves off as boys. A spectator to-day cannot help wondering how it is that Orlando fails to see that the self-styled Ganymede is a woman, and how it is that Portia was able to fool the Duke into a belief that she was a lawyer of the sterner sex. In Shakspere's time, this difficulty did not exist. Then a boy impersonating a girl could disguise himself as a boy without too great a strain upon the spectators' willingness to accept fiction for fact. Yet even in Shakspere's time, there may have been a puzzling complexity in the performance of "As You Like It," when a boy-actor played the part of a girl who gave herself out for a lad, and who then as a lad was willing to let Orlando pretend that she was his lady-love.

III

Many critics have expressed wonder at the violence and coarseness of "Titus Andronicus"; and they have been unable to reconcile these crudities with the gentler spirit and loftier view of life revealed in the later tragedies. Here again an explanation may be found in a consideration of the playwright's relation to the players. The "Titus Andronicus," which we have in Shakspere's works, is now believed to be his revision or amalgamation of two earlier dramas dealing with the same subject, both of which had been often performed, and both of which had then come into the control of the company of actors to which Shakspere belonged.

He was at that time only a beginner, with none of the authority which is the result of a series of successes. He was but a prentice playwright, whose task it was to patch up old pieces and to make them more worthy of performance by his comrades. Even if he had revolted against the inartistic vulgarity of the earlier tragedies-of-blood which he had to make over, even if he had wished to modify and to soften their harsh and repellent features to accord with his own finer taste, he would not have been permitted to do so, because the associated actors who were his employers would not have accepted his new version, if they found it shorn of the bombast and of the brutal extravagance which characterized the two old plays and which gave the performers occasions for overacting, the effect of which had been tested by long usage. Perhaps one reason for the rant and the violence that strikes us in the plays of Shakspere's immediate predecessor, Marlowe, especially in his "Jew of Malta" and in his "Tamburlaine," is that he wrote the chief parts in these pieces for Alleyne, a most robustious actor, who was nearly seven feet in height and who possessed a proportionate physical energy.

Charles Lamb, who had a humorous relish for paradox, once ventured to suggest that Shakspere's plays can be appreciated better in the study than on the stage. He held that it was a disadvantage to have Hamlet, for example, forever associated with the person of John Philip Kemble. Now, it may be admitted at once that there are many things in Shakspere's plays which we can best taste as we study them reverently, book in hand. But there are also many things which affect us far more powerfully in the theater than in the library, — and these are the essentially dramatic things. These are the things which we can be sure that Shakspere meant us to feel when we are witnessing his plays. He wrote them to be acted; and it is only when we see them performed that we are enabled to see them as their author intended us to see them. It is to be noted also that Lamb did not follow his own advice; he was a most assiduous theatergoer, as almost every essay of his testifies. We shall do better if we are guided rather by his practice than by his precept. Indeed, one of the first rules which every student of the drama ought to lay down for himself is not to neglect any opportunity to see any play of Shakspere's which may happen to be announced, even if the performance does not promise to be entirely adequate. Nothing furnishes the memory more satisfactorily than a collection of Shaksperian performances.

Molière, whose name must always be linked with those of Sophocles and Shakspere, was the most accomplished comic actor of his day; and, of course, he devised a leading character in all his comedies for his own acting. To certain of these characters he gave his own physical characteristics, his cough, for example, just as he gave lameness to other characters intended for the acting of his lame brother-in-law, Béjart. He wrote the gay serving-maid in the "Bourgeois Gentilhomme" to utilize at once the infectious laughter of Mlle. Beauval, who had only recently joined his company. For his own wife, the fascinating Armande Béjart, he composed a succession of brilliant parts, varied and veracious. Chief among the characters he wrote for her are the charming Elmire in "Tartuffe" and the witty Célimène in the "Misanthrope." And the tragic heroines of Molière's younger contemporary, Racine, were the result of his intimate knowledge of the power of personation possessed by Mlle. Champmeslé.

IV

Accepting the fact that Sophocles and Shakspere, Molière and Racine, and all the chief dramatists in the long history of the theater, have always composed their plays with a keen appreciation of the histrionic ability of the actors by whom their pieces were to be performed, there is interest and profit in an inquiry as to the exact measure of the influence which the actors may have exerted upon the authors. And here we can find help in considering the performers of our own time, since the histrionic temperament as such probably varies very little with the lapse of centuries. The actor is apparently to-day the same kind of human being that he was yesterday and the day before yesterday. In his attitude toward his own calling, toward the exercise of his own art, Roscius probably was not unlike Garrick and Coquelin. What they wanted, each of them, was a play in which he had a good part, — and in his eyes a good part was one in which he could act to his heart's content. A good part is one in which the actor has something to do or somebody to personate. He demands action and character, — and these are precisely the qualities which the playgoer also demands.

Therefore, the influence of the performers on the playwright has been wholesome in so far as their desire for good parts has tended to stiffen the dramatic action, to intensify the passionate climax of the play. And this pressure of the actors on the author has tended also to persuade the poet to a larger and a deeper reproduc-

tion of human nature, so that he could provide the
performers with characters that richly rewarded their
faculty of impersonating creatures wholly unlike themselves. No doubt, the playwright has not infrequently
yielded too much to the wishes of the players and has
been satisfied merely to compose a vehicle for the self-
exhibition of the actors. Of course, the author can
claim no mercy if he is willing to subordinate himself
wholly to the actor and to put together what is but little better than a framework for the display of some
special actor's tricks. This is what Sardou did not disdain to do more than once for Mme. Sarah-Bernhardt,
surrendering the proper independence of his art so that
she could show off all the artificialities of hers. "Fédora," for example, was so tightly adjusted to the cleverness of the French performer that it lost the most of
its effect when acted by Signora Duse, because the
Italian actress found in its tricky ingenuity no opportunity for the poignant veracity she revealed in a simpler and sincerer study from life, like Verga's "Cavalleria Rusticana."

Yet an adroit and self-respecting dramatic poet can
get the utmost out of the varied powers of an actor of
versatile genius without any enfeebling complaisance
and without any unworthy self-surrender. And if
proof of this assertion were needed, it could be found
in "Cyrano de Bergerac." It is not too much to say
that if the masterpiece of M. Rostand had never been
acted or published and if it were suddenly to be discovered after its author's death, the general opinion
would then be that it was a most ingenious specimen
of the dramatic poem, probably composed without any
expectation that it could ever be performed, since the

central figure was so various and so many-sided, now grotesque, and then lyric, now broadly humorous, and then loftily heroic, that the author could never have hoped to find any actor multifarious enough to impersonate the character and to reveal its contrasting aspects. But we happen to know that this brilliant play was written especially for a brilliant actor, and that it was put together with an eye single to his extraordinary range of personation. Coquelin was an incomparable comedian, who had played countless parts, some lyric and heroic, some humorous and grotesque. He had a variety so marvelous that "he seemed to be not one but all mankind's epitome." There was in "Cyrano de Bergerac" no demand made on the actor that Coquelin had not already met in some one of the hundred dramas he had appeared in; and many of the separate effects he had achieved in his best parts were carefully combined in this one character. There was never a more skilful example of theatrical tailoring than M. Rostand's cutting and fitting of his poetic fabric to the exact size and shape of Coquelin's histrionic accomplishments, yet this did not in any way detract from the originality and the charm of the play itself. Although it is a fact that "Cyrano de Bergerac" is what it is solely because Coquelin was what he was, nevertheless the play was performed by many other actors; it was translated into half a dozen different languages; it was read with delight by all who appreciate pointed and polished verse; it lost nothing of its literary value from the circumstance that it had its origin in the poet's desire to write a great part for a great actor. Other comedians may attempt to act Cyrano — indeed, a score of other actors have been tempted to do so; but Coquelin's performance of the part remains inimitable and unapproachable. He was the best Cyrano because Cyrano was measured to fit him. There is excellent excuse for the French phrase which declared that the actor who first plays a part "creates the character." This, at least, is what Coquelin did with Cyrano.

The knowledge we chance to possess that M. Rostand composed this play specially for Coquelin will explain the final act, which puzzled not a few critics. Why does the hero die at the end of the play? Why should he die? The piece is called a "heroic-comedy," and we do not expect to have a comedy end with a death-scene. On the other hand, there is no real reason why Cyrano should not die, — that is to say, there is no logical and necessary conclusion of the highly artificial story which would require the hero either to pass away in the fifth act or to survive to fight again some other day. This being the case, it is easy to see why M. Rostand chose to let the spectators behold the last moments of his hero. It gave him as fine a finish as any other possible termination; it enabled him to touch lightly the chords of pathos; and, above all — it supplied Coquelin with a death-scene, more or less of a novelty even for that marvelous comedian, who may often have envied Mme. Sarah-Bernhardt the many death-scenes which she has presented and which have permitted her to draw easily upon the tears of all who heard her dying speech and confession.

Perhaps a few of those who have been surprised that this heroic-comedy should end as sadly as a tragedy, may have wondered also why the old soldier Flambeau was allowed to occupy a disproportionate place in M. Rostand's other poetic drama, the "Aiglon," wherein he was not the chief figure, — with the chief figure of which, indeed, his connection seems almost episodic. Could not the story of the masterful Napoleon's weakling son have been set forth without dragging in this ancient and loquacious warrior? Here, again, the explanation is easy when we are aware that Flambeau, although not originally acted in Paris by Coquelin, was actually written for him; and that the origin of the play is to be found in the fact that the actor had expressed to the poet his desire to appear as one of the faithful old guard of the great Emperor. The stalwart figure of the veteran, loyal to his master's memory, thus suggested by Coquelin, fascinated M. Rostand; but when the poet sought for a plot in which to set this character to work, he was led irresistibly to the feebler form of the puny King of Rome, the impotent heir of a mighty name. As the playwright worked out his story in scenes and acts, he found the princeling taking the center of the stage and the old soldier becoming inevitably a subordinate character, full of color, no doubt, and very useful in building up the situations of the play, but no longer the focus of interest.

v

When we peruse Legouvé's "Memories of Sixty Years," we learn how "Adrienne Lecouvreur" came to be composed especially for Rachel, and we see why the heroine does not appear in the opening act of the play to which she gives her name, and why she first comes in view clad in the costume of one of Racine's characters. And in the same interesting and instructive reminiscences, M. Legouvé also records how he wrote a certain speech in his earlier piece, "Louise de Lignerolles," half a dozen times because Mlle. Mars insisted that it was not what it ought to be, until finally she told him that what she wanted was something like "la-la-la — là." That is to say, her histrionic instinct made her feel the emotional rhythm of the proper speech for the character at that moment in the play; and Legouvé, having full confidence in her judgment, promptly set fit words to the tune she had indicated. Every other dramatist could recall instances of the unpremeditated effects he has achieved, now and again, by thus accepting the hints of his actors. Many a great drama is the greater because of practical suggestions made by the actors, just as many a great drama has been due to the desire of the poet to profit by the rich gift of some contemporary performer. There is characteristic shrewdness in a remark which Augier once made to the comedian Regnier: "My experience has taught me that an actor deprives me of all that he does not add to the part I have written."

We may read in the life of Bulwer Lytton how he listened to the advice of Macready and made over both the "Lady of Lyons" and "Richelieu" in accordance with the valuable advice which the actor gave him. So Mr. Bram Stoker has told us how Henry Irving felt that Tennyson's "Becket," in the form in which the poet had published it, was not likely to succeed as a play, although it contained the superb figure of the martyred prelate which the actor-manager was longing to personate. Finally, Irving saw the practicability of a few rather radical alterations, the suppression of a scene here, and the writing of a new speech or two there. With fear and trembling, he took these suggestions to Tennyson; and the poet, longing for success on the stage, accepted them gladly, writing at once the added lines that the actor wanted and giving permission for the omissions and transpositions that Irving believed to be necessary.

Here we find the actor rising almost to the level of the poet's collaborator; and it would be easy to collect many another illustration of this harmonious partnership between the creative and the interpretative artists. The plot of "Gringoire," Banville's charming little play, was changed for the better by the author in consequence of suggestions from Coquelin, who created the part of the starving poet. The ingenious turn of the story toward the end of the piece was the invention of the comedian; and when he proposed this to the author, Banville asked scornfully: "Do you want me to write a play like Scribe?" Coquelin laughed and replied that this was just what he did want. "Very well, then," said Banville, smiling in his turn, "that is just what I will do!"

Not only does the wise dramatist profit by every available suggestion of the actors, and not only does he take advantage of the special capabilities of the performers he may have in mind for this part or that, he is also moved sometimes to refrain from putting into his play scenes which are not likely to be properly acted by the special comedians whom he expects to personate certain characters. Sheridan was the manager of Drury Lane when he brought out his own "School for Scandal." Every part in that glittering comedy was written particularly for the performers who first played it; and so admirably was it then per-

formed as a whole that Charles Lamb thought it some
compensation for growing old that he had been born
early enough to see the "School for Scandal" in its
glory. Indeed, the several performers were so closely
fitted that when a friend asked the author-manager
why his comedy did not contain a love-scene for the
two characters whose marriage brings it to an end,
Sheridan was ready with the obvious answer that
Smith and Miss Hopkins could not make love. Now,
Smith was the original Charles Surface, and Maria was
first acted by Miss Priscilla Hopkins (afterward the
wife of John Philip Kemble).

Evidence of this adjustment of the story of a play
to the limitations of the performers for whom it was
intended, can be found abundantly in certain of the
comedies of John Lyly, written for the Children of
Paul's, one of the companies of boy-actors in vogue
in the earlier days of Queen Elizabeth. In these polished pieces of suave rhetoric and artificial sentiment,
there is nothing of the terror and of the horror which
characterized many of the contemporary plays written
for the full-grown performers of the regular theaters.
There is no rude power, no rant, no bombast; all is
decorous, and everything is suppressed which is likely
to be too exacting for their youthful inexperience of life.

And this same artful adaptation of a plot to the
performers for whose use it was devised can be seen
also in the earliest of English comedies that has come
down to us, "Ralph Roister Doister," written by
Udall, the master of Eton, for performance by his own
pupils. For all its imitation of Plautus in its external
form, this English comic play smacks of the soil; and
it has an obvious likeness — in its robust fun, in its

frequent horse-play, and in its occasional snatches of song — to the nondescript pieces which undergraduates undertake for their own pleasure to-day. "Ralph Roister Doister" is just the sort of bold and hearty farce which mature schoolboys could perform with zest and with unfailing effect. And its successive episodes made no demands upon the original performers to which they were not likely to be equal. In fact, a careful examination of this unpretending little play seems to suggest that the Eton schoolmaster had a premonition of the truth which the later Scribe once expressed to Legouvé. The wily French playwright declared that dramatists did well to study the qualities of the contemporary actors, but that there was a more constant advantage in availing one's self also of the defects of these performers, — "since their merits might abandon them, whereas their faults would never leave them."

This may have been said more or less in jest; and yet it has a kernel of truth. The playwright needs to take stock of his performers, and if he can find his advantage in utilizing their failings, so much the better for him, — although, of course, it is their real endowment that he will utilize the more often. And he may gain by considering special actors while he is composing his play, even if he may not actually expect that they will be employed in the performance of that piece. Although these special actors may be unavailable, perhaps because they are engaged elsewhere or because they have retired from the stage, the dramatist may find a stimulus to his invention, if not to his imagination, in keeping in mind the personality of these performers while he is composing his play.

In fact, the more closely we study the history of dramatic literature, and the more sharply we analyze the structure of the masterpieces of the drama, the more firmly we become convinced that the dramatic poets of every age and of every race have never failed to weigh scrupulously the gifts, the deficiencies, and the special qualities of the various performers upon whom they had to rely for the proper presentation of their plays to the public. And this has been for our pleasure as well as for their profit. Mme. de Sévigné accused Racine of "writing plays for la Champmeslé, and not for posterity." No doubt Racine was guilty of the charge; but as it has happened, the plays that fitted Mlle. de Champmeslé have succeeded also in retaining the admiration of posterity. They survive as the unexcelled masterpieces of French tragedy.

CHAPTER III

It is obvious that the general spectacle presented by the interior of a Greek theater during the representation of a drama must have been quite unlike anything we are accustomed to in modern times. The open-air buildings, the performance in broad daylight, the vast crowds of spectators, the chorus grouped together in the center — all these characteristics of a Greek theatrical exhibition must have combined to produce a scene to which there is no exact parallel at the present day. This fact should be kept clearly in view. — A. E. HAIGH, *The Attic Theater.*

I

IN every period when the literature of any language has been characterized by abundant dramatic productivity, the playwright will be found to have composed his plays in accordance with the conditions of the actual theater of his own time. He may not have liked these conditions and he may have believed that they could be bettered; but he has always begun by accepting them, whatever they might be. He has done this necessarily and inevitably, whether he himself was truly a dramatic poet like Sophocles and Shakspere or merely an ingenious stage-craftsman like Kotzebue and Scribe. What the playwrights of every age have done instinctively and without hesitation, the historians of literature are now beginning to perceive; and only a few of them have yet grasped the full significance of the fact that it is impossible justly to appreciate the art of the truly dramatic poet, Sophocles or Shakspere,

Molière or Ibsen, without a clear understanding of the chief circumstances of an actual performance in the particular theater for which the dramatist prepared his plays, and to the size and shape of which, and to the scenic appliances of which, he had to adjust the construction of his story.

We are now well aware that there have been many types of theater in different countries and at different times, most of them varying very widely from our snug modern playhouses. We all recognize that the immense outdoor theater of the Athenians was as unlike as possible to the smaller half-roofed cockpit of the Londoners under Elizabeth, and also to the long narrow tennis-court of the Parisians under Louis XIV. But while these differences between the theaters of earlier periods may be a matter of common knowledge, we do not always apply our information when we undertake to discuss the dramaturgic skill of the playwrights of these several epochs. We must always keep in mind the extent to which the theater has often dictated to the author what he could put into his play and what he had to leave out, and how he had to present what he desired to set forth. We ought to give full weight to the pressure exerted on the playwright by the changing conditions of the playhouses of successive centuries, — by the size of the theater, for one thing, which may be so huge as to forbid the author's choice of any but broad and simple themes, — by the elaboration of heavy scenery, which may impose on him the duty of compacting his plot so that he will need few changes of place, — or by the improved modern modes of artificial illumination (candles first, then oil-lamps, after a while gas, and finally electricity), all of which have wrought in turn significant modifications of dramaturgic method. For example, it is only as we come to a realizing sense of the influence exerted upon the art of the dramatist by the specific conditions of each of the special types of theater which have existed each in its own time and place, that we can measure the wisdom of Shakspere in rejecting the advice of Sidney to model his plays after those of the Greek dramatists; and that we can gage also the unwisdom of Tennyson in taking Shakspere's histories as the pattern of his own poetic dramas, composed centuries later, when the conditions of the English theater had entirely changed.

The critics of any particular period of the drama have not always been familiar with the conditions existing during other periods. The historians of Greek literature are acquainted with our modern playhouses and they are now studying the ruins of the theaters still accessible in Greece and in the Grecian colonies; but they have paid little attention to the methods of presenting plays in the Middle Ages, at first in the churches, and later, on platforms in the market-places. The historians of English literature have scarcely yet attained to a fairly clear perception of the way in which plays were acted under the Tudors, and they have not yet seized the full significance of the changes which resulted during the Restoration from the introduction of painted scenery and of artificial light. The scholars who knew only one manifestation of the drama have rarely possessed the perspective which would be supplied to them by a knowledge of other aspects in the other periods when the drama was flourishing. There is a striking unity in the drama as we trace its

development down through the ages; its essential principles are always the same, since the aim of the real
dramatist has varied little, whether he was a Greek
of old, a Frenchman of the seventeenth century or a
Scandinavian of the nineteenth. And his methods were
affected by traditions still surviving from the playhouses of an earlier generation. These traditions the
dramatist profits by even if they are no longer in exact
accord with the actual conditions of the theater for
which he is writing; and so we find the Elizabethan
playwrights making use of the two doors on opposite
sides of the stage to indicate two wholly distinct places,
— a device which is apparently a survival from the
several "mansions" of the French miracle-plays. In
fact, it is impossible really to understand the dramaturgic methods in vogue at any particular period without taking into consideration the circumstances of performance at least half a century earlier.

No one, it may be noted, has undertaken to trace
the slow development of the art of the scene-painter,
distinguishing sharply between true scene-painting as
we now know it, a realistic perspective intended to re-
produce the place itself, and that very different thing,
the building up in miniature of the house or of a part
of the house (such as we find in the Middle Ages and
again in the Italian comedy-of-masks), which is the
work of carpenters completed by the work of house-
painters. No one has collected the many references
which make it plain that properties of all sorts —
altars, thrones, arbors, etc. — were in use long before
there was any attempt at true scene-painting. And no
one has ever made a collection of plans of theaters,
all drawn to the same scale, so that we could see at a

glance how immense was the theater of Dionysus at Athens and how small the tennis-court wherein Molière acted. With the aid of a collection of these plans and with the collateral information now available, we could follow the changes in the method of performance from Sophocles to Ibsen, and we should be led to one interesting conclusion, — that instead of there being only two types of theater, as is often assumed, the ancient and the modern, there are in reality many, of which the medieval is not the least important.

We should be induced to acknowledge that the theater in England for which Marlowe and Shakspere and Jonson wrote, and the theater in Spain for which Lope de Vega and Calderon wrote, were neither of them really modern; and they were both medieval in their methods or at least semi-medieval. We should be made to see that Molière is apparently the earliest of the moderns, in that his plays now need no readjustment, no editing, no transposing of any kind, to fit them for the playhouses of to-day. And we should discover that a very striking change in the practices of the playwrights was brought about in the second half of the nineteenth century, when the stage was at last abundantly lighted in every part by electricity and when the curving bow of the footlights was cut back to the curtain, which thereafter rose and fell inside a picture-frame.

II

The difference between the playhouse in which we can to-day see one of Mr. Clyde Fitch's plays and the playhouse in which Sheridan's comedies were originally given, is greater than the difference between Sheridan's Drury Lane and the house for which Congreve wrote

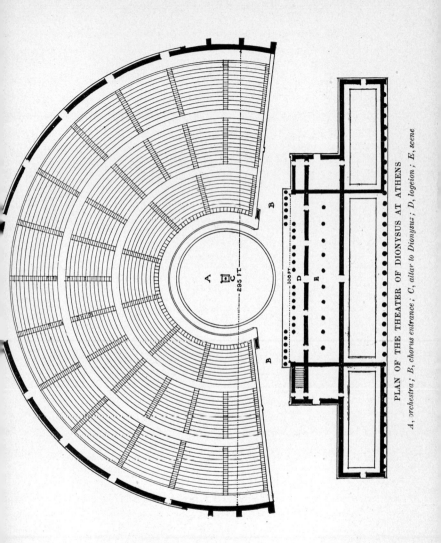

PLAN OF THE THEATER OF DIONYSUS AT ATHENS

A, orchestra; B, chorus entrance; C, altar to Dionysus; D, logeion; E, scene

and in which Betterton acted. And in its turn, this
Restoration playhouse was very unlike the Elizabethan
theater for which Shakspere wrote and in which Burbage acted. Even more apparent is the difference
between the theater of Dionysus at Athens and the
Roman theater at Orange, in the south of France.
These several theaters, ancient and modern, are sharply
distinguished from one another by their size, by their
shape, by their method of illumination, by the absence
or presence of real scenery, and also by the arrangement of the seats for the spectators; and as we study
these successive changes, we are confirmed in the conviction that the physical conditions of the playhouse
must always have exerted a powerful influence upon
the dramatic poets who followed each other down
through the centuries.

The theater of Dionysus at Athens is accepted as
the earliest of the great Greek theaters, yet it is so well
preserved that it is possible for a traveler now to sit
on its marble benches and look down into the orchestra
where the chorus circled with solemn chant about the
altar of the god in whose honor the drama had come
into being.[1] For a long time, the primitive Greek plays
were acted in the market-place, and the spectators sat
on temporary benches. After one of these rows of
seats had broken down, a space was leveled at the foot
of the Acropolis, and the spectators grouped themselves on the hollow hillside above. In time, the slope
was rounded out, and from the level space where the
actors stood, tiers of marble seats rose high up the
shoulders of the mountain. The orchestra itself was
paved; and some kind of low structure must have been

[1] See illustration facing page 74.

erected behind the semi-circular space of the orchestra
to serve as a background for the movements of the
actors and for the evolutions of the chorus. It is generally admitted now that there was no elevated stage
in the Attic theater; and the acting took place in the
orchestra itself, the semi-circular level space which
bowed out into the curving tiers of seats. It is coming
to be admitted also that there was no scenery, although
there may have been properties. Of course, the author
was free to avail himself of the doors and of the roof
of the low structure which shut in the orchestra, and
which probably served also for a dressing-room for all
those who took part in the performance.

The arc of the semi-circle, where this structure
stood, was seventy-two feet long; and the farthest
point of the prolonged semi-circle was about the same
distance away. And above this level space, there rose
nearly eighty tiers of seats. It has been asserted that
more than twenty thousand spectators could be present
at a performance. As we sit on those benches to-day,
and glance down to the orchestra and see how small a
single figure looks so far away, and how impossible it
is to perceive any play of feature, we are not surprised
that the Greek actors were raised on lofty boots and
wore masks that towered above their heads, increasing
their apparent stature. We recognize that under such
circumstances the dramatist was wise to avoid all acts
of physical violence impossible to performers thus
accoutered. We perceive that he was well advised
when he preferred a plot already familiar to his spectators, so that they would not lose the thread of the
story, even if a sudden gust of wind from the Ægean
might now and again wrap the floating draperies about

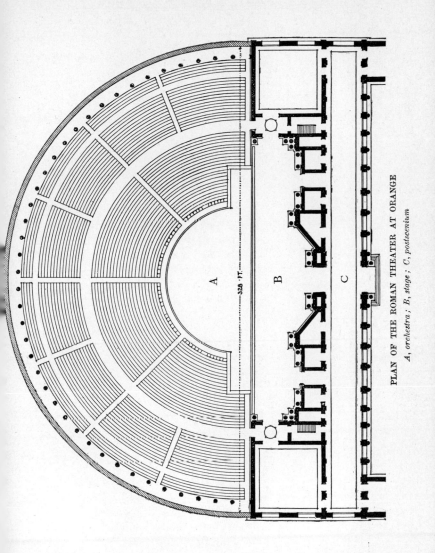

PLAN OF THE ROMAN THEATER AT ORANGE

A, orchestra ; B, stage ; C, postscenium

325 FT.

the heads of the performers and for a moment deprive the audience of the spoken words. We can approve also his practical shrewdness in choosing a theme not only already known in its outline, but also possessing a bold simplicity, which demanded a massive treatment. We can understand more clearly the function of the chorus, which supplied a restful lyrical variety, and also that spectacular element which appeals to the eye and which seems to be required to hold the attention of an immense gathering in the open air. And we end by seeing the obvious likeness which exists between one of the old Greek tragedies and one of our broader modern music-dramas of the Wagnerian type, if this should be performed out-of-doors.

In building their playhouses, as in most of their other artistic endeavors, the Romans followed in the footsteps of the Athenians.[1] They modified the Greek theater to suit their own needs. Giving up the seats on the curving hillside which enabled the audience to look down on the actors, they filled the orchestra with benches, and they were therefore forced to raise up a stage so that the spectators could see the performers. This stage was a long and narrow shelf; and it had behind it a high wall, pierced with doors and richly decorated with columns and statues. This stately piece of ornate architecture was the unchanging background for every play; and its doors were utilized as the plot might demand. In the theater at Orange in the south of France, the stage was about one hundred and ninety feet wide. The radius of the auditorium was more than one hundred and eighty feet. There was accommodation for six thousand spectators. Although this

[1] See illustration facing page 140.

theater at Orange is a little late, the earlier Roman playhouses were not unlike it in size and in shape.

Such a theater seems to be better suited for pantomime and for the feats of acrobats than for a drama dealing truthfully with the pathos and the humor of life. Perhaps we can catch a glimpse of one reason why the delicately polished comedies of Terence failed to please his contemporaries when they were performed. The style of that accomplished man of letters could hardly be expected to convey much pleasure to the audience collected in a very large theater of this type. The Comédie-Française, on one of its visits to Orange, ventured to perform there a neo-Greek playlet, the "Ilote" of M. Paul Ferrier; but although this had been successful in Paris at the Théâtre Français, it was found to evaporate into immediate insignificance in the vast space of the old Roman theater. On the other hand, the "Œdipus" of Sophocles, and one or two other French versions of massively planned Greek tragedies, were really more effective when performed at Orange than they ever had been in Paris, as though they demanded a larger frame than any modern theater could provide.

Gaston Boissier, who was not only one of the most learned students of Latin literature but also one of the acutest of critics, visited the substantial ruin at Orange and also most of the other surviving Roman theaters. As a result of these investigations, he declared that when he sought to evoke a vision of the spacious Latin playhouse and to reconstruct a mental image of it as it must have been in the full splendor of the imperial period, he believed that he was enabled thereby better to understand the pieces which were performed in these stately edifices. "No doubt, this theater was made for these plays, but they were also made for this theater; they were instinctively accommodated and appropriated to the place where they were to be represented. The actual circumstances of their performance imposed on them certain necessities, which they had to accept and which in time erected themselves into rules. It would be easy to prove that many of their qualities and of their defects, for which subtle explanations have been sought, have, in fact, no other origin than this obligation of the dramatist to conform to the conditions of performance in the only type of theater with which the Latin dramatists were familiar." And the shrewd Frenchman then pointed out the skill with which the artful Plautus "solved the problem of getting himself listened to (in a vast uncovered space) by inattentive and noisy spectators, who had at bottom little real liking for the entertainment which was offered to them."

III

In the Middle Ages, the tradition of the Greek theater, and even that of the Roman, seems to have been lost; and we find a new dramatic form evolved spontaneously out of the ritual of the church. Just as the Ara Cœli in Rome still exhibits at Christmas a waxwork reproduction of the infant Jesus cradled in the rude manger of the inn, so the medieval priests put into dialogue and presented in action other episodes of the Birth and also of the Resurrection. Choristers, with shepherd's crooks in their hands, came in by the eastern portal and advanced through the congregation, singing the glad tidings, until they drew near to the manger within the chancel, in front of which they might meet other officials of the church, representing the Three Wise Men. Later, a place apart was found for Herod and his soldiers; and other places, here and there, in the vast cathedral, were assigned to other actors in other episodes of Christ's career, — the Temple, for one, and, for another, the house of the High Priest.

These several places were called "stations." When the swollen mystery was turned out of the cathedral, and when its presentation was undertaken by laymen, the traditions established in the church were carefully preserved with only the necessary modifications. In one manuscript of a mystery acted in Valenciennes in 1547, there is a miniature of the stage on which it was acted; and from this picture a model has been made, which gives us a good idea of a medieval performance in France.[1] The stage was a shallow platform about one hundred and thirty feet in length; and at the back, in a long line, were little houses representing each of the several stations, the various places required in the course of the drama. At the extreme right of the spectators is Heaven, raised high on pillars; and at the extreme left is Hell-mouth. Ranged between were the Inn, the Temple, the House of the High Priest, and the other necessary "mansions" (as the French termed the stations), used only when they were called for by the special episodes of the story, the rest of the acting taking place anywhere on the stage, which was accepted as a neutral ground whereon anything might be represented.

In England, instead of massing the stations at the back of a long stage, the more general practice was to set them up separately on wagons, like the floats of a Mardi Gras parade, and they were called "pageants."

[1] See illustration facing page 292.

But even in England, more or less of the acting was done, not on the floats, but in the street itself, in the midst of the assembled spectators, just as had been the case when the earlier performances were given in the church itself. The street was then the neutral ground which might be supposed to be anywhere, — the shore in front of Noah's Ark, or the space between the palace of Herod and the house of the High Priest (these two dwellings being represented by two pageants brought forward at the same time). This is the tradition which survived in the Elizabethan theater, where the acting took place also on a neutral ground. The stage was only a platform unincumbered by scenery, and it was therefore free to represent any needed place. At right and left, there might be two doors, which properly labelled, could stand, if need be, one for Asia and the other for Africa.

Under the later Tudors, there sprang into being several companies of actors, patronized by the great nobles. They went about acting where they could, in palaces and in townhalls, on village greens and in the courtyards of inns. They carried a few properties, swords and scepters, and the like; but they knew nothing of scenery painted on frames. When at last they were forbidden to act in the inns of London, they went a little outside the city and put up playhouses of their own. They had no models to go by, for they knew as little about the theaters of Greece and Rome as their medieval predecessors had known. But they had found that the courtyards of inns, hollow rectangles girt with galleries, were suitable for their purpose; and so it is that the playhouses that they built were very like the inn courtyards, — with the inn itself omitted. They put up a square or circular or oval structure, open to the sky, except over the galleries, and except also over the back part of the platform which jutted into the yard where the groundlings stood.

We have the contract for the building of one of these playhouses, from which we learn that it was square, eighty feet on each side, and that the platform-stage was forty-three feet wide.[1] Two pieces of arras (or of cloth painted like tapestry) were hung from the gallery at the back where it crossed the platform. It was through these curtains, or through the two doors one on either side, that the actor made his entrances and his exits. The draperies could be looped back to reveal a supposed cave or study, while the gallery above could serve as a balcony or as the outer wall of a castle, or merely as another place from which some character could oversee what took place on the stage below. The platform, although it had no painted scenery, was often enriched with properties, — thrones and arbors and wells, — as these might be called for by the story.

This platform-stage was the neutral ground whereon any character might meet any other character without any question as to the exact spot where the meeting was supposed to take place. If the action of the play could be made clearer by particularizing the special place, then one of the characters was careful to say where they were supposed to be. But the spectators, some of them seated on stools on the stage itself and almost mingled with the actors, some of them standing in the yard on three sides of the platform, and some of them accommodated more comfortably in the private boxes of the galleries, asked no questions about

[1] See illustration facing page 238.

place or time; they wanted to see a story set forth in all its phases, and they cared nothing to know just where it was that any two characters were supposed to be at the very moment when the plot was thickening to a crisis. The playwright had the largest liberty of time and place, a larger license than was good for most of the Elizabethan dramatists, who did not compact their plots and who were amply satisfied if they succeeded in interesting their unexacting audiences. And when we contrast this London theater for which Shakspere wrote with the Athenian theater for which Sophocles wrote, we get a glimpse of the gulf that yawns between the English drama and the Greek. We perceive one of the chief causes of the differences between them; and we see at the same time how distinctly the form of each was conditioned by the circumstances of its performance.

In his ample and acute study of the "Tragic Drama of the Greeks," Haigh called attention to the fact that one of the chief characteristics of the Shaksperian drama, "the calm and tranquil manner in which the scenes were brought to a close, originated in the casual circumstance that the old English theater had no dropscene; the successive portions of a play were terminated, not by a curtain, but by the actors walking off the stage; and for this reason it was impossible to finish up with a climax, as is now the invariable custom." And Haigh then remarked that the unity and simplicity of Greek tragedy were due to the force of circumstance, especially to the influence exerted by the constant presence of the chorus, which prevented any change of place.

In one respect, similarity in the circumstances of performance brought about a significant similarity of treatment in the Greek drama and in the Elizabethan. In the theater of Dionysus at Athens, as in the Globe Theater in London, there was no painted scenery, a theatrical adjunct as unknown to Shakspere as to Sophocles; and therefore the dramatic poet was not only tempted to put into his dialogue the description of any special place which he wished to call up in the minds of the spectators, he was actually compelled to do this, since he could accomplish his purpose in no other way. From the descriptions of the wild and lonely spot where the hero is fixed to the rock, given by one or another character in the earliest episodes of the " Prometheus Bound " of Æschylus, some commentators have chosen to assume the existence of some sort of scenery which would suggest to the assembled multitude the gloom and horror of the spot. But this is an unwarranted inference, for if an adequate scenic representation of the place had been possible, the poet would not have felt called upon to put its description into the mouths of his characters. We do not find Ibsen or Rostand delaying the action of their dramas by any detailed description of the background which the spectators have now before their eyes. For the modern dramatic poet, any such digression would be an impertinent superfluity, since he knows that he can rely on the skilful scene-painters to represent pictorially the outward aspects of the place where the action passes. To the audience of Æschylus, as to the audience of Shakspere, poetic description was not superfluous or impertinent; it might be helpful. And we all know how freely Shakspere availed himself of this privilege of pictorial description, a privilege denied to the dramatic poet of to-day.

IV

In France, the strolling companies had become accustomed, not to the courtyards of inns, but to tennis-courts; and it is in an altered tennis-court that we find Molière acting more than once. A tennis-court was a rectangle of a little less than one hundred feet long by a little less than forty feet in width. It had galleries along the sides; and it had a solid roof, and therefore it had to be lighted by candles. A stage was easily put up at one end, shut in by a proscenium arch, in which a curtain probably rolled up at the beginning of every act. But here again we have spectators seated on the sides of the stage, not on separate stools, but on benches perpendicular to the footlights; and again we find the actors surrounded by the audience as in England and in Greece. Behind these benches there might be painted scenery, although this was at first little more than a drop-cloth. The French dramatists, following Corneille's example, had accepted the so-called "unity of place"; and in most of Molière's plays, he confined all his acts to a single and unchanging scene.

It is true that certain of his earlier plays, on the model of the Italian comedy-of-masks, were probably performed in a set representing a public square with houses (solidly built of wood) on each side, into the doors of which the characters went and from the windows of which they could lean out.[1] This set was familiar to Molière and to his audiences, as it was that used by the Italian comedians who played in the same theater on alternate nights. And thus we see that we need to know the earlier Italian conditions to understand how it was and why it was that Molière was able

[1] See illustration facing page 172.

to put on the stage the story of the "School for Husbands" — which, as Voltaire said, seems to be all in narrative, although it really is all in action. After a while, Molière dispensed with the convenient devices of the Italians; but his set is always very simple, as had to be the case when the stage was encumbered with spectators. His characters always stand, except when chairs are absolutely necessary; and the action is adroitly arranged so as to be easily presented in a neutral ground, the narrow space between the spectators on the stage and the painted drop-scene which hung at the back. This is one reason why his plays can now be performed in any modern theater. They do not need elaborate scenery, although elaborate scenery can be used without doing them any harm.

Molière is in reality the earliest of modern dramatists, since Shakspere's conditions were at least semimedieval. Shakspere's courtyard playhouse was unroofed and lighted only by the sun, and it had no scenery, whereas Molière's tennis-court playhouse was roofed and artificially lighted and had painted scenery. And Molière did not always act in a tennis-court playhouse. He was allowed to move his company into the stately theater built by Richelieu on the model devised by the Italian architects after their study of the ruins of the Roman theaters still surviving here and there in the peninsula.[1] Palladio had even attempted at Vicenza what he believed to be a reproduction of a Roman theater. Under this Italian influence, the tennis-court playhouse was given up in France, as the courtyard playhouse was given up in England; and everywhere there were erected theaters externally not unlike

[1] See frontispiece.

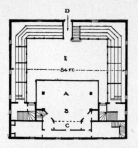

**PLAN OF THE FORTUNE THEATER,
LONDON**

*A, front stage; B, back stage; C, inner
stage; D, entrance; E, courtyard*

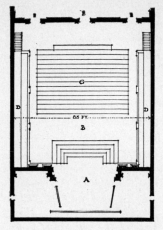

**PLAN OF THE RICHELIEU-MO-
LIÈRE THEATER, PARIS**

*A, stage; B, parterre; C, seats; D, D,
galleries; E, E, E, entrances*

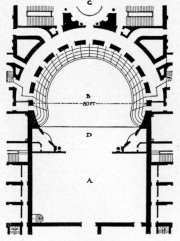

**PLAN OF THE DRURY LANE THEA-
TER, LONDON**

*A, back stage; D, front stage, or apron;
B, auditorium; C, entry*

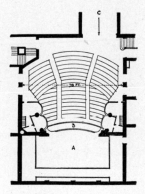

**PLAN OF THE EMPIRE THEA-
TER, NEW YORK**

*A, stage; B, orchestra; C, entrance;
D, auditorium*

our modern places of amusement, — although in Paris, a portion of the audience continued to have seats on the stage until the middle of the eighteenth century, — and when Voltaire's "Sémiramis" was produced, the ushers had to beg these spectators to yield a passage for the Ghost of Ninus. As many of these Italianate theaters were intended to serve also for the performance of opera with its customary spectacle, they were much larger than the buildings which had been earlier found satisfactory. It was difficult to light the stage adequately with the sputtering candles or the feeble oil-lamps which were then the only means of illumination. Probably this is one reason why the stage was made to curve out into the audience far beyond the proscenium-arch in which the curtain rose and fell. In England, this projecting area between the bow of the footlights and the line of the curtain was called the "apron," and the best lighted central spot was known as the "focus." It became the habit of the actors to present every important moment of the piece out on the apron, and as near to the focus as possible, because it was only there that there was sufficient light to enable the spectators to perceive their play of feature. This brought them very close to the audience, and they actually turned their backs on the spectators who sat in the boxes nearest to the stage.

This was the prevailing type of theater for two centuries after the Restoration; and there is no better example of it than the Drury Lane, which Sheridan managed and for which he wrote the "School for Scandal." [1] The proscenium-arch was about seventy feet wide; the stage was about the same depth; and there

[1] See illustration facing page 192.

was an apron of eighteen feet in front of the curtain. The scenery was very much what we are still permitted to see in the present performance of the earlier and simpler Italian operas, — that is to say, there was a drop-scene at the back, and there were on each side, and parallel with the drop, five or six "wings," representing trees or columns or side walls. It was through the broad openings between these wings that the performers came out on the stage. The place of the action could be shifted any number of times by merely pushing out half-scenes which met in the middle of the stage, and by sliding back the wings of the first set and sliding forward those of the second.

This is the method of presentation which allowed Sheridan to put two or three different places into a single act of the "School for Scandal" and to display his characters first at Lady Sneerwell's and then at Lady Teazle's. It was the only method known to Shakspere's earliest editors, from Rowe and Theobald down; and in their ignorance of the more primitive Elizabethan theater, they assumed, naturally enough, that this was the method employed by Shakspere; and so they divided the text of his plays into acts and scenes, whenever they thought they could detect any indication of a change of place. This division into acts and scenes conveys a wholly false impression of Shakspere's real method. He conceived his play as a story told in action in a series of dialogues, many of which were held on the neutral ground that might be anywhere. Only where there was an advantage to be gained by particularizing the exact spot where the action lay, did Shakspere take trouble to indicate it; and we may be sure that nothing was further from his thought than that his story should be cut up into the snippets of scenes that we find in the ordinary library editions of his plays.

V

Toward the end of the two hundred years which extended from the Restoration to the middle of the nineteenth century, the conditions of performance began to change. The art of the scene-painter became more elaborate; and the box-set was devised, whereby a room could be shown with its walls and its ceiling. The influence of the realistic movement of the middle of the nineteenth century imposed on the stage-manager the duty of making every scene character-istic of the period and of the people, and of relating the characters closely to their environment. The facil-ities for lighting were greatly improved, first by the introduction of gas, then by the invention of the lime-light, and finally by the perfecting of the electric light. It was found to be possible to illuminate the stage so as to show the expression on the actors' faces, even in the remoter corners of the stage. The apron behind the curving footlights was no longer necessary or even useful; and the stage was therefore cut back to the proscenium-arch, which became a frame for the stage-opening. Sir Hubert Herkomer declared the modern practice when he asserted that "the proscenium should be to the stage-picture what the frame is to the easel-picture; it should separate the stage-picture from the surroundings, just as a painted picture should reach the frame."

It is for this picture-frame stage that every dramatist of to-day is composing his plays; and his methods are of necessity those of the picture-frame stage; just as the methods of the Elizabethan dramatic poet were of necessity those of the platform-stage. Probably we have not yet seen all the consequences of this striking change in the physical conditions of the theater; and probably we have not yet seized the full significance of the transformation. For example, as the actor is no longer partly surrounded by the audience, as the performers are now withdrawn beyond a magic line of separation, the drama is certain hereafter to be less oratorical, less rhetorical, less bombastic; it is bound to be simpler in its language, more "natural." The long soliloquy, the confidential self-revelation, which was not out of place on the platform-stage, when a character was on the neutral ground that might be anywhere, and when he was so close to some of the spectators that he could put out his hand to touch them, — this is obviously inappropriate now when the actor is remote behind the proscenium, and seated on a real chair in what looks like a real room.

The assertion has been made that the relinquishing of the soliloquy is to be ascribed to the influence of Ibsen; and it may be admitted that the Norwegian dramatist has been masterly in his adjustment of his methods to the conditions of the picture-frame stage. But we can shift the real responsibility for the banishing of the soliloquy a little further back; it does not lie on Ibsen's shoulders, but on Edison's, — since it was an inevitable consequence of the incandescent bulb. Here we find the confirmation of a remark made by Ludovic Celler in his account of stage-conditions in France in the seventeenth century: "Artificial light creates a realm of convention, where an imitation is more easily accepted and where the eyes are less exacting; a compromise is attained between fact and fiction; and artificial light is what has most contributed to the progress of theatrical representation."

Upon the picture-frame stage of the twentieth century, it is now possible to present, without any alteration or transposition, the tragedies of Sophocles, composed in accordance with the conditions of the immense open-air theater of Athens, and also the comedies of Molière, composed in accordance with the conditions of the tennis-court playhouse of Paris. But the plays of Shakspere and of Sheridan can be put on this picture-frame stage of ours only after they have been rearranged, because Shakspere's were composed in accordance with the wholly different and absolutely incompatible conditions of the courtyard theater, and Sheridan's in accordance with the conditions of the post-Restoration playhouse. The picture-frame stage may be superior to its several predecessors, or it may be inferior to them, but it is at all events different from them; and it is the stage to which we are nowadays accustomed. If Shakspere and Sheridan were writing plays to-day, it is the picture-frame stage that they would write for; and we should find them so arranging the episodes of their stories that these could be presented with only a single set in each act, since the elaboration of our modern scenery makes it disadvantageous to attempt a change of place during the act. This is a technical difficulty to be vanquished, which could not fail to affect their method of treatment, and even to some extent their choice of theme. The technical possibilities of any art at any moment must more or less determine and may more or less limit, not only how the artist shall express what he has to say, but also what he shall attempt to express. And it is only after we have analyzed these technical possibilities that we are really prepared to appreciate what the artist has actually accomplished.

Attention must be called also to one other point, — to the fact that since the scene-painters have gained the skill needful for the satisfactory and more or less realistic representation of interiors and of exteriors, and especially since the invention of the electric light has made it possible to illuminate every corner of the stage on which these interiors and exteriors are set, the conditions of performance are now very similar throughout the civilized world, differing only in minor and unimportant details. A modern theater in Paris or in London is structurally very similar to a modern theater in New York or Melbourne, in Budapest or Buenos Ayres. This standardizing of the playhouse is a new thing in the history of the drama. There may have been a general resemblance between the conditions under which Shakspere worked and those under which Lope de Vega worked; but these early English and Spanish conditions are wholly unlike those of the Greek theater, of the Roman theater, of the French theater of Molière's time, and of the English theater of Sheridan's day, which all varied widely from one another. Now at last, out of all these contending traditions there has been evolved the type of theater best suited to the circumstances of our modern civilization; and the plays written to-day in any one of the modern languages can be transported anywhere and translated for performance without any structural modification.

The world-wide uniformity of theatrical conditions

has brought with it a substantial identity of drama-turgic method. In its framework, a French play is now closely akin to a German play, an Italian play to an American. And as a result, the modern dramatist is enabled to make a cosmopolitan appeal, not possible to any of his predecessors in any of the earlier periods when the drama has most abundantly flourished. The plays of Ibsen, of Rostand, of d'Annunzio, and of Echegaray have passports permitting them to go any-where and everywhere. The method of any one of these dramatists is fundamentally the method of every other, however national and individual may be his material. And it is curious to note that this acceptance of a cosmopolitan form has been accompanied by a deeper appreciation of local color, of racial types of character, and of themes peculiar to the several races. The form is cosmopolitan, but the content is increas-ingly national. Ibsen is intensely Scandinavian; Verga is immitigably Italian; Sir Arthur Pinero and Mr. Henry Arthur Jones are rigorously British; Mr. Au-gustus Thomas and Mr. Clyde Fitch are thoroughly American; and yet each of them, whatever his stock, has built his plays in accord with the same interna-tional formula, the only formula which is really satis-factory in our uniform theaters.

CHAPTER IV

THE INFLUENCE OF THE AUDIENCE

Shakspere, we know, was a popular playwright. I mean not only that many of his plays were favorites in his day, but that he wrote, mainly at least, for the more popular kind of audience, and that within certain limits, he conformed to its tastes. — A. C. BRADLEY, *Oxford Lectures on Poetry*.

I

THE shape of the special theater for which a dramatist has composed his plays, its size, its scenery, and its lighting, all exert an influence upon the playwright and combine to condition the form which his work must take, even if they do not more or less modify its content also. But the strongest pressure upon the content of the drama of any special period and of any special place is that of the contemporary audience for whose delight it was originally devised. How any author at any time can tell his story upon the stage depends upon the kind of stage he has in view; but what kind of story he may tell depends upon the kind of people he wants to interest. As Dryden declared in one of his epilogues: —

> "They who have best succeeded on the stage
> Have still conformed their genius to the age."

And this couplet of Dryden's recalls the later lines of Johnson: —

> "The drama's laws the drama's patrons give,
> And we who live to please, must please to live."

In other words, the dramatic poet is not independent of his audience, as the lyric poets may be, since he can never be satisfied with mere self-expression. His work depends for its effect upon his hearers, and he has to take them into account, under penalty of blank failure. He must give them what they want, even if he gives them also what he wants. The author of a drama cannot labor for himself alone; he has to admit the spectators as his special partners. There is ever a tacit agreement, a quasi-contract between the playwright and the playgoers. As the ingenious and ingenuous Abbé d'Aubignac asserted, more than two centuries ago, when he was laying down laws for the drama: "We are not to forget here (and I think it one of the best Observations I have made upon this matter) that if the subject is not conformable to the Manners as well as the Opinions of the spectators, it will never take." And a later remark of his proved that he possessed the prime requisite of a dramatic critic, in that he had worked out his principles not merely in the library but also in the theater itself: "For if there be any Act or Scene that has not that conformity to the Manners of the spectators, you will suddenly see the applause cease, and in its place a discontent succeed, though they themselves do not know the cause of it."

Just as the theater for which Sophocles wrote differed in almost every way from the theater for which Shakspere wrote, so the audience that the Greek poet had to please, if he was to win the awarded prize, was very unlike the audience that the English poet had to please, if he was to make his living as a professional playwright. There is not a wider difference between the theaters of Louis XIV's time, wherein Molière's comedies were first produced, and the cosmopolitan modern playhouses wherein Ibsen's dramas are performed, than there is between the burghers of Paris, whom the French humorist had to amuse, and the narrow-minded villagers of Grimstad, whom Ibsen had always before him as the individual spectators he wished to startle out of their moral lethargy.

Even though the playwright has ever to consider the playgoers, their opinions and their prejudices, he is under no undue strain when he does this; and the most of his effort is unconscious, since he is always his own contemporary, sharing in the likes and dislikes of his fellow-countrymen, the very men whom he hopes to see flocking to the performance of his plays. Sophocles did not need to take thought to avoid what would be displeasing to the thousands who sat around the hollow slope of the Acropolis; he was an Athenian himself; and yet, no doubt, he acted always on the advice Isocrates used to give to his pupils in oratory, who were told to "study the people." Shakspere did not have to hold himself in for fear of shocking the energetic Elizabethans; he was himself a subject of the Virgin Queen, one of the plain people, with an instinctive understanding of the desires of the playgoers of his age. As M. Jusserand has acutely asserted, the English playgoing public of Shakspere's time demanded "nourishment suited to its tastes, which were spontaneous and natural; it imposed these on the playmakers; it loved, like all peoples, to see on the stage, made more beautiful or more ugly, that is to say, more highly colored, what it found in itself embryonically, what it felt and could not express, what it could do and yet knew not how to narrate."

Molière was able to choose themes to interest his contemporaries because he was himself a Frenchman, sympathizing with the sentiments of his time and governed by the same heredity as the spectators of his plays. He is himself the superb example of the truth of Nisard's assertion that "in France the man of genius is he who says what everybody knows; he is only the intelligent echo of the crowd; and if he does not wish to find us deaf and indifferent, he must not astonish us with his personal views — he must reveal us to ourselves." And as Molière is the type of the urban and urbane French dramatic poet, guided by the social instinct, ever dominant in France, so is Ibsen rather a rural type forever preaching individualism to the dwellers in the tiny seashore village where he spent his youth, and giving little thought to the inhabitants of the larger world where he had lived since his maturity. Although cosmopolitan audiences have appreciated Ibsen's power and skill, it was not for cosmopolitan audiences that he wrote his social dramas, but for the old folks at home in Norway, whom he wanted to awaken morally and mentally. And here, in his memory of the feelings and of the failings of the men and women among whom he grew to manhood, we can find the obvious explanation of that narrow parochialism which is sometimes revealed most unexpectedly in one or another of his plays.

II

A certain knowledge of the people to whom the playwright belonged, and for whom he wrote, is a condition precedent to any real understanding of his plays. And, on the other hand, a study of the drama of any period or of any place cannot fail to supply interesting information about the manners and customs, the modes of thought, and the states of feeling of the people of that country at that time. For example, the medieval drama seems to have had its earliest development in France, and perhaps for this reason one mystery is very like another mystery all over Europe, whether it is French or English, Italian or German; but one of the variations from this monotony is to be found in the scene between Joseph and Potiphar's wife, which the English redactors treated in outline only or omitted altogether, but which the French compilers elaborately amplified for the greater joy of their compatriots. To this day the French are willing to laugh loudly at the humorous side of conjugal infidelity, whereas, we who speak English are unwilling to take this other than seriously. Here we can see reason why many a skittish farce, which has amused thousands in Paris, has failed to please in New York and in London.

The lack of popular appreciation about which Terence often complained bitterly was due to his incompatibility with the only audiences which Rome then knew. He proportioned his intrigues and polished his dialogue when his spectators were accustomed to coarse buffoonery. Terence was born out of his time; and he might have been a really successful writer of comedies had he lived in the Italian Renascence, when he could hope for an audience of scholars swift to enjoy his delicate finish and his delightful felicity of phrase. As it was, Terence, refusing to gratify the tastes of the populace of his own time, had to confess failure. The more practical Lope de Vega accepted the audiences of his day for what they were, less vio-

lent than Terence's, but quite as robust and wilful as
Shakspere's; and the Spanish playwright made the
best of the situation, disclosing his marvelous inventiveness and his splendid productivity in countless
pieces of the widest variety. In his apologetic poem
on the "New Art of Making Plays," he pretended that
he composed these pieces against his own better knowledge of the so-called "rules of the drama," and that
before he sat down to write, he was careful to put Terence and Plautus out of the room; but he was probably too completely his own contemporary, too much
a man of his time and of his race, to have been forced
to any great sacrifices of his artistic code. In reality,
he seems to have felt no awkward restraint as a result
of his desire to please his public; and apparently he
was able to express himself freely and fully in his plays,
even if he also took care to have them conform to the
likings of the populace of Madrid. So Shakspere was
careful to have his plays conform to the likings of the
populace of London; and he also was able to use his
dramas for the amplest self-expression. Here we may
observe once more that the true artist unhesitatingly
accepts the conditions imposed on him, whatever they
may be, and that he is often able to turn the stumbling-
block in his path into a stepping-stone to higher things.

Even if a Greek dramatic poet could by his prophetic power have foreseen the potency of modern romantic love, he could never have dared a "Romeo and
Juliet," because the contemporary spectators would
have failed to understand the swift and sudden emotion which is its mainspring. And, on the other hand,
the Greek dramatic poets dealt with many a motive
with which the modern audience can have no sym-

pathy. For us the beautiful pathos of the "Alcestis" of Euripides is spoilt by the contemptible alacrity with which the husband allows his devoted wife to die for him, although his conduct did not seem at all reprehensible to the Greeks, who held so exalted an opinion of the value of the young male citizen to the state, that they saw no impropriety in his accepting his wife's lovely sacrifice of herself. The "Antigone" of Sophocles turns also on a Greek sentiment very remote from our modern feeling, a sentiment which has to be explained to us before we can grasp its significance or understand its importance to the noble heroine. And again, in the "Medea" of Euripides, the wrathful heroine's slaughter of her children to revenge herself for their father's abject desertion of her seems to us unendurably repugnant.

At the period when the Homeric poems were composed, there still survived among the Greeks a belief that the sacrifice of a virgin before a fleet set sail would bring favorable winds. At the period when the Attic tragedies were written, this superstition had probably passed away; but the memory of it lingered. The Athenian spectators who sat in the theater of Dionysus were well aware that their ancestors had held this belief; and therefore they were not unwilling to accept the legend of Iphigenia, when it was presented in a play by Euripides. But we moderns can have no sympathy with a superstition like this; and we do not easily understand how it could ever have been accepted. And as a result, Racine and others have wasted their efforts trying to interest us in a subject which is to us inconceivable, not to say, abhorrent.

Shakspere may not himself have had any belief

REMAINS OF THE THEATER OF DIONYSUS AT ATHENS

either in witches or in ghosts, but he knew that his contemporaries had no doubt about these weird creatures
and these spectral beings. And he had therefore no
hesitation in making effective use of them whenever
occasion served. No modern dramatist dealing with a
modern theme would dare to invoke the aid of a ghost
or of a witch, because the belief in them is no longer
a common possession of his contemporaries. Nowadays, we may be willing to accept stranger things, —
telepathy, for example, mental healing, and the like;
but we are not willing to believe that the slaying of a
maiden will have any influence upon the storms of the
sea, or that a sheeted ghost will walk the earth to bid
his son avenge his taking off or to fright his murderer
with his gory locks.

It would not be difficult to adduce examples of the
effect exerted on the dramatist, not by the lapse of time,
but by the change of country, by the divergence of
racial points of view even in the same period. For
instance, in Sudermann's strong drama, "Heimat,"
known to us by the name of the heroine Magda, the
unbending rigor of the aged father and his violent
harshness are almost repulsive to us in America, where
we are not accustomed to yield so blind a deference to
the head of the family as the old colonel insists upon
in Germany. But there is no need to multiply these
examples, since we all know the divergent attitudes of
different peoples toward the social organization. In
this divergence we can find the explanation why more
than one excellent play is little known outside the land
of its birth. The finest of French comedies of the
nineteenth century is the "Gendre de M. Poirier" of
Augier and Sandeau; and although it has been trans-

lated into English or adapted more than once, it has failed to interest our audiences, because it is fundamentally French both in theme and in treatment. Its appeal is fundamentally local; and the veracity of its interpretation of characters essentially French has prevented its acceptance in Great Britain and the United States. The more truthfully a dramatist reproduces the life about him, the more sincerely he presents the special types his countrymen will most surely appreciate, the more he subordinates plot and situation to the revelation of character, the less likely he is to see his plays successful outside of his own language. The ingenious complications of the inventive Scribe, in which the characters were only puppets in the hands of the playwright, were performed all over the world, while the rich and solid comedies of Augier have rarely been exported beyond the boundaries of France.

There are striking differences to be observed even between the playgoers of two countries speaking the same language and inheriting the same social opinions; such differences are discoverable sometimes between the audiences of London and the audiences of New York. For example, in Bronson Howard's "Banker's Daughter," the young artist to whom the heroine is engaged when the piece begins and whom she thinks she then loves, even when she marries another man to save her father, has to be eliminated in the course of the action, so that she may find herself absolutely free to give her true love to her devoted husband. Therefore, one act took place in Paris, and a noted French swordsman was introduced to force a quarrel on the young painter and to kill him in a duel. Although the duel is no longer possible in the United States, Ameri'

can audiences know that it still exists in France, and
we are familiar with the feud of the southwest and
with the street-shooting of the mining-camps. But
when Bronson Howard's play was adapted for London,
with its characters localized as British subjects, his
London collaborator protested against the duel, on the
ground that a British audience would not accept it.
If the young artist was to become an Englishman, then
he would laugh at the suggestion of crossing swords.
So the artist ceased to be, and in his stead there was a
young soldier; and the act in Paris took place at the
British embassy, where the officer had to appear in
uniform. There the French swordsman insulted him
and his uniform, and in his person the whole army of
the Queen, until the British spectators fairly longed
to see the Englishman knock the Frenchman down.
And when the stalwart young fellow was goaded at last
to this violence, the London audience could not thereafter object to his giving to the French swordsman
"the satisfaction of a gentleman."

This shows the difference between the two audiences
speaking the same language; and another illustration
will serve to show the difference that may exist between
two audiences in contrasting quarters of the same
American city. When Mr. Clyde Fitch's "Barbara
Frietchic" was produced at the Criterion Theater in
New York (where the best seats sold for two dollars),
the Southern heroine, in her quarrel with her Northern
lover, tore the stars-and-stripes into tatters, only to
sew the flag together later that she might be shot beneath its folds. But when this play was taken to the
Academy of Music (where the best seats sold for fifty
cents), the heroine was no longer allowed to destroy

the national flag, for fear that an act so unpatriotic would forever alienate from her the sympathy of the spectators in that popular playhouse. This anecdote is not well vouched for and it may not be a fact; but perhaps it is quite as significant even if it chances to be only an invention.

These may seem but trifles, after all; and no doubt they are. But they serve to make clear how dependent the dramatist is upon the unreflective sympathy of the spectator. This the practical playwrights of every epoch and of every clime have always felt. Sometimes they have been tempted to take advantage of it un-worthily by crude appeals to the prejudices of the play-goers they were seeking to please; sometimes they have even descended to overt claptrap. On occasion, they have not been ashamed to bring in the national flag to capture unthinking applause. Some of them have not hesitated to seize every opportunity to praise their own country and to contrast their own countrymen favor-ably with foreigners. In French plays, the British and the Americans are almost unfailing subjects for satire and for caricature; and, on the other hand, the French-man has been a butt in countless comedies in the English language.

Even the foremost of dramatic poets have now and again been glad to voice eloquently their own patriotic sentiments, certain that these would prove welcome to their audiences. Shakspere, for example, let slip no opportunity to praise England, precious stone set in the silver sea; and he was so subdued to what he worked in that he revealed no insight into the nobility of Jeanne d'Arc. Euripides, so Professor Mahaffy has pointed out, was prone to make his Athenian heroes paragons of perfection, while going out of his way to blacken the legendary heroes of rival cities like Sparta and Thebes. And in his "Medea," the same dramatic poet seized a very slim excuse to insert a superb choral ode to the glory of Athens.

III

These are merely more or less unfortunate illustrations of the inevitable dependence of the dramatist upon the spectators whose sympathy he must capture and whose interest he must awaken. A play must please the people for whom it is composed; and if, for any reason, it is unable to do this, then it has missed its mark. The final verdict has been rendered; and there is no hope of moving for a new trial. And it must please the whole people, the crowd at large, for the strength of the drama lies in the breadth of its appeal. It misses its purpose unless it has something for all, — for young and old, for rich and poor, for men and women, for the educated and for the uneducated. More than any other literary form, it has preserved the communal quality which characterizes all primitive poetry. Of all the arts, the drama is essentially the most democratic, for it cannot exist without the multitude. It has been called "a function of the crowd." It cannot hope for success when it seeks to attract only a caste, a coterie, a clique; it must be the art of the people as a whole, with all their divergencies of cultivation. And this it has been whenever it achieved its noblest triumphs, — in Greece, when Sophocles and Euripides followed Æschylus; in England, when Shakspere succeeded Marlowe; in Spain, when Lope de Vega and Calderon worked side by side; and in France, when Molière came as a connecting link between Corneille and Racine.

Any attempt to organize the drama on an aristocratic basis is foredoomed to failure; and every effort to make it independent of the average man has resulted in sterility. Just as it is unfortunate for dramatic literature that poets have sometimes been unwilling to master the form which was suited to the theater of their own times, and have let themselves lazily descend to the lower level of the so-called "closet-drama," so it would be unfortunate also if they had the privilege of composing their plays for a theater set apart from the plain people, appealing only to the dilettants, and independent of the takings of the door. It is good for every man, even if he is truly a poet, and especially if he is truly a poet, that he should go down into the arena and meet his fellow-men face to face. There is mischief in any attempt to found an endowed theater which shall not rely for the major part of its support upon the public as a whole.

This is an experiment which has been tried more than once, notably when Goethe had sole control of the court-theater at Weimar. He chose the plays; he trained the actors; he was the autocrat even of the audience, for when the students from Jena expressed their feelings, he rebuked them with an Olympian frown until they ceased coming. And the result was what might be expected. Of the plays which were prepared specially for the Weimar theater, only those written by that born dramatist, Schiller, have kept the stage. And Goethe himself, in his old age, seems to have seen the futility of his efforts, for he told Eckermann that "nothing is more dangerous to the well-being of a theater than when the director is so placed that a greater or less receipt at the treasury does not affect him personally." Probably Goethe would have admitted without hesitation that the theater is a function of the crowd. The drama is not for the selfish delight of the poet alone, who must never neglect his duty of revealing the people to themselves.

The Comédie - Française is not supported by the French government; it is only helped out by the gift of the theater itself rent-free and by a subsidy which makes possible a proper pension-fund and which frees the manager from any temptation to produce the coarser types of popular melodrama. It has to reckon with the people and it depends for its prosperity upon the sale of its seats. This is the case also with the court-theaters of Germany and with the subsidized opera-houses as well. Although these opera-houses and these theaters are aided by subsidies, either public or private, they are never rendered independent of the box-office. They have to rely for support on the whole body of play-goers and opera-lovers; and if they do not succeed in attracting these, then their bankruptcy is unavoidable. And this is as it should be, for no art is ever prosperous when it is aristocratic, since the basis of every art is our common humanity.

It is possible that those superfine spirits who culti-vate an aristocratic aloofness from their fellow-men may be tempted to assert that if the theater is a function of the crowd, then the drama must be of necessity the vulgarest of the arts, incapable of delicacy of analysis, of subtlety of expression, and of any higher poetic flight than can be appreciated by the common herd. But this assertion is based on a confusion be-

tween the residuum of the populace and the whole
body of the public, including the most intelligent and
the most cultivated. It is to the whole public that the
dramatist must appeal; and he mistakes his larger
opportunity if he prefers to attract only the residuum.
If the theater is to-day a function of the crowd, so it
always has been; and there is a patent absurdity in
suggesting that the necessity of pleasing the people as
a whole prevented Racine from delicacy of analysis,
Molière from richness of expression, and Shakspere
from exalted flights of poetic self-expression.

Even the vulgar residuum of the populace is often
warmly responsive to loftiness of theme and to largeness of treatment. "Hamlet" is ever one of the most
popular plays which can be presented on the English-
speaking stage; and "Tartuffe" is unfailingly attractive to French audiences. The intellectual aristocrat is
often tempted to underestimate the good sense of the
plain people as this is displayed in art and in politics.
President Butler, in his suggestive discussion of
"True and False Democracy," has warned us never
to forget "that the same individuals constitute both the
mob and the people. When their lower nature rules,
these individuals are a mob; when their higher nature
guides, they are the people. The demagogue makes
his appeal to the mob; the political leader, the states-
man, to the people." So in the theater, even though
the cheap playwright may prefer to put together pieces
good enough only for the mob, sometimes even pander-
ing to their baser instincts, the true dramatist never
fears the result of a lofty appeal to the people as a
whole. He knows, even if others forget, that the
poetic dramas which the literary critics now most

esteem, were widely successful when they were first produced in the theater. He would echo the opinion of Cicero, an artist in letters if ever there was one, that "given time and opportunity, the recognition of the many is as necessary a test of excellence in an artist as that of the few."

It is a significant fact that the real dramatist, tragic or comic, has never expressed that contempt for the mere multitude which sometimes falls from the mouth of the dilettant and of the amateur. He does not express this sentiment because he does not feel it; indeed, he could not feel it without self-betrayal. It is his duty to understand the multitude, to sympathize with it, to reveal it to itself. Molière was frank in his declaration of his reliance on the common sense of the plain people. "I hold it to be as difficult to attack a work which the public approves," so he declared in a preface, "as to defend one which it condemns." Success on the stage is probably impossible to a dramatist who really has a contempt for the crowd. Dryden, for example, was free in voicing his distaste for the comic drama of his own day, and he seems to have despised the contemporary playgoers he strove to please by labored attempts at fun. And Dryden is not one of the masters of English comedy; in fact, his fame might be fuller if he had never adventured himself into the comic drama. It is related that a distinguished contemporary novelist once remarked that whenever he wrote in a play any passage which made him tingle with shame, then he knew he had done something the theatrical public would like. But his knowledge of the theatrical public was apparently insufficient, since no one of the plays containing these passages has succeeded on the

stage. He might think the public foolish, but he failed
to appreciate its shrewdness. It may be foolish, in certain ways and to a certain extent; but it knows what it
likes, — and above all else, it likes sincerity.

IV

Probably the cause of this novelist's error can be
found in the fact that he was a novelist, and that he
believed that the drama was only another form of fiction, in which he could put the same things that he had
put into his novels. But a play is not a novel; and it
has to be something wholly unlike a novel. Its methods
are not the same, and its subject-matter is also differentiated from that proper enough in a narrative to be
read by the fireside. There are themes which the novelist can treat and from which the dramatist is de-
barred, because his work is to be set before men massed
together, and not before scattered individuals. But
what the dramatist may lose from the duty of taking
into account the spectators in the theater, he more
than regains by the greater impressiveness of the play,
by its more direct effect on those who see it, an effect
far more powerful than that of the novel, just as the
influence of the orator is deeper than that of the es-
sayist. The French government permitted the publi-
cation of "Oncle Sam" and of "Germinal," but it
forbade the performance of Sardou's play and the
dramatization of Zola's novel. There is no need of denying that the drama has its limitations, for so has
every other art; and effects possible to one art are not
possible to another. There is no need of denying even
that the novel has its own advantages over the play, just
as the play in its turn has its advantages over the novel.

Théophile Gautier, who disliked the stage, perhaps because he had to earn his living as a theatrical critic, used to disparage the drama as lagging far behind fiction in that it never dealt with a new idea until long after this had been exploited in newspapers and in prose-fiction. Perhaps he would have found it difficult to prove his assertion; but it would be easy to give a good reason why there might be some warrant for it. It is because the drama must appeal to the people as a whole, and not merely to the more intelligent, the more cultivated, the more advanced. Until an idea has sunk into the popular consciousness, until it has been absorbed by the main body of a playwright's contemporaries, he can put it into a play only at his peril. What Wordsworth said of the poets is true especially of the dramatic poets, — that they write under the restriction of hoping to give "immediate pleasure to a human being, possessed of that information which may be expected from him, not as a lawyer, a physician, a mariner, an astronomer, or a natural philosopher, but as a Man." In other words, the dramatist has ever to find the greatest common denominator of the public as a whole, whereas the lyric poets and the novelists can, if they choose, narrow their appeal to a single caste or a single class. Here we can perceive the justice of the general feeling that partisan politics and sectarian religion are, both of them, totally out of place on the stage.

The theater is a function of the crowd; and the work of the dramatist is conditioned by the audience to which he meant to present it. In the main, this influence is wholesome, for it tends to bring about a dealing with themes of universal interest. To some extent, it may be limiting and even harmful, — but to what extent we cannot yet determine in our present ignorance of that psychology of the crowd which Le Bon has analyzed so interestingly. We are only beginning to appreciate the fact that a group of men and women gathered together has a psychic unity of its own, a consciousness of itself as an entity, a soul which is not merely the sum total of the souls of the men and women present. No one has asserted this more sharply than Professor Hibben. He declared that a patent fallacy underlies the saying that "the whole equals the sum of the parts." Although the saying may be sound in mathematics it is false in sociology : —

"In any group of men, in a clan, a tribe, a society, in church or in state, the whole is more than the sum of its parts. The parts may be seen, they may be counted. We find them in registers, in rosters, in tables of census statistics, and yet the communal spirit which makes for unity and solidarity is unseen. It is the *esprit de corps*, without which the body dies and returns to its elemental parts. And, within the still larger range which embraces the circle of mankind in general, the several parts are bound together as members one of another, because they are united in a common ancestry and a common destiny, a common weal or woe. The spirit of humanity makes all one."

Thus it is that, in the playhouse, every successive audience has an individuality of its own, differing collectively from other audiences, seeing the same performance in the same theater in the same week. An afternoon audience, composed mostly of women, will take the points of a play in quite different fashion from an evening audience, in which there is a larger proportion of men. Humorous speeches and effects which bring hearty laughs at night will sometimes scarcely evoke even a condescending smile in the after-noon.

An audience is a crowd, and it has the special char-acteristics of any other crowd, of the spectators at athletic sports, of the participants in a camp-meeting, of the delegates to a political convention. And it has also certain characteristics peculiar to itself, to the fact that it is gathered in a theater, that it is composed of a group of playgoers. Every crowd consists of hu-man beings who, when they are a part of the crowd, and in consequence of that fact, have each of them lost consciousness of certain of his individual mental char-acteristics. On the other hand, every one of them has acquired a keener consciousness of certain mental and emotional qualities which he has in common with the other members of the audience. M. Le Bon's doc-trine has been neatly condensed into this series of statements : —

"The mental qualities in which men differ from one an-other are the acquired qualities of intellect and character; but the qualities in which they are at one are the innate basic passions of the race. A crowd, therefore, is less intellectual and more emotional than the individuals that compose it. It is less reasonable, less judicious, less disinterested, more credulous, more primitive, more partisan; and, hence, a man, by the mere fact that he forms a part of an organized crowd, descends several rungs on the ladder of civilization. Even the most cultured and intellectual of men, when he forms an atom of a crowd, loses consciousness of his acquired mental qualities and harks back to his primal nakedness of mind. The dramatist, therefore, because he writes for a crowd, writes for an uncivilized and uncultivated mind, a mind richly human, vehement in approbation, violent in disapproval, easily credulous, eagerly enthusiastic, boyishly heroic, and carelessly thinking."

And Mr. Clayton Hamilton, from whom this extract is quoted, added that

"both in its sentiments and in its opinions, the crowd is hugely commonplace. It is incapable of original thought and of any but inherited emotion. It has no speculation in its eyes. What it feels was felt before the flood; and what it thinks, its fathers thought before it. The most effective moments in the theater are those that appeal to commonplace emotions — love of woman, love of home, love of country, love of right, anger, jealousy, revenge, ambition, lust, and treachery."

This is what underlies Victor Hugo's assertion in the preface of his "Ruy Blas," that there are three classes which go to the theater, — the "main body of spectators who demand action, women, who desire emotion, and thinkers who look for character." In other words, story, plot, incident, is of primary importance in a play, since this is what is most pleasing to the largest number; and delicacy of character-delineation and veracity of psychology are only secondary. This truth was seized long ago by Aristotle; and it was as imperative in Athens then as it is now in Paris and in New York. It seems to explain the boast of the elder Dumas that all he required for success on the stage was "four boards, two actors and a passion."

The audience in a theater is first of all a crowd, with the characteristics it has in common with all crowds. But it is also a crowd of a special type, in that it has come together with the desire of recreation, of amusement, of pleasure. Its purpose is not serious, like the purpose of the camp-meeting or of the political convention. It is inclined to resent instruction or edification, since it feels that the theater is not the fit place for either of these useful things. This is one reason why the chief dramatists have rarely attempted to preach or to assume the attitude of the instructor; they have been satisfied to present life as they saw it with their own eyes, to mirror one or another aspect of the infinite complexity of human existence, leaving the spectator free to draw his own moral from the picture.

This is the reason also why no great dramatic poet has ever been a pioneer in philosophic speculation. It has been the strength of the great dramatists that they were not too far in advance of their time, that they held most of the opinions of their contemporaries, contenting themselves with restating the eternal commonplaces of life in imperishable phrase for immediate effect on their contemporaries. And thus in not striving strenuously to be up-to-date, they have largely escaped the peril of being out-of-date. "Dramatic art," so Professor Letourneau has asserted, "being an essentially collective sort of literature, addressing itself to the multitude, can not express more than the average of the prevailing opinions, of the ideas current in the surrounding social medium; too original views, too special feelings, are not in its domain."

V

As a result, we can see that any people is likely to have, at any period, the drama that it deserves, since it can have only the kind of play that it is willing to accept. In the golden days of Athens, the Greeks had tragedy of the noblest type; and in the decadence of Rome, the drama was degraded to vulgar and violent pantomime, which had to compete for popular favor with the brutal sports of the arena. And even a spectator to whom these were abhorrent had to yield to the infection that emanated from his fellows, massed all around him in the amphitheater. Saint Augustine tells us of an acquaintance of his who had renounced gladiatorial shows, but who yielded to the solicitation of friends. For a while he sat with closed eyes, refusing to witness the deadly combats, but when he relaxed his guard over himself and opened his eyes, he was soon caught by the contagion, and he swiftly found his soul filled with sanguinary joy.

In the Colosseum, the crowd had the baser instincts of the mob; and even to-day, in places of amusement of the lower sort, we can discover not a little of a similar brutality. Yet these are exceptions. In the theater nowadays, the crowd is not to be confounded with the mob; it is representative of the average of the community and not of the inferior elements only. It is representative of the main body of men and women; and at bottom, the instinct of the main body is to be relied on. Burke, who is not to be suspected of undue partiality to democratic ideals, did not hesitate to assert that "man is a most unwise and a most wise being. The individual is foolish. The multitude for the moment is foolish, when they act without deliberation; but the species is wise, and when time is given to it, as a species it almost always acts right."

It is to the species that the dramatist addresses himself; and the history of the drama affords abundant evidence not only that the species acts right, but also that its judgment is sound. The great dramatists whose works we study reverently to-day were the most popular playwrights in their own times. The plays of Sophocles and Shakspere, of Calderon and of Molière, filled the theaters when they were first produced. The spectator of these masterpieces may not have suspected that they were masterpieces; he may not have appreciated the rare qualities in them which the student discovers now; but they gave him the specific pleasure he was seeking in the theater, and he was ready to return there again and again when they were acted.

We may go further and assert that this broad popular acceptance is far more significant of abiding merit than the laudation of any minority of professed critics. Whenever there has been a divergence of opinion about a play between the classes and the masses, time has generally proved that the masses were wiser than the classes. When Shakspere was a young man, Sidney published his "Defence of Poesy," in which he poured scorn upon the plays that then held the English stage; he besought poets to take pattern by the drama of Greece and of Rome. But the playgoing public of London would not accept sterile imitations of this sort; and it gave a warm welcome to the large and free dramas Shakspere wrote in accord with the bolder sentiment of the Elizabethan age. In France, again, the French Academy, at Richelieu's request, condemned the "Cid" of Corneille for its violation of the so-called "rules of the drama." But the playgoing public at Paris knew what it wanted, and in despite of the academicians, it flocked to the theater whenever the "Cid" was performed. The true dramatic poet puts into his plays many things which the public as a whole may not appreciate; but it is always for the public as a whole that he writes his plays.

CHAPTER V

THE LAW OF THE DRAMA

It is sometimes supposed that the drama consists of incident. It consists of passion, which gives the actor his opportunity; and that passion must progressively increase, or the actor, as the piece proceeded, would be unable to carry the audience from a lower to a higher pitch of interest and emotion. A good serious play must therefore be founded on one of the passionate *cruces* of life, where duty and inclination come nobly to the grapple. — ROBERT LOUIS STEVENSON, *Memories and Portraits.*

I

THE literary drama has grown out of the folk-drama; and it is composed to be performed by actors, in a theater, and before an audience. But what is its essential quality? In what vital way does the drama differ from the epic of old or from the novel of our own day? What are its necessary characteristics? What specific quality is it that sets the drama apart from all other literary forms? To attempt to define this differentiation by saying that the drama has to tell a story by means of dialogue is inadequate, since dialogue is often used for story-telling in poetry and in prose-fiction, in the idyls of Theocritus, for example, and in the social satires of the French lady who has chosen to call herself Gyp. We approach nearer to a satisfactory definition when we say that a drama is a story in dialogue shown in action before an audience. Its essential quality is due partly to the fact that it is to be performed by actors in a theater, but mainly to the fact that it is intended for the public as a whole and not for the separate constituent elements of the public. Its specific characteristic is the result of its appeal to the throng and not to the individual. Its appeal is to the mass, and to the communal desires of the main body. What does the mass wish to see when it comes together to behold a story in dialogue shown in action by performers on the stage? What does the crowd demand, under these circumstances, which the individuals taken severally would not insist upon?

It is the late Ferdinand Brunetière who has most clearly declared the distinctive element of the drama. To the volume of the "Annales du Théâtre" for 1893, the French critic contributed a preface, which he called the "Law of the Drama." In this essay, he formulated more elaborately a theory which he had already summarily suggested and casually applied in the series of lectures on the "Epoques du Théâtre Français (1636–1850)," delivered at the Odéon Theater in the winter of 1891–2. This theory had there emerged into view in his opening lecture on Corneille's "Cid"; and it had been a little more fully stated in his final lecture on Scribe and Musset. As Brunetière pursued his task, the importance and the utility of this theory seem to have impressed him more and more; he considered it anew, and in its remoter implications, before setting it forth by itself in his contribution to the "Annales du Théâtre" for 1893.

In this prefatory essay, he began by pointing out that the so-called "rules of the drama" are evidently invalid. By the rules of the drama, he meant the code of restrictions which were held to give correctness to comedy and especially to tragedy. This legislation was the

result of the amplification (by La Harpe and Népomucène Lemercier) of principles laid down by Boileau and
d'Aubignac, and derived directly from the Italian the-
orists of the Renascence, Castelvetro and Robortello.
The decisions of these critics have been overruled by
the authority of the great modern dramatists who have
unhesitatingly violated these alleged rules.

Yet since the drama differs fundamentally from
the epic and from prose-fiction, it must have some
essential principle of its own. If this essential principle can be discovered, then we shall be in possession
of the sole law of the drama, the one obligation which
all writers for the stage must accept. Now, if we
examine a collection of typical plays of every kind,
tragedies and melodramas, comedies and farces, we
shall find that the starting point of every one of them
is the same. Some one central character *wants* something; and this exercise of volition is the mainspring
of the action. In Corneille's "Cid," Chimène wishes
to avenge her father. In Molière's "School for Wives,"
Arnolphe wishes to marry Agnès, whose ignorance
seems to him a guarantee of fidelity. Even in a farce
of Labiche's, the hero wishes to get out of the awkward
complications in which he is involved. But Labiche's
hero is opposed in his desires by the fear of reprisals;
Molière's elderly hero is unable to achieve his desire,
because love for Horace awakens the unbending resolution of Agnès; and Corneille's heroine is thwarted
in the attaining of her desire by the opposition of a
stronger will than her own. In every successful play,
modern or ancient, we shall find this clash of contending desires, this assertion of the human will against
strenuous opposition of one kind or another.

Here, then, we have what Brunetière declared to be the law of the drama. He made it plain that the drama must reveal the human will in action; and that the central figure in a play must know what he wants and must strive for it with incessant determination. This is what differentiates the drama from the novel, "Figaro," for instance, from "Gil Blas." The hero of Beaumarchais has a will of his own and fights for his own hand; he knows what he wants and he knows why he wants it. The hero of Le Sage drifts through life along the line of least resistance; he has no plans of his own and he takes what chances to come his way. Figaro acts; Gil Blas is acted upon. The play of Beaumarchais may be made into an acceptable novel; but the novel of Le Sage cannot be made into an acceptable play. A novel may be dramatized successfully only when it is inherently dramatic, — that is to say, only when its central figure is master of his fate and captain of his soul. Action in the drama is thus seen to be not mere movement or external agitation; it is the expression of a will which knows itself.

The French critic maintained also that, when this law of the drama was once firmly grasped, it helped to differentiate more precisely the several dramatic species. If the obstacles against which the will of the hero has to contend are insurmountable, Fate or Providence or the laws of nature, — then there is tragedy, and the end of the struggle is likely to be death, since the hero is defeated in advance. But if these obstacles are not absolutely insurmountable, being only social conventions and human prejudices, then the hero has a possible chance to attain his desire, — and in this case, we have the serious drama without an inevitably fatal

ending. Change this obstacle a little, equalize the
conditions of the struggle, set two human wills in opposition, — and we have comedy. And if the obstacle
is of a still lower order, merely an absurdity of custom,
for instance, we find ourselves in farce. Of course,
these several dramatic species rarely exist in complete
purity of type; comedy often declines into farce, for
example, and farce not infrequently elevates itself
toward comedy.

Brunetière found a confirmation of his theory in the
fact that the drama has most amply flourished when
the national will has stiffened itself for a magnificent
effort. Greek tragedy is contemporary with Salamis;
and the Spanish drama is contemporary with the conquest of the New World. Shakspere was a man when
the Armada was repulsed; Corneille and Molière were
made possible by the work of Henry IV and Richelieu; Lessing and Goethe and Schiller came after Frederick. And the Orientals have no vital drama because
they are fatalists, because they do not believe in that
free will without which the drama cannot exist. It
is significant that men of action, Richelieu, Condé,
Frederick, Napoleon, have ever been fond of the
theater. A belief in free will is always favorable to the
drama, whereas a belief in foreordination may be not
unfavorable to the novel, the chief figures of which are
not required always to know their own minds.

Here Brunetière rested his case. He concluded by
calling attention to the difference between the so-called
rules of the drama — which are always narrow, always
rigid, and always certain to be broken sooner or later
because of this narrow rigidity — and this one single
law of the theater, as he stated it, large, supple, flexible

in its application, simple in itself and yet general, rich in
its consequences and ever ready to enrich itself still
further by all the confirmations which experience and
reflection may supply.

II

It is not too much to say that this statement of the
law of the drama is the most suggestive and the most
important contribution to the theory of the theater
which has been made for many years. It is as significant as any of Lessing's contributions to the theory
of art. The more clearly it is perceived, the more illuminating it will be found. Brunetière has here given
us the key to many an obscurity. He has provided us
with an instrument for gaging the true dramatic value
of a play. He has put into our hands the means whereby we can explain difficulties otherwise very puzzling.
For instance, he has enabled us to see why it is that
the medieval mysteries, and also the English chronicle-plays (which more or less follow the medieval
model) are not so interesting as the tragedies in which
we find the hero "at war with the words of fate."
To the central figure of the chronicle-play things
merely happen, and while we may be interested now
and again in the separate episodes, our attention is
only languidly held by the story as a whole; whereas the
central figure of any one of the tragedies stands forth
the embodiment of will, knowing what he wants and
bending all his powers to the accomplishment of his
purpose. This law of the drama explains also why
novels, full of bustle and abounding in variety of incident, have often failed to attract the public when
they were dramatized.

If any cavil must be made, it is that Brunetière took upon himself to lay down the law somewhat arbitrarily. Perhaps it might have been better to say that a consideration of all the masterpieces of the drama, and of all the plays of less value which have now and again achieved a fleeting success on the stage, discloses the fact that the attention of an audience in a theater can be aroused and retained only by an exhibition of the human will. As individuals, we can find pleasure in reading about the misadventures of characters with no minds of their own; but when we are massed together as spectators in the playhouse, these nerveless creatures no longer satisfy us, and we demand men of a sterner sort, with iron in the blood to struggle valiantly for the desire of their hearts. The career of a character to whom things merely happen seems to us insufficiently interesting when it is represented in action on the stage before us collectively, although we may severally follow such a career more or less eagerly when we read about it in the study. Now and again, of course, a piece may delight some few of us solely by its subtle revelations of character or by its ironic picture of life; but the plays which have pleased long and pleased many have always an essential struggle to serve as a backbone. In other words, what Brunetière promulgated as a hard and fast decree may be set forth, if we prefer another statement, as a logical deduction from the accumulated experience of mankind.

While the credit for declaring this law thus clearly, and of applying it so as to bring out the special quality of the drama, and to make plain the fundamental difference between a play and a novel, is undoubtedly due to Brunetière, he had not a few predecessors who

had caught sight of the theory which he was to iso-
late sharply. It is impossible that so pregnant a truth
about one of the foremost of the arts should not have
been perceived by earlier critics. Voltaire, for example, in one of his letters, asserted that every scene in
a play should represent a combat; and Stevenson declared that "a good serious play must be founded on
one of the passionate *cruces* of life, where duty and
inclination come nobly to the grapple." This coin-
cides with Schlegel's assertion that tragedy deals
with the moral freedom of man, which can be displayed only "in a conflict with his sensuous impulses."
So Coleridge emphasized the fact that accidents ought
not to be introduced into tragedy, since " in the tragic
the free will of man is the first cause." And in "William Meister," Goethe had gone so far as to say that,
while the hero of a novel might be passive, the hero
of a play must be active, since "all events oppose
him, and he either clears and removes every obstacle
out of his path, or else becomes their victim."

Goethe's opinion reappears more elaborately stated
in Hegel, who treated tragedy at length and with his
customary subtlety. In setting forth compactly Hegel's
opinions, Professor Bradley noted that "in all tragedy
there is some sort of collision or conflict — conflict
of feelings, modes of thought, desires, wills, purposes;
conflict of persons with one another, or with circumstances or with themselves." Then the British critic
brought out the German philosopher's insistence on
the essential point that "pity for mere misfortune, like
fear of it, is not tragic pity or fear, since these are due
to the spectacle of the conflict and its attendant suffer-
ing, which do not appeal simply to our sensibilities or

our instinct of self-preservation, but also to our deeper mind or spirit." This truly tragic conflict appeals to our spirit because it is of the spirit, being a conflict "between powers that rule man's spiritual life and have the right to rule it. They are the substance of humanity, and especially of man's ethical nature. The family and the state, the bond of parent and child, of brother and sister, of husband and wife, of citizen and ruler, or citizen and citizen, with the obligations and feelings appropriate to these bonds; and again the powers of personal love and honor, or of devotion to a great cause or an ideal interest like religion or science, or some kind of social welfare — such are the forces exhibited in tragic action." And as these are all acknowledged to be " powers rightfully claiming human obedience, their exhibition in tragedy has that interest, at once deep and universal, which is essential to a great work of art."

III

But is Brunetière's law of the drama really contained in Hegel's theory of tragedy? After all, Hegel is dealing with tragedy only and not with the whole range of the drama; and he is but giving his own analysis of the old theory of the tragic conflict. Brunetière went much further; he declared a principle by which the drama as a whole is differentiated absolutely from the epic and prose-fiction. His law governs comedy and farce as well as tragedy. Furthermore, even in considering tragedy, Brunetière laid stress not so much on the circumstances of the conflict, of the struggle in which the hero is involved, as on the stark assertion of the hero's will. He made plain the fact that the truly dramatic element does not lie in the mere clash of contending forces, but rather in the volition of the hero himself, in the firm resolution which steels a man for the struggle. This is a most significant simplification of the older idea; and it is most helpful.

In this simplification, Brunetière has gone behind Hegel; indeed it may be said that he has gone back to Aristotle. The "master of all that know" was ever the ardent champion of free will against determinism; and perhaps this sympathetic advocacy of a principle which is the fundamental characteristic of the drama is added evidence that Aristotle was not only the first but also the foremost of dramatic critics. He held Sophocles to be the mightiest of the three great Greek dramatic poets; and one reason for this preference is probably his keen appreciation of the dramaturgic dexterity of the author of "Œdipus," the faculty of construction, the sheer playmaking skill revealed again and again; but another reason might be found in the fact that Sophocles never allowed his hero to be a mere plaything in the hands of fate, and always so contrived his story that the impending curse did not become operative except by the volition of the individual.

Aristotle anticipated Coleridge in ruling out accidents and in declaring that poetry rebels against the rule of chance. And he emphasized the necessity of plot, that is, of a story guided by the human will. "Without action there cannot be a tragedy," he asserted; "there may be without character." As Professor Butcher has explained, "the drama not only implies emotion expressing itself in a complete and significant action and tending toward a certain end, it also im-

plies a conflict." The British scholar has also suggested that "we may even modify Aristotle's phrase
and say that the dramatic conflict, not the mere plot,
is 'the soul of tragedy.'" And we may in turn modify
Professor Butcher's phrase and say that the soul of the
drama is not in the dramatic conflict so much as in the
naked assertion of the human will which is the cause
of the conflict.

That these modifications are necessary is evidence
that Brunetière's law of the drama is not explicit in
Aristotle's treatise, any more than in Hegel's, although
it may be a development of their kindred theories
which they would both of them accept. It was Brunetière who shifted the emphasis from the more or less
external conflict to the internal act of volition which
determines the struggle. It was the French critic who
first made it unmistakably plain that the drama depends on man's free will. He supported his doctrine
by examples drawn mainly from the French drama;
but other illustrations as striking can be found in
other literatures.

The development of English tragedy, for example,
out of the lax chronicle-play, which was only a straggling panorama of the events of a reign, was due largely
to the influence exerted by Seneca's tragedies, poor
enough as plays, but vigorous in the stoical assertion
of man's power over himself and of his right to control his own destiny. This development of English
tragedy may even have been helped a little by the remoter influence of Machiavelli, traces of which are
abundant throughout Elizabethan literature. The so-
called Machiavellian villains of the tragedy-of-blood
may reveal a total misconception of the acute Italian's

principles; and yet none the less the sharpening of
the dramatic conflict may have been helped at least a
little by Machiavelli's reiterated emphasis on the duty
of the strong man to work his will as best he can, deciding all doubtful points in his own interest.

The chief advantage of Brunetière's law is that it
enables us to set off the true dramatic conflict from
the grosser forms of combat. The drama cannot exist
without the theater; and the theater is only a little
differentiated from the amphitheater. The stage is
first cousin to the arena; and Professor Groos was on
safe ground when he asserted that " the pleasure afforded by the drama has one very essential feature in
common with ring-contests, animal fights, races, etc.,
— namely, that of observing a struggle in which we
may inwardly participate." That is to say, we want to
take sides; we long to see one or the other of the two
parties gain the victory; we have a communal instinct
to sympathize with some one strong, central character
battling against odds, with whom for the moment we
may even identify ourselves more or less.

In the ancient arena, the gladiators fought to the
death; and with so poignant a presentation of the dramatic conflict as this no Roman playwright could hope
to compete. In the modern circus, the bloodless effort
to overcome difficulty has often an element of lurking
danger which supplies an added piquancy. Even at
its loftiest elevation, the drama cannot help having an
obvious kinship with the " show-business"; and as we
climb steadily from the cruel and deadly sports of the
Colosseum, past the startling exploits of the circus, up
to the sumptuous spectacle of the ballet, and then, at
last, aloft to the subtlety of comedy and the serenity

of tragedy, we find the several steps of our ascent so close together we cannot tell exactly where it is that the true drama actually emerges into view. Here Brunetière's law may serve as a test, in that it shifts the emphasis from the outer struggle to the inner stiffening of the human will, which controls the combat.

Even in the cheaper kinds of melodrama, when we behold the rivalry of a villain absolutely villainous with a hero entirely heroic, apparently only a bald antithesis of black and white, both the villain and the hero want the same thing, — usually this is the possession of the heroine; and there is therefore a tense conflict of contending determinations. In plays of a higher class, especially in the social drama, dealing with themes of contemporary importance, with the burning questions of modern life, the opposition is not between a bad man and a good man; it is between two opinions, between two men each of whom believes that he is in the right, — each of whom, in fact, is in the right from his own point of view. And the true dramatist does not take sides; he holds an impartial attitude, letting both his characters express themselves honestly. Perhaps there is no better example of this than the "Gendre de M. Poirier" of Augier and Sandeau; and probably the spectators of this comedy sympathize some of them with Poirier and some with his son-in-law.

It may not be easy always for the spectator to declare exactly what the struggle is, but he can always recognize the desire of the central figure. In "Hamlet," for instance, externally the struggle may seem to be between Hamlet and Claudius, or between Ham-

let and his own weakness of will, or between Hamlet
and an overmastering fatality which broods over him
from the beginning. But there is no doubt about the
desire of Hamlet himself; he wants to do what is
right, even if he is ever in doubt as to what he ought
to do and even if he finds it hard to make up his mind.
And in "As You Like It," the strife between Orlando
and his brother, between Rosalind and her uncle, —
these are only necessary elements of the mechanism
of the story. Orlando knows what he wants; he wants
Rosalind; and Rosalind wants him to want her.

IV

When we have once accepted and assimilated
Brunetière's law of the drama, we can utilize it to interpret a principle laid down by Sarcey. That very
practical critic, who passed all his evenings in the
theater and who deduced all his theories from observation of the effect of the acted drama upon audiences,
declared that in every story which is fit to be set on the
stage, there are certain episodes or interviews which
must be shown in action and which cannot be narrated
by the characters. He called these the "scenes that
must be treated," the *scènes à faire*. If any one of
these essential scenes is shirked by the playwright, if
he describes it in his dialogue, instead of letting the
spectators see it for themselves, then the audience will
be disappointed and their interest will flag.

The spectators may not be able to declare the reason for their dissatisfaction; but they will be vaguely
aware that they have been deprived of something to
which they were entitled. They feel that they have
been defrauded of their just expectations, if they are

not made eye-witnesses of a vital incident which the inexpert dramatist has chosen to bring about behind closed doors or during one of the intermissions between the acts. Sarcey insisted that here was a certain test of the born playwrights, of the artists who have an instinctive mastery of the theater, that they have always an unerring intuition as to the meetings which the spectators will expect to see.

Now, what are the essential scenes without which a play will fail to impress the audience? What are these scenes which must be shown in action? Obviously, they are the scenes in which we can see the struggle of contending wills. They are the episodes wherein the dramatic conflict enters on its acutest stage, the interviews wherein there is the actual collision of the several resolves, the clash of volition against volition. They are those wherein "passion must appear upon the scene and utter its last word," — to borrow Stevenson's apt phrase. Thus we see that Sarcey's theory links itself logically with Brunetière's. The essential characteristic of the drama is that it deals with the human will; and a play therefore loses interest for the audience when the playwright fails to let us see for ourselves the acute crisis of this clash of contending determinations.

Brunetière and Sarcey derived their theories from observation of the practice of the great dramatists; and there is no difficulty in adducing illustrations from the masterpieces of the drama in support of these theories. All the great dramatists, ancient and modern, have done instinctively what Brunetière and Sarcey declared to be necessary. In the "Agamemnon," for example, Æschylus lets the murder of his chief character take place out of sight, for that is only the inevitable consequence of the meeting of Agamemnon and Clytemnestra which he sets before us. In "Macbeth," Shakspere shows us the guilty determination of Macbeth and Lady Macbeth just before the murder of Duncan, which is itself all the more impressive because it is not shown. In "Othello," we are made witnesses of the working of the poison of jealousy in Othello, as this is distilled by Iago.

In "Tartuffe," Molière puts before us the attempt which the sanctimonious rogue makes upon the virtue of Elmire; just as Sheridan sets on the stage the assault of Joseph upon Lady Teazle. In the "Doll's House," Ibsen lets us hear all that Nora has to say after she has discovered the depths of her husband's pettiness. The expert playwright of every age has been aware that spectators are interested only in what they can see for themselves and that they remain but tepidly attentive to what is told them. It is the special privilege of the theater that it can make a visible appeal, with all the impressiveness of the thing actually seen and not merely narrated. And it is only at his peril that the playwright fails to profit by this privilege.

The validity of the principles laid down by Brunctière and by Sarcey we can all of us test for ourselves when we analyze the impression made upon us in the theater. If we have found ourselves languid and bored, we have only to analyze the conduct of the story to discover the cause of our dumb dissatisfaction and to assure ourselves that the playwright failed to present before us the essential scenes of the essential struggle. On the other hand, when a play, tragedy or comedy, melodrama or farce, has held our attention, a little analysis will reveal to us that this is because the dramatist has made us spectators of the scenes that must be treated to bring out the full value of the clash of contending volitions.

CHAPTER VI

A CHAPTER OF DEFINITIONS

A country may be overrun by an armed force, but it is only conquered by the establishment of fortresses. Words are the fortresses of thought. They enable us to realize our dominion over what we have already overrun in thought; to make every intellectual conquest the basis of operations for others still beyond. — SIR WILLIAM HAMILTON, *Lectures in Metaphysics and Logic.*

I

IN the mechanic arts, and in the market-place, the need of new words is met by the swift selection of the term nearest at hand, ill-chosen it may be, but filling an immediate want and thereby at once justifying its use. For example, in the art of electricity, their convenience forced promptly into circulation such a misbegotten word as "cablegram" and such a startling combination as "separately excited boosters." But in the library and in the lecture room, higher standards obtain, and the rough-and-ready methods of the machine shop are unacceptable. As a result of our squeamishness in the manufacture of the new terms needed, and in consequence also of the difficulty in winning general acceptance for those which we do venture to make, the vocabulary of criticism lacks many a word which it ought to have. For instance, there is no satisfactory way of distinguishing the true short-story from the casual narrative which happens to be brief, although it might have been long. And there is no single word for that most precious gift to humanity

known as the sense-of-humor, the negative quality
which prevents a man from taking himself too seriously, and which is often lacking even in those who
possess abundantly the positive quality known as
humor.

In the liberal arts, wherein emotion dominates and
individuality is all-important, we cannot hope for the
exact vocabulary of the sciences, wherein fact rules
and the personal equation is cautiously eliminated.
Horse-power, foot-tons, kilowatts, — these are all terms
of precision absolutely independent of the user's own
feelings, whereas *tragedy, romance, imagination* are all
words which may call up different ideas in the mind
of every individual writer and reader. A writer cannot make sure that any reader will take any one of
the words in the same sense that he himself employs
it. Professor Gummere, tracing the history of the
popular ballad, had to devote many of his early pages
to the definition of the type itself, pointing out clearly
just what he holds it to be. Probably he would be the
first to admit that he has no right to impose all the
elements of his definition upon every other historian
of literature who shall hereafter consider the subject;
and certainly the other historians would be emphatic
in denying his claim if he had insisted on it. In like
manner, we find the opening chapter of Professor
Thorndike's illuminating history of English tragedy
occupied by the author's effort to arrive at a definition of the type, as it arose in Greece and as it has
developed in Great Britain.

There is an advantage in insisting upon resolute
definitions. Even if scientific precision is not to be
hoped for, every writer gains by the sturdy struggle to

make sure that at least he knows exactly what he himself intends by the words he employs. He cannot be certain that the majority of his readers will always take these words in his sense; but if he can impose his definition upon only a few, others will follow in due season, until the terminology of the art is made more precise. We all recognize now the value of Coleridge's distinction between imagination and fancy. We can all appreciate the distinction between true romance, perennial and eternal, and the neo-romanticism which was aping it a century ago. We are most of us ready now to admit that the short-story is a type by itself, differing from the novel, as the lyric differs from the epic, not in its brevity only, but also in its object. We have been led to a clearer understanding of the development of the Elizabethan drama by the devoted labors of the scholars who have revealed to us the existence of the special types which they have called the chronicle-play and the tragedy-of-blood. These names for groups of plays, hitherto lost in the immense mass of our older drama, are not merely convenient, they are positively helpful to every student of the stage.

When we set out to investigate the slow evolution of the drama in our language, we are entitled to feel that we have taken a long step in advance as soon as we have attained to a knowledge of the special characteristics of the mystery, the morality, the chronicle-play, the tragedy-of-blood, tragi-comedy, the comedy-of-humors, the heroic-play, the ballad-opera, sentimental-comedy, the closet-drama, and the problem-play. We have gone still further forward when we have learned how tragedy was developed out of the tragedy-of-blood, as the tragedy-of-blood had been developed out of the

chronicle-play. And in like manner, any one under-
taking a study of the history of fiction cannot fail to
find profit in the history of the rise and fall of the
pastoral-romance, the romance-of-chivalry, the picaresque-romance, the oriental-tale, the short-story, the
detective-story, the sea-tale, and the novel-with-a-pur-
pose.

These names may mean little or nothing to the several authors, each bent on expressing his vision of life
as best he could; nor need they be pressed unduly on
the attention of ordinary readers, content to enjoy
without question. Every student can find his profit
in keeping them in mind; but he must remember always that we have no right to assume that the author
ever gave a thought to the specific name the historians
of literature might one day bestow on his masterpiece.
Often he would have been puzzled himself to declare
the literary type to which it properly belonged. Rare
indeed is the writer who has set himself down deliberately to compose a chronicle-play or a tragedy-of-
blood which should be only and strictly a chronicle-play
or a tragedy-of-blood. These questions of terminology
are for critics only. The creators are careless in the
matter; they are seeking to express themselves in one
of the forms popular at the moment, never hesitating
to stretch this form till it cracks, or to contaminate it
with some other type.

If any one had told Molière that his two masterpieces, the " Misanthrope" and " Tartuffe," stepped out
of the domain of pure comedy and crossed over into that
of tragedy, it is probable that this revelation would
have worried him very little; and Shakspere made fun
of the mania for classification when he had the pedantic

Polonius present to Hamlet a company of actors the best in the world for " tragedy, comedy, history, pastoral, pastoral-comical, historical-pastoral, tragical-historical, tragical-comical-historical-pastoral, scene undividable or poem unlimited." And in Professor Baker's "Development of Shakspere as a Dramatist," he makes the point that the tragedies of the English dramatist may have seemed to the public of their own day "not tragedies at all but merely more masterly specimens of dramatic story-telling than the things that had preceded them." The Elizabethan audience, accustomed to the loosely knit chronicle-plays, found the tragedies more interesting without ever stopping to think that they were different in kind as well as in degree. To Shakspere, it is possible that "Macbeth" may have been only a chronicle-play more effectively constructed.

When M. Rostand had written a part around M. Coquelin and had invented a story to carry the part, he found himself confronted by the difficulty of classifying his drama; and he solved the puzzle by reviving an old name for the new type. He declared that " Cyrano de Bergerac" was a heroic-comedy. Goldsmith called "She Stoops to Conquer" a comedy; and when certain critics insisted that it was only a farce, and that it contained some scenes "too mean even for farce," he may have shrugged his shoulders, since the public had laughed at his play, not asking whether their risibles had been excited by a farce or a comedy. And Mark Twain would probably be surprised if it should be pointed out to him that "Huckleberry Finn" is really a picaresque-romance, a direct descendant of " Gil Blas" and "Lazarillo de Tormes." Very likely

the statement would not interest him, since "Huckleberry Finn" would remain thereafter just what it had
been before.

II

But if those labels matter little to the creators, they
have their importance to the investigators of literary
evolution. We may modify Pascal's dictum and declare that half of the art of criticism lies in the precision of the definitions. And to the student of any art,
there is unfailing profit in a firm grasp of classification.
When he has really apprehended the essential characteristics of any special type, he is likely to be surprised to discover it unexpectedly turning up in periods when it has been supposed to have practically
disappeared. There is the chronicle-play, for example,
which flourished abundantly in Shakspere's youth.
Professor Schelling thinks that it died out when it had
run its course in the seventeenth century, and no doubt
the name has departed from ordinary speech; but the
thing itself can be found again and again in the dramatic literature of the nineteenth century, and two
striking examples are visible already in the first decade
of the twentieth century. The writer of a chronicle-
play applied to a lay subject the practices of the mystery which set forth the gospel-story; and he sought
to put into action and dialogue all the episodes of the
career he dealt with. He took it as a whole and presented it as it came to him, with little selection, suppression, or climax. He felt no call to focus interest on
an essential struggle and to make every scene con-
verge toward a central point. His method was only
externally that of the drama; for what he wanted to do
was only to show a narrative in action for the benefit

of those who could not or would not read the original story. When we have once grasped the characteristics of the type, we can see easily enough that this is in fact the method of the elder Dumas in his "Napoleon" and of Giacommetti in his "Marie Antoinette." It is the method also of Mr. Stephen Phillips in his "Ulysses" and of Mr. Percy Mackaye in his "Jeanne d'Arc." Tennyson's "Queen Mary" and "Becket" are both of them chronicle-plays, — histories, if we prefer the Shaksperian term. They are modelled on the loose and straggling pieces written by Shakspere before he had learnt how to compact a tragic plot. And there is no denying that the chronicle-play is likely to reappear again more than once in the coming century, since it is a lax and easy form, forever tempting to poets who are unwilling to take the trouble to master the technic of the theater of their own time.

It has been a distinct advantage to the student of the drama that the terms, chronicle-play and tragedy-of-blood, have won general acceptance to describe special types of the drama. It would be a far greater advantage if we were able to use with equal precision two more important terms. These are comedy and tragedy, both of them words of loose meaning, which cannot be applied with any rigorous exactness. Even when taken together, they fail hopelessly to cover the field, which seems to be divided between them. The setting up of these two words over against each other would appear to imply that any play which is not a tragedy must be a comedy, and any play not a comedy must be a tragedy. But this is obviously absurd, for there are plays a-plenty which are neither tragedy nor comedy, and which also are not even tragi-comedy,

in any of the many shifting meanings of that bastard
term.

The word tragi-comedy seems to have been first
used by Plautus in his "Amphitryon," because he combined serious and comic effects, setting gods by the
side of slaves. Sidney declared that its distinguishing
quality was to be found in its "mingling kings and
clowns," and in that its author was willing to "match
hornpipes and funerals." Here we perceive a survival
of the now exploded belief that tragedy could properly
present only exalted personages and that it ought to
be free from all admixture of the comic, — although
the "Alcestis" of Euripides has both a humorous
character, the intoxicated Heracles, and a happy ending. Nowadays we take a larger view of tragedy, and
are ready to see it even in the humblest of families.
Few would be disposed to-day to deny the term to the
somber "Ghosts" of Ibsen; although this drama is
in plain prose, although it presents plain people, and
although it does not actually end in death, we feel in
it the largeness of a truly tragic theme.

Both in English and in French, tragi-comedy had
a long struggle for life; and finally failed to establish
itself in either language, although Corneille used it
to describe his "Cid" and Fletcher to describe his
"Faithful Shepherdess." Even in Fletcher's time,
three centuries ago, its proper application was so
doubtful that he was forced to declare his own definition in his preface to this pastoral play: "A tragi-comedy is not so called in respect of mirth and killing, but
in respect that it wants death, which is enough to make
it no tragedy, yet brings some near it, which is enough
to make it no comedy, which must be a representation

of familiar people." To-day we have no special term to apply to a piece such as Fletcher here describes, and the best we can do is simply call it a "play." Yet Mr. Henry Arthur Jones chose to revive tragi-comedy as the proper designation for his "Evangelist," and it would have been convenient to be able to use tragi-comedy to describe Mr. Clyde Fitch's "Climbers," which although satiric in intent, skirted the edge of tragedy; indeed, it is said that one manager declined this drama because he did not believe that the public would take any interest in a play "which began with a funeral and which ended with a suicide."

For a variant of the type of play which Fletcher and Beaumont originated and which Shakspere took over from them (in the "Winter's Tale," for example), Professor Thorndike has suggested the appropriate term of dramatic-romance. And here again is a convenient term to describe certain modern pieces only too prevalent in our theaters of late, most of them dramatizations of pseudo-historical or wholly fantastic tales of adventure, such as "When Knighthood Was in Flower" and the "Prisoner of Zenda." The word tragedy seems to convey a fairly simple idea; but, as Fletcher remarked, it connotes a deadly termination of the story, and so it apparently excludes all those serious dramas which fail to end fatally. On the other hand, the word comedy has been broadened to include all the manifestations of the comic spirit on the stage — the lyrical-burlesque of Aristophanes and the acrobatic farce of the Italians, which we know as the comedy-of-masks, as well as the brilliant satires of contemporary society such as Sheridan and Beaumarchais gave us. That is to say, tragedy is applied strictly to only one of the several types of serious drama, the one in which death rings down the curtain; whereas comedy is stretched to include every kind of humorous piece. As a result, we have no name for the special type of comedy which corresponds to the special type of tragedy — the comic play which deals with life sincerely and satirically, without exaggerated caricature in the character-drawing and without extravagant fun-making in the episodes. High-comedy is what one might call the play of this class, taking as our typical specimens the "Femmes Savantes" of Molière, the "Way of the World" of Congreve, the "School for Scandal" of Sheridan, and the "Gendre de M. Poirier" of Augier and Sandeau. In this wise and witty comedy-of-manners, — to give it another name, more widely used but less exactly descriptive — the action, however serious it may seem, never stiffens into serious drama; and, on the other hand, however amusing it may be, it never relaxes into the robust and boisterous mirth of mere farce. Rich as is the dramatic literature of the world, the plays worthy to be classified under this head are surprisingly few. Modern British dramatists have given us occasional specimens of this difficult form, Oscar Wilde's "Lady Windermere's Fan," for example, and Mr. Henry Arthur Jones's "Liars." The Greeks, from whom we have perfect examples of pure tragedy, left us not a single specimen of high-comedy — although, of course, it is possible that one may yet be discovered amid the plays of Menander, if we can replevin them from oblivion.

What is even more curious is that there is not really a satisfactory specimen of high-comedy to be selected

out of the immense mass of the Elizabethan drama.
No one of Shakspere's comedies and not one of Ben
Jonson's conforms to this special type. The comic
dramas of Ben Jonson belong to the class known as
the comedy-of-humors; and the most beloved of Shakspere's lighter plays, the "Merchant of Venice" and
"Much Ado about Nothing," are best to be described
as examples of romantic-comedy, the form which the
great dramatist specially affected and which he improved for his own use, even if he took the suggestion
of it from Greene. In this romantic-comedy, we find
Shakspere sustaining the interest of the more playful
theme, with which he is chiefly concerned, by the
powerful episodes of an underplot which is allowed
at times to become almost tragic in its intensity.

However delightful may be the romantic-comedies
of Shakspere, with their unceasing poetic charm and
their unfailing contrast of character, they have not
afforded a model to modern dramatists, who seem to
have felt that this type of play was a special product
of the semi-medieval, semi-renascence theater of the
Elizabethans, and that it would not flourish on our
modern stage, set with realistic scenery. Indeed, the
only poet of the nineteenth century who was attracted
to this Shaksperian form was Alfred de Musset; and
it must be remembered that the most of his dramatic
fantasies, passionate yet mocking, were not originally
intended for the actual theater.

On the other hand, the high-comedy of Molière,
prepared for a playhouse which was modern in the most
of its conditions, has served as a model for Congreve
and Sheridan, for Augier and Sandeau, and for all
who have since essayed the comedy-of-manners. That

only a few have been able to handle this form successfully is evidence that it is inherently difficult. Apparently the danger is twofold, and it is very like that
which confronts the lyrist who ventures upon the true
vers de société. The playwright, who ought to make
his plot the result of the clash of character on character, is tempted either to surcharge his story with sentiment or to permit his sense of fun to run away with
him. In the one case, the plot ceases to be comic and
becomes unduly emotional, as happened in "Frou-
frou," which begins in the best vein of high-comedy
only to sink at last submerged in sentiment. And in
the other case, the play becomes wholly comic, and
abandons sentiment for breadth of humor, as happened in "She Stoops to Conquer," which fails somewhat to justify its claim to be considered strictly as a
comedy-of-manners. In fact, if we closely scrutinize
Goldsmith's dramatic masterpiece, we find in it what
may fairly be called fun for its own sake. An element
of frank farce makes itself evident; and a similar farci-
cal excess is discoverable also in the "Rivals." Probably
this is what Sir Arthur Pinero had in mind when he
ventured to define a comedy as "a successful farce
written by a deceased author."

III

Often has farce been seized as a term of reproach to
hurl in the face of a living playwright; and melodrama
has also served many times as a missile of offense. But
even if they are less noble, farce and melodrama are
types of plays quite as legitimate as comedy and tragedy,
and, to the student of the development of the drama,
each of them has an interest of its own. All the more

reason is there that the two words should be defined,
and that we should be able to see why farce and melodrama are properly held to be inferior to comedy and
tragedy. The cause of this inferiority is simple and it
may be stated simply. In high-comedy (the comedy-of-
manners) and again in the serious drama (of which true
tragedy is one class) we perceive that the plot is made
by the characters, that the characters dominate the plot,
and that the plot is what it is solely because the characters are what they are. But in farce, and again in
melodrama, the reverse is seen to be the case; the
plot, the situation, the incidents are the controlling
factors, and the characters are only what the plot
allows them to be or forces them to be; they exist
solely in order that they may do what their maker
bids them, instead of going forward, apparently of
their own volition, impelled by the logic of their own
individuality. In high-comedy (in "Tartuffe" and
in the "School for Scandal"), and in true tragedy (in
"Œdipus" and in "Othello"), the successive events
of the story are brought about almost inevitably, as
though they could not happen otherwise; whereas in
farce and in melodrama, the action of any character
may be arbitrary at any moment.

If the characters seem to lead an independent life
of their own, existing apart from the circumstances
in which they happen to have been presented, if they
linger in our memories as fellow human beings, whose
course of conduct we can venture to predict from what
we already know of them, then the play in which they
appear is not fairly to be classified as farce or as melodrama. But if the characters fade into nothingness,
when we seek to separate them from the events in

which they took part, and if their movements have been so illogical and so completely controlled by another will than their own, that we are ever left in wonder as to what they will do next, then the play in which they are puppets is farce or melodrama.

If we apply this test sincerely, we shall find ourselves declaring that at least a dozen of Molière's most joyous pieces are farces — excellent farces, beyond all question, but farces nevertheless. Furthermore, we shall find ourselves putting the same label on at least two of Shakspere's plays, the "Comedy of Errors," and the "Merry Wives of Windsor"; while yet another of his so-called comedies, the "Taming of the Shrew," is not only farce, but often farce of a violent type, of the slapstick and knockabout variety. And we shall be forced also to record that "Titus Andronicus," the rank tragedy-of-blood, revised by Shakspere in his dependent youth, and also the "Cymbeline" of his later years, are both of them melodramas, and that neither of them is a masterpiece of plot-making.

When two surviving comrades of Shakspere, years after his death, piously gathered his plays into a single folio volume — the most precious possession of all modern literature — they risked a rough-and-ready classification into three groups, comedies, tragedies, and histories; and even then they could find no fit place for that nondescript narrative in dialogue, "Troilus and Cressida." Later criticism has accepted as fairly accurate the grouping together of the so-called histories, since the loosely knit pieces thus assembled are all of them chronicle-plays. The group of tragedies is now seen to include not only true tragedies, like "Macbeth" and "Othello," but also at least one specimen of the tragedy-of-blood. But the designation of the plays in the third group is unsatisfactory and misleading, however wide an extension may be given to comedy. Even if we might fairly include under this head the romantic-comedies, the farces, and such humorous fantasies as the "Tempest" and the "Midsummer Night's Dream," wherein we find fairy folk commingled with our grosser humanity, and the dramatic-romances (of which the "Winter's Tale" is an example), even then we cannot but feel that comedy is absolutely the one word most inapplicable to "Measure for Measure" and "All's Well that Ends Well," those dark plays of unlovely intrigue wherein Shakspere dealt with themes which were unworthy of him and which not even he could make worthy.

IV

We may rest certain that if Shakspere were to return to life to-day, he would waste little of his time on the immense mass of contradictory criticism with which commentators have obscured his works. When he was alive, he never took himself too seriously; and if he came back to this modern world of ours, he would find many things to do more interesting than to grope through guesses of all sorts about his intentions in this or that play, which he wrote primarily to please the theatergoers of his own time, and secondarily to express himself as he was at that particular period of his life. Probably it would surprise him hugely to learn that the plays, which he did not even take the trouble to have printed, were deemed worthy of study in our universities, and that critics were engaged in classifying them, setting down this as a tragedy-of-blood and that as a dramatic-romance, a third as a romantic-comedy, and a fourth as merely a farce. If asked whether "Troilus and Cressida" ought to be grouped with the tragedies or with the comedies or with the histories, he might answer only with a shrug of the shoulder.

We may smile at the long list which Polonius rattles off glibly, and we may be sure that Shakspere meant us to smile at it; but none the less is classification the beginning of knowledge. The student has got hold of something solid when he finds out for himself what need there was for a term like tragi-comedy in both England and France in the seventeenth century, and why the eighteenth century saw in France the development of the *comédie-larmoyante* (known in English as sentimental-comedy), and of the *tragédie-bourgeoise* (known in German as tradesman's-tragedy). He has made an advance in knowledge when he ascertains just what a ballad-opera is and a musical-comedy, an *opéra-comique* and an *opéra-bouffe*, and when he can trace the influence they have exerted on one another. He will find a profit in grasping the exact scope of the English heroic-play, and the Spanish comedy-of-cloak-and-sword. He will gain if he keeps clearly in mind a working definition of farce and of melodrama, to enable him to perceive more swiftly the relation of the former to comedy, and of the latter to the serious drama.

Of course, it is needful for us always to remember that classification is a means only; it is never an end in itself. It is useful only in so far as it enables us to appreciate the exact position of the more important plays which have come down to us from the past, and to measure the value of the more important of the plays which are now proffered to us in the present day. It is a constant aid to the apprehending of the significant fact that the development of the drama has been continuous, and that it is subject to laws which reveal themselves at work in every period. Although the past and the present may seem very unlike, they have many aspects in common; and therefore it is an advantage to the critic of the acted drama of our own time, as well as to the historian of the dramatic literature of other centuries, to be able to explain the one by the aid of the other.

The likeness of certain ancient manifestations of the drama to certain modern manifestations is as easy to exaggerate as it is impossible to deny; and there is no occasion to give undue weight to the suggestion that the lyrical-burlesque of the Greeks reveals a certain similarity to the nondescript medley made familiar of late in America by Messrs. Weber and Fields, just as the comedies of Plautus show a certain likeness to the plays of tenement-house life in New York, put together by Mr. Edward Harrigan. So in Calderon's day, there were Spanish analogues to the modern swashbuckler romanticist pieces, just as there were, in Shakspere's time, English analogues of the modern Bowery melodrama. The precursor of the problem-play of Ibsen can be found more than once in the list of Molière's works, where it is possible also to discover an anticipation of our latter-day musical-comedy. And for a final illustration of these survivals of form and of these reincarnations of spirit, take the comedy-of-humors, which Ben Jonson built up solidly with his imaginative exaggerations, and set it by the side of any dramatization of a loose-jointed serial story by Dickens, in which we cannot fail to find the same violent distortion of character into caricature. A dramatization of any one of Dickens's novels can hardly help being a comedy-of-humors.

v

The French, among whom the critical faculty is more acutely developed than among other peoples, have a larger vocabulary of critical terms than there is in any other language; and they have devised a classification of certain of the effects of dialogue which are common to every type of comic play. They call a jest which evokes laughter a *mot*, and they make a distinction which is not easy to render in English between *mots d'esprit*, *mots de situation*, and *mots de caractère*. The *mot d'esprit* is the witticism, pure and simple, existing for its own sake, and detachable from its context — like the remark of one of the characters in "Lady Windermere's Fan": "I can resist everything — except temptation." The *mot de situation* is the phrase which is funny, solely because it is spoken at that particular moment in the setting forth of the story, like the "What the devil was he doing in that galley?" which is not laughter-provoking in itself and apart from the incident calling it forth, but which arouses peals of merriment in its proper place in Molière's "Scapin." And the *mot de caractère* is the phrase which makes us laugh because it is the intense expression, at the moment, of the individuality of the person who speaks it — like the retort of the wife to her sister in the "Comedy of Errors," when she has been roundly abusing her husband. Luciana satirically comments that a man no better than this is no great loss to be bewailed. Whereupon Adriana, smiling through her tears, returns: "Ah, but I think him better than I say" — a line which gets its laugh, of course, but which lingers in the memory as a sudden revelation of the underlying character of the speaker.

It is with the *mot d'esprit* that we must class the most of the so-called epigrams which glisten on the surface of the dialogue. They are mere jokes, smart sayings, and ingenious aphorisms, taken out of a notebook and pinned into this play or that, as appropriate to the one as to the other. They offer to a clever young man a short and easy way to attain the brilliancy and the verbal glitter which we have been accustomed to expect in English comedy, since the author of the "Way of the World" sent up his Congreve rockets. They delight us at first, even though at last they fatigue us a little, in the comedies of Sheridan and in the comedies of Oscar Wilde; and yet neither of these ingenious dramatists relied for success upon this superficial flashing of brisk witticisms, being very careful, in "Lady Windermere's Fan," as well as in the "School for Scandal," to construct a solidly framed plot, with a clearly defined struggle of contending desires, to sustain the interest of the spectators. Underneath the crackling of artificial wit, there is a well-built play, the story of which would please in the theater, even if the spoken words were absolutely commonplace.

This device of sprinkling detachable witticisms throughout the dialogue has the obvious disadvantage that it forces the author to endow his empty-headed characters with his own alertness of intelligence. For instance, Mrs. Malaprop's blunders are far too felicitous to be natural in the mouth of a lady so limited in understanding; and the elaborate system of swearing expounded by Bob Acres is far too clever for that rather fat-witted country squire. Sheridan, who had not only humor, but also the rarer sense-of-humor, did not fail to detect the weakness of his practice, and in the "Critic," when one of the spectators of the play, which is being rehearsed, ventures to suggest that a certain speech is rather above the capacity of the character who had just delivered it, the author promptly retorts that he is "not for making slavish distinctions, and giving all the fine language to the upper sort of people."

The temptation to attain brilliancy of dialogue by the use of these portable witticisms projected into the play by main strength is one which the true dramatist outgrows as he gains in years. It was in their youth that Congreve and Sheridan gave their comic masterpieces to the stage. It was in his youth that the younger Dumas displayed the facets of his wit in the "Demi-Monde," which bristles with obvious *mots d'esprit*, surface adornments lacking in the "Francillon" of his maturer years, in which there are few quotable phrases, but in which the wit is incessant, pervasive rather than paraded, integral, and not external. This later comedy of Dumas's deserves the praise which Mr. William Archer once bestowed on a play of Bronson Howard's, whereof the dialogue abounded in witty speeches which belonged there, "like blossoms on a laburnum," instead of being stuck on, "like candles on a Christmas tree."

VI

Closely akin to the *mot d'esprit* are the longer passages, also existing for their own sake, and enriching
the dialogue, it may be, but not serving to help along
the action of the play. There is no logical necessity
for Jaques to set forth the seven ages of man, or for
Touchstone to nominate in order the seven degrees of
the lie. Even though we cannot wish either of these
speeches away, we cannot deny that the one, as well
as the other, is an excursus. Touchstone's explanation
seems doubly out of place, in that it is inserted in the
last scene of all, when the comedy is hastening toward
its happy end. Perhaps it was written to fatten the
clown's part, and perhaps it was put precisely where
it is to give Rosalind time to change from the boyish
costume of Ganymede into the ampler habiliments of
her own sex. Jaques's cynical denunciation of his fel-
low-man can easily be defended, it is only fair to note,
by the plea that it is the completest revelation of its
speaker's character; in other words, that it is in fact to
be classed not only with *mots d'esprit* but also with *mots
de caractère*. And a like defense might be proffered
for the hunting speech of Lady Gay Spanker in "London Assurance," a highly artificial tirade.

But every one of these glittering passages bears a
striking likeness to a tenor or soprano solo in Italian
opera, devised to exhibit the accomplishments of the
performer rather than to contribute to the rounding
out of the play. Such bravura passages are common
also in later Roman tragedy, when the dramatic poet
steps aside for a moment to air his eloquence at greater
length than is necessary. This is one of the vulnerable
spots in the armor of the dramatists, pierced by the keen

wit of the authors of the "Rehearsal," the attack on
Dryden (the framework of which Sheridan borrowed
when he wrote the "Critic"). When one of the bystanders remarks that a certain passage in the piece
that is being rehearsed is "not to the purpose, for the
play does not go on," since "the plot stands still," the
irritable author promptly retorts with the unanswer-
able query: "What is the plot good for but to bring in
fine things?" It deserves to be noted that Shakspere,
who indulges freely in these pleasant digressions in his
comedies, is chary of them in his tragedies, as though
the severer tragic mold forced him to strive for the
loftiest standard, such as he found no need to impose
on himself in comedy, which seemed to him a form
looser and less clearly defined.

The *mot de situation* is far more valuable to the playwright and far more mirth-provoking to the audience
than the *mot d'esprit*. But it is less easy to illustrate
because it is part and parcel of the story of the play,
and it is therefore not quotable without an explanation
of the incident which evokes it. As good an example
as any is the "sister, sister, every way" of Congreve
in "Love for Love," which owes its point to the attempt
of Mrs. Foresight to corner Mrs. Frail by producing
unexpectedly a gold bodkin and by asking where the
other lost it; "oh, sister, sister!" Taken aback for a
moment, Mrs. Frail collects her wits quickly and retorts: "If you go to that, sister, where did you find this
bodkin? Oh, sister, sister, every way!" But the great
master of the *mot de situation* is Molière, who always
scornfully refrained from the easier *mot d'esprit*. Without descending to the mechanical trick of the catchword, Molière more than once redoubles the effect

of a *mot de situation* by carefully calculated repetition. And the trick of the catchword, mechanical as it is, can be varied adroitly. In "Lady Windermere's Fan," for example, a young girl, whom we see taking part in the general conversation, and after a while wooed and finally engaged to be married, is never heard to say anything except "Yes, mamma."

As for the *mots de caractère*, there is no need to say much, for examples will spring swiftly to the minds of all lovers of Molière and of Shakspere. Falstaff abounds in them: "I think the devil will not have me damned, lest the oil that is in me should set hell on fire," which is a *mot d'esprit* as well as a *mot de caractère*. Indeed, it would not be difficult to pick speeches out of Falstaff's which combine the merits of the *mot d'esprit*, the *mot de situation*, and the *mot de caractère*. And the characteristics of all three types are united also in the speech of Sir Peter to his wife in one of the famous quarrel scenes of the "School for Scandal," when Lady Teazle says: "I should think you would like to have your wife thought a woman of taste"; and the husband explosively retorts: "Taste! Zounds! madam, you had no taste when you married me!"

CHAPTER VII

TRADITIONS AND CONVENTIONS

Tragedy or comedy, every stage-play is, in a certain sense, only a tissue of conventions. It is a convention to compact into a few hours of time the whole drama of an existence or the duration of the catastrophe which historically brought it to an end; it is a convention to lend to the persons of this play the language of verse or even that of a prose which is generally neither their maternal tongue nor the speech of their condition. — F. BRUNETIÈRE, *Histoire de la littérature française classique.*

I

As the dramatist writes for the theater of his own time, he begins always by accepting the theatrical traditions which he finds established, and as he seeks to interest the spectators, he has no hesitation in utilizing the conventions which he finds in favor with his audiences. Art exists only when the artist in his search for truth is allowed to depart from the mere facts of life. Painting "steals but a glance of time," and represents as motionless that which we know to be vibrating with movement. Sculpture is not only motionless, it is also monochrome; and the sculptor transmutes into the uniformity of marble or bronze the varied hues of the human figure and sometimes even the variegated tints of customary costume. To deny to the painter or to the sculptor the privilege of thus ignoring the accidental facts of life, is to refuse him the right to delight us with his work. Strictly speaking, of course, the immobility of a picture or of a statue is not "natural"; but unless we grant at once this departure from nature, we deny ourselves the enjoyment of painting and of sculpture. Underlying every one of the arts, there is a kindred departure from "nature," which we must tolerate before we can give ourselves up to the pleasure which that art offers us. Even in the primitive ballad, we find the characters talking in rime, which was never the practice of mortal man. But we like rime, in its proper place, and we gladly allow the lyrist to assume that he is setting before us beings who are wont to express themselves in rime as well as in meter.

A convention is thus seen to be a denial of the actual fact, known to us all, a denial which we permit for our own profit. In most of the arts, we have accepted these necessary conventions so completely that we are wholly unconscious that they authorize the artist to be "unnatural." We are so constituted that what is familiar tends to be received as right and proper — in a word, as rational. But what is familiar to us is not necessarily familiar to others; and the American Indians, when they first saw a portrait in profile, used to ask where the other side of the face was, — a question which would never occur to any of us, accustomed as we are to frequent the picture galleries. Indeed, we are so familiar with the art of the draftsman that we recognize a portrait in black ink on white paper, or in white chalk on a blackboard, although we have none of us either a black or a white line around our faces.

The conventions which underlie each of the arts are permanent, for without them the art could not exist. They are tacit agreements between the artist and the public that if he shall be authorized to ignore certain of the mere facts, he will do his best to present the truth as he sees it. A convention is an implied contract between two parties; and neither party has a right to violate the conditions of the treaty. It is the convention of opera, for instance, that there exists a race of human beings, whose natural speech is song; and the opera-goer has no right, therefore, to object to the death-song of Tristan on the ground that a dying man would not have the physical strength to sing for half an hour on his death-bed. It is the refusal of Tolstoy to abide by this implicit contract which invalidates his contemptuous attack on the opera. So the convention which underlies pantomime is that there exists a race of human beings, whose natural speech is gesture, and who are able to employ it to express all those emotions which the rest of us would translate into spoken words. To be willing to accept this contract is a condition precedent to our enjoyment of pantomime. We may, if we choose, refuse to be parties to this agreement; but then there is nothing for us to do but to keep out of the theater whenever a pantomime is represented, as Tolstoy should have kept away when an opera was performed.

Besides these permanent conventions which are the basis of each of the several arts, we can discern others which are temporary and accidental, accepted in only certain places and only for certain periods, but not prerequisite to the existence of the art. For example, in the wall-paintings of the royal tombs of Egypt, men are depicted in ruddy brown and women in pale yellow, while the Pharaoh is always very much larger in proportion than are his subjects. So in the Pompeian pictures of mythological themes, the less important figures are painted upon a smaller scale. Tem-

porary conventions of this sort are due sometimes to
special conditions. A sculptor who intends to repro-
duce his clay model in bronze can rely upon the firm
supports to be concealed inside that metal; but if he
expects to make a statue of marble he has to introduce something, a falling drapery or an arbitrary
column, which will add strength to the ankles, where
the marble would be most fragile. There are even
Roman sculptures, in which the body of a horse is
frankly sustained by a wholly impossible trunk of a
tree projecting up from the ground into the belly of
the animal.

II

The drama, being an art, has its necessary conventions, like all the other arts; and it has also its temporary and accidental conventions, often due to special
circumstances of a particular theater. The necessary
conventions of the drama are the result of three conditions of theatrical performance. The first of these is
that the dramatist has at his disposal only a limited
time — two or three hours at the most; and he is therefore compelled to select rigorously the vital elements
of his theme and to compact his dialogue out of all
resemblance to the ample and repetitious speech of
ordinary life. The second and the third are the obligation so to handle his story that everything done on
the stage can be seen by the spectators in the theater,
and that everything said on the stage can be heard by
the audience. The playgoer wants to have as much
as possible packed into the "two hours' traffic of the
stage"; he wants also to see everything and to hear
everything; and he is therefore ready to grant to the

playwrights every privilege which will help them to give him what he wants.

First of all, of course, he insists on understanding the story; and therefore the dramatists always employ the language which they and the spectators have in common. This is so needful that we take it for granted; and yet it is not "natural" that the Persians in the tragedy of Æschylus should speak Greek, that Julius Cæsar and Hamlet and Romeo should speak English and not Latin and Danish and Italian; and that the Cid of Corneille and the Don Juan of Molière should speak French. In "Henry V," Shakspere pushes this convention still further; the English characters speak English, of course, and so also of course do the French characters among themselves — except in one scene; but when Henry V is wooing Katherine, she uses the hesitating broken English of a learner of our tongue.

It is true that condensation is also necessary in the dialogue of prose-fiction, a rigorous selection of significant remarks. The most realistic novelist, striving to echo the accent of contemporary triviality, has never dared to let his characters discourse at one half the length to which their chatter would run in real life. The pressure of time forces the playwright to compact his dialogue to an extent never dreamed of by the novelist. This is one reason why the dramatizer of a novel has to rewrite its dialogue in conformity with the different scale demanded by the theater. On the stage, a love-scene of supreme importance may be so artfully condensed that it does not last more than five minutes, although in real life it might have taken at least one hour.

Not only does the dramatist condense the speech

of his characters, but he clarifies it also. Every person in a play is supposed to be capable of saying just what he means the first time of trying, and in the fewest possible words; and this is a very violent departure from the practice of everyday life, where our speech is uncertain, halting, and ragged. Every character also uses the best possible words to voice his thought, and every other character immediately takes his meaning without hesitancy; and this is again a variation from the fact, since we are continually failing to catch the exact intent of those with whom we are talking. Praise is abundant for the verisimilitude of the dialogue of Ibsen's social dramas and for the skill with which Ibsen has given to every one of his characters the actual vocabulary which that character would use.   Yet his compact and polished prose rests as frankly on a convention as the song of the operatic hero or as the all-sufficient gesture of the pantomimist.

The convention underlying Shakspere's tragedy is that the characters belong to a race of human beings whose habitual speech is blank verse, the unrimed decasyllabic iambic. Yet in some of his earlier plays, Shakspere varies from this convention, frequently dropping into rime, while in certain of his other plays, notably in " Julius Cæsar," he makes another departure, and we find the heroic figures employing blank verse, the less distinguished characters using a stately rhythmic prose, while the populace appropriately sinks into the every-day speech of the common folk. The corresponding convention underlying the tragedies of Corneille and Racine and the comedies of Molière is that the characters belong to a race of beings whose habitual speech is the alexandrine, with

alternating couplets of masculine and feminine rimes.
As we who speak English are used to blank verse,
Shakspere's lines seem to us "natural"; and as we
are not accustomed to hear rime on the stage, Corneille's lines often seem to us "unnatural." But both
are departures from the actual facts of human speech;
each is a convention accepted willingly by the compatriots of the author. So in the Spanish drama, we
find *asonantes* relieved by an occasional sonnet, with
its complicated metrical construction. But this is
scarcely a bolder contradiction of the mere facts of life
than the convention which obtains in the comedies
of Congreve and of Sheridan, where all the characters,
even illiterate servants, are endowed with the keen and
finished wit of the author.

III

It is imperative that we should approve of the essential conventions of the drama, or we must deny ourselves the pleasure of the theater. We may not even
be aware that they are conventions, but we permit
them none the less. Almost any non-essential convention we are willing also to accept, if its acceptance
is helpful, even though it contradicts all our habits.
We moderns are accustomed now to realistic scenery
and characteristic costumes in the theater; the Greeks
of old and the Elizabethans after them had the full
pleasure of the drama without these accompaniments.
And yet we are willing enough to get along without
either of these accompaniments, if the bargain is
frankly presented to us beforehand. Henry Irving
once performed the "Merchant of Venice" at West
Point in the mess-hall, on a platform draped with

flags, without any scenery; and Edwin Booth once gave "Hamlet" at Waterbury, the whole company appearing in their traveling clothes, because their stage-costumes had miscarried. In both cases, the spectators were warned in advance; they knew what to expect and they speedily adjusted themselves to the novel conditions. Molière's "Misanthrope" was once performed before Louis XIV in the marble court of Versailles without any attempt at an appropriate background.

In a play, all the details of action and of speech must be significant, or else the playgoer is misled and his interest distracted. He wants to see everything that is done; and therefore the fourth wall of every room is removed, so that he can behold what takes place on the stage. He wants to hear everything that is said; and therefore a character whispering a sharp warning to another character, in the presence of a third, so pitches his voice that it carries to the back of the auditorium, although it is supposed to be inaudible to a third character only a few feet distant.

In the English playhouses of the eighteenth century and of the early nineteenth, the most important episodes of a play were acted in the "focus" close to the pit, and remote from the scenery, for it was only here that there was light enough for the spectators to see the changing expression on the faces of the actors. This was a convention then acceptable to the playgoer, since it increased his pleasure; but it is unacceptable in our smaller theaters wherein the electric light illuminates every part of the stage. To-day we expect an actor to remain "in the picture." Acting in the focus was a temporary convention due to temporary conditions; and when these conditions ceased, the convention was no longer tolerable, although it survived the conditions out of which it arose. We are still willing that the lilting lyric trolled by Rosalind in the Forest of Arden shall be accompanied by the full orchestra of the theater; the arrant absurdity of this does not annoy us, partly because we are used to it, and partly because we prefer it.

But we should resent immediately any similar absurdity to which we were not accustomed. It is a little difficult for us to understand how it was that the massing of spectators on the right and left of the stage when Shakspere's and Molière's plays were first acted, did not interfere with the verisimilitude of the performance. This is a state of affairs which would strike us now as very strange, although it seemed natural enough then to the rest of the audience, as they were used to it and knew no other device. These spectators on the stage were supposed not to be there, and therefore they did not interfere with the pleasure of the others. A similar convention still exists in the Japanese theater. One American visitor to the playhouse in Tokio has recorded his impressions of the performance with significant analysis of the ultimate effect: —

" The prompter sat on the stage in view of the audience, and the fact that he was dressed in a skin-tight suit of black with a black hood, like a chimney sweep or a goblin, and that he kept his face always from the spectators, was supposed to render him invisible. Another black imp remained on the scene to act as dresser and stage manager. It was his duty to assist an actor in making any alteration in his costume, and to carry away any prop that had been used: a letter, fan, or tea-tray. If he thought an

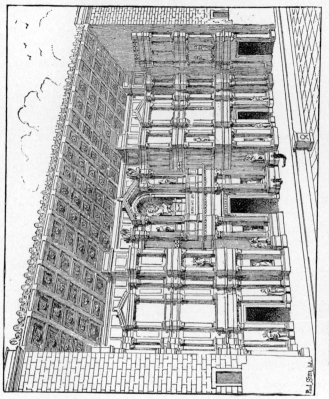

RESTORATION OF THE STAGE OF THE ROMAN THEATER AT ORANGE

actor's sash was not properly fastened, he would creep up behind him, even though the actor were speaking, and tie it properly. We were not supposed to see him do this. As a matter of fact, it was curious how soon one failed to note his presence."

Just as the Japanese attendants in black are supposed to be invisible, like the spectators on the English stage, so we can find analogues to Shakspere's medley of prose and verse in the classic Sanskrit drama, in which the heroes speak the nobler Sanskrit, while the women and the servants are allowed only the humbler Pali. In the medieval Portuguese passion-plays, the devil often spoke Spanish; and in the more modern pieces written for the east side Jewish theaters of New York, it is only the broadly comic characters who are frankly Yiddish in their vocabulary.

It is not easy always to distinguish between a convention and a tradition. Strictly speaking, a convention is a departure from the fact in order to give the spectator something he would otherwise have to forego. A tradition is an accepted way of doing things, which may or may not be completely "natural." Conventions are all traditions, but not all traditions are conventions. In the Latin drama, we find a tradition taken over from the Greek drama, the frequent employment of an intriguing slave, who plots for his master's benefit. This scheming servant may be truthfully portrayed along the traditional lines; but when he reappears in Molière, he has no longer any relation to real life; he stands forth as a tradition which has become a convention. In the Greek drama, again, we find the "recognitions" which Aristotle discussed, such as the sudden discovery by parents of long-lost children. Now, in

Greece, where there was ever intermittent war and casual piracy, children were captured and sold as slaves; and it was always possible that they might be restored to their parents at the end of the play. But when the Latin drama took over this tradition of the Greek drama, it became only a convention, since the conditions of life had changed and there was little likelihood that sons might be sold into slavery and bought by their own fathers, as in the "Captives" of Plautus. And when this Greek tradition, which had hardened into a convention in Rome, is transplanted into Italian comedy and into French, its conventionality is seen to be flagrant, — a fact which did not prevent Molière from employing it.

When Molière borrows plots from the Italians, he is forced to make a convention out of another tradition. In Southern Italy, where the comedy-of-masks flourished, people live out of doors; and the traditional scene of the Italian improvised play is a public square, in which all the characters meet to talk about their private affairs. But when Molière transplanted this tradition to Paris, where the climate is colder and damper, and where business is transacted indoors, when he represented M. de Pourceaugnac and the two doctors sitting down for their comic consultation in chairs set out in the street, he was obviously transforming the Italian tradition into a mere convention.

The traditions of the medieval stage survived for a long while, and they are visible abundantly in Shakspere's plays and even in the earlier pieces of Corneille. In our modern theaters, the changes of scenery are consecutive; the scene of the second act may be different from that of the first act, and the later acts may each have its own set. But on the medieval stage, especially in France, the traditions of the earliest performance of the passion-play in the church had led to a wholly different arrangement. In the church, the several episodes were acted in several places, each of which was known as a "station"; and in France, when the mystery was thrust out of the church, these stations were all erected in one long line at the back of the platform on which the performance took place, and they were known as "mansions." Thus it was that the French theater came to have the "simultaneous set," all the places needed in the action being then in sight at once, not displayed consecutively, as is the custom to-day. It is this tradition of bringing together places actually remote, which Shakspere follows in "Richard III," when he sets on the stage at the same time the tent of Richard and the tent of Richmond. Probably these tents were represented in the Globe Theater only by a looping back (at the extreme right and at the extreme left) of the tapestry pendant from the upper gallery. When Corneille adapted the "Cid" from the Spanish, he employed this simultaneous set, erecting on the stage the mansions required for his plot, and letting the stage itself serve as a neutral ground where all the characters might meet as they entered each from his own dwelling. This was absolutely in accord with the medieval tradition.

IV

Of all the conventions of the drama, none has a more interesting history than the soliloquy, the speech in which a character talks aloud, not to any person on the stage with him, but directly to the audience. And one of the most striking changes which have taken place in the drama of our own time is the sudden disappearance of the soliloquy. In the final decades of the nineteenth century, the leading playwrights of every modern language began to display a distaste for this monologue, with Ibsen setting the example of renunciation. Time was, and not so long ago, when the playwright found it very convenient to have the villain lay aside his mask and bare his black soul in a speech to himself. But now this device, convenient as it may be, is discarded. No longer does a character come down to the footlights for a confidential communication to the audience, telling them his thoughts, declaring his intentions, and defending his acts. So sharp is the reaction against the practice, that the French writer of a eulogistic study of the later German naturalistic dramatists, after praising the technic of Hauptmann, asserts positively that the soliloquy and the aside are hereafter banished from the stage.

Yet this abandonment of these conventions, however complete it may seem now, is very recent indeed. Ibsen made a frank use of these devices in his earlier dramas. In Sudermann's "Honor," one character, Trast, talks aloud to himself, and then still soliloquizing, rebukes himself for talking aloud. In Mr. Henry Arthur Jones's "Middleman," the soliloquy and the aside are used without question, and with no anticipation that they were so soon to fall out of fashion. In these modern plays, they are employed as they had been utilized in the medieval drama, as well as in the tragedies and comedies of the Greeks and Romans.

Perhaps the French writer on the German drama is justified in believing that the doom of the soliloquy is sealed and that the sentence of banishment has been pronounced on the aside. But his dislike for them expressed in 1905 is diametrically opposed to the liking confessed in 1684 by the English translator of the Abbé d'Aubignac's "Pratique du Théâtre." The translation is ingenuously entitled "The Whole Art of the Stage, containing not only the Rules of the Dramatick Art, but many curious Observations about it"; and one of these curious observations is the confession "that it is sometimes very pleasant to see a man upon the Stage lay open his heart and speak boldly of his most secret thoughts, explain his designs, and give a vent to all that his passion suggests." The French author had deduced his principles of the dramaturgic art, partly from the practice of the ancients, and partly from his own examination of what gave pleasure to a French audience in the days of Louis XIV. He had noted that the soul-unveiling soliloquy was welcome in the dramas of his own contemporaries, and he had discovered it to be freely employed in the plays of Plautus also. And for two centuries or more, this convention was found convenient by the composer of plays and acceptable to the audience. Then, in the final years of the nineteenth century, we observe the dramatists discarding it hastily, and the spectators crying out against an outworn trick unworthy of a self-respecting workman. Why this unexpected change of attitude on the part of playwright and playgoer alike? What had happened to open their eyes to the obvious fact that the soliloquy was "unnatural"? Now, to find the answer to these questions we need to take a long glance back over the history of the theater. As the drama of the Greeks was an outgrowth of their song, we might expect to observe in their plays a freedom of lyric self-expression; and in Æschylus, for example, we hear the bound Prometheus proclaim his woes to the wintry sky, before the winged chariot brings the daughters of ocean to comfort his windy solitude. Even in Sophocles, certain of the longer speeches of the chief characters, although delivered after the chorus has circled into the orchestra, are rather spoken at large than addressed directly to this band of courteous listeners. In the classicist tragedy of the French, the chorus has shrunk to a single attendant for each of the chief figures. Thus in Racine's masterpiece, Phèdre is ever accompanied by Œnone, Aricie by Ismène, and Hippolyte by Theramène, and to these they can unbosom themselves freely, the wily poet thus avoiding the semblance of the soliloquy while profiting by all its advantages. These confidants are colorless creatures, sketched in vague outline only and existing for the sole purpose of being talked to. Mere shadows of their masters and mistresses, they share the same fate; and in the tragedy which is rehearsed in Sheridan's "Critic," where the heroine goes mad in white satin, the confidant unhesitatingly goes mad in white muslin. The confidant was one of the outward and visible signs which excited the special detestation of the ardent romanticists of 1830. Victor Hugo dismissed these pale figures from his dramas; and the exuberant lyrist was thereby driven back to the soliloquy. The argumentative monologue which he bestowed on the king in "Hernani" is one of the longest soliloquies discoverable in all dramatic literature. This introspective oration is a superb specimen of Hugo's swelling rhetoric, splendid and stately with soaring figures of speech.

In his "New Art of Making Plays," Lope de Vega discussed the various stanzas and suggested that the sonnet was suitable for a soliloquy, — a suggestion which raises a very pretty question as to whether the artificiality of the soliloquy itself might not be disguised by the artificiality of the form in which it was presented. An arbitrary interweaving of rimes recalling the structure of the true sonnet is to be found more than once in the earlier plays of Shakspere, wherein we may readily detect the delight of the young poet in mere verbal ingenuity. But Shakspere was a practical playwright, up to every kind of trick of his trade, and making his profit out of every convention acceptable to his audiences. The soliloquy was far too convenient a device to be given up; and probably the thought never entered Shakspere's head that he could get along without it.

In scarcely any of his strongest plays, has he taken more trouble with his plot, with its structure, with its conduct, than he has in "Othello"; and in scarcely any other is the soliloquy more frequently employed. He uses it again and again to let Iago reveal his own villainy, as though he did not want the turbulent groundlings to be in any doubt as to the wickedness of his honest Iago. And so it is that at the end of the first act, Iago simply talks aloud to the audience, frankly taking them into his confidence and exposing his own dark designs. In the middle of the second act, and again at the end of that act, Iago explains his schemes to the spectators, as his plans take shape in his foul brain.

As Iago is the incomparable villain of the master of the English stage, so is Tartuffe the incomparable villain of the master of the French stage; and it must be confessed that Molière is able to make his hypocrite transparent without the aid of a single soliloquy or a single aside. Disclaiming these artless devices, he so contrives his story that we cannot help knowing Tartuffe for what he really is, long before we first hear his voice, and here Molière reveals himself as truly modern, whereas Shakspere, having accepted the Elizabethan tradition as he found it, is perforce semi-medieval in his methods.

But often Molière is no more logical in his use of the soliloquy than Shakspere is. Neither the French dramatist nor the English made any distinction between that soliloquy which reveals the character and that which informs us as to the facts of the plot. Both held that the soliloquy was equally pleasing, no matter whether it was merely supplying information which a more scrupulous playwright would have conveyed to the audience by some less arbitrary contrivance, or whether it displayed before us the conflicting emotions of a hero at the crisis of his fate, not possible to be made known except out of his own mouth. Yet the distinction between these two purposes for which the soliloquy may be used, ought to be obvious enough, even if it was not seized by Molière and Shakspere.

v

Nowadays, playwrights are forced to find a better way for a character to "explain his designs" than to leave him alone on the stage, so that he can tell the spectators what he is going to do. Such a proceeding seems a little too easy to be quite worth while; and the soliloquy which merely transmits information to the

audience can be defended only with difficulty. But
the soliloquy in which a character speaks "boldly of
his most secret thoughts" stands on a higher plane.
It lets a tortured hero unpack his heart; it opens a
window into his soul; and it gives the spectator a pleasure not to be had otherwise. It allows us to listen to
the communing of a character with himself, as though
we were not overhearing what he is saying. Professor
Bradley has remarked, in his stimulating discussion of
"Shaksperean Tragedy," that "in listening to a soliloquy we ought never to feel that we are being addressed." He declared that in this respect, as in others,
many of Shakspere's soliloquies are masterpieces; but
he admitted that "in some the purpose of giving information lies bare, and in one or two the actor openly
speaks to the audience." And Molière is as vulnerable
to this reproof as Shakspere.

The fact is that when Shakspere and Molière came
to the theater, they found the soliloquy a labor-saving
contrivance that they took over without bestowing a
thought on the principle underlying it. This principle,
if formally declared, would be that the soliloquy is a
means of exposing to the spectators the actual thoughts
of a character when he is alone. In other words, an
actor soliloquizing must be supposed to be thinking
aloud. But so little did either Shakspere or Molière
care for the principle involved, that both of them
unhesitatingly set before us a character soliloquizing
and yet overheard by some other character. This is
a contradiction in terms, if we analyze it philosophi-
cally, — but that is exactly what was not attempted by
either of these great dramatists or by any of the playgoers of their times. What to us may seem an arrant

absurdity is to be found as early as Terence and as late as Beaumarchais. Shakspere lets Romeo overhear Juliet's soliloquizing on the balcony; and Molière is as careless in the "Miser."

There was a clever man once who justified his habit of talking to himself by two good reasons, — he liked to talk to a man of sense and he liked to hear a man of sense talk. It is in the "Misérables" that Victor Hugo tried to justify the monologue by one bad reason; he declared that it was an error to believe that the soliloquy was not natural, since "often a strong agitation speaks out loud." But a strong agitation does not speak out loud a speech of a hundred lines and more, as the King does in "Hernani." There is no advantage in maintaining that the soliloquy is "natural." It is not; and no more is blank verse or highly condensed prose. As Professor Bradley has remarked: "Neither soliloquy nor the use of verse can be condemned on the mere ground that it is unnatural. *No* dramatic language is natural."

It may seem strange that audiences which still admit without protest many another convention quite as contrary to the actual fact, should have awakened suddenly to the lack of verisimilitude in the soliloquy. They accept it without cavil in "Rip Van Winkle," in one act of which no voice is heard but Rip's talking to himself or speaking to the dumb specters. They accept it again in a protean piece like the one act "Dick Turpin," in which all the parts are assumed by the same actor, and which is necessarily nothing but a succession of monologues. But they are annoyed when the characters in a modern play of real life take the liberty of soliloquizing, because both authors and audiences have discovered that it is out of place on the picture-frame stage of to-day, however appropriate it may have been to the platform-stage of yesterday. The dramatist can utilize it now only at his peril; at best he can use it on rare occasions and very briefly, merely to give a fleeting glimpse of the speaker's deeper emotion. If it is boldly employed in the fashion formerly acceptable, it will revolt us by what we now see to be its flagrant incompatibility with the conditions of the modern theater. It will probably survive as a tradition in the poetic drama, where we are glad always to listen to noble thoughts loftily phrased. It may even linger also in the lighter forms of comedy, where we shall not sharply feel its incongruity, because we do not take these humorous pieces seriously.

CHAPTER VIII

DRAMATIC CHARACTERIZATION

Hamlet is a name; his speeches and sayings but the idle coinage of the poet's brain. What, then, are they not real? They are as real as our own thoughts. Their reality is in the reader's mind. It is *we* who are Hamlet. This play has a prophetic truth, which is above that of history. Whoever has become thoughtful and melancholy through his own mishaps or those of others; whoever has borne about with him the clouded brow of reflection, and thought himself "too much i' th' sun"; whoever has seen the golden lamp of day dimmed by envious mists rising in his own breast, and could find in the world before him only a dull blank with nothing left remarkable in it; whoever has known "the pangs of despised love, the insolence of office, or the spurns which patient merit of the unworthy takes"; he who has felt his mind sink within him, and sadness cling to his heart like a malady, who has had his hopes blighted and his youth staggered by the apparitions of strange things; who cannot be well at ease, while he sees evil hovering near him like a specter; whose powers of action have been eaten up by thought, he to whom the universe seems infinite, and himself nothing; whose bitterness of soul makes him careless of consequences, and who goes to a play as his best resource to shove off, to a second remove, the evils of life by a mock representation of them — this is the true Hamlet. — WILLIAM HAZLITT, *The Characters of Shakspere's Plays.*

I

FOR immediate success on the stage, a play must have a story strong enough to arouse and retain the interest of the spectators; and it is characteristic of Aristotle's shrewdness that he seized this fact firmly, and declared it sharply more than two thousand years ago, with only his experience in the Attic theater to guide him. But while a sufficient story is a prerequisite to

immediate success, it will bestow only a fleeting popu-
larity, if the play is not peopled by characters that linger in the memory independently of the action in which
they have been presented. Taste in stories varies from
century to century and from country to country, and the
number of possible situations is so strictly limited that
the most the new dramatist can do is to shuffle the old
plots and to carry them on with new characters. But
human nature is much the same the wide world over,
and generation after generation. A character which
has once impressed itself upon the contemporaries of
the author as vital and significant has a chance of long
life; and in the final analysis, it is by his power of projecting characters that the dramatist survives.

On the plot, on the situations, on the sequence of
events, which the playwright needs first of all to win
the favor of the throng, he must expend his invention,
and he must be as ingenious as may be in adroit devices to sustain the interest of his story. On the characters who live and move inside this plot, he must
bestow the best of his imagination; and into them,
he must breathe the breath of life, so that they will
exist for us long after we have lost our liking for the
kind of story in which they originally figured. To us
nowadays, the central incidents of the " Merchant of
Venice" are unconvincing, not to call them puerile; but
Shylock is an unforgettable figure, as alive to-day as
when he first strode on the stage of the Globe Theater.
The plot of the "Winter's Tale" is a tissue of absurdities; but the young loves of Perdita and Florizel still
enchant us because they are eternally human. In the
"Merchant of Venice," we tolerate the impossibility
of the situations for the sake of the central character;

and we are almost as lenient toward the "Winter's Tale," although its characters do not loom so large in our memories. A story of some sort, there must be; but we reserve our warmest regard for the men and the women who carry it on. It is by veracity of character delineation, by subtlety of psychology, that the great plays are great. It is by this power of creating living and breathing human beings, recognizable fellow-creatures with ourselves, that the playwright establishes his title to be considered truly a dramatist. If he lacks this power, if he cannot leave behind him characters that the next generation will recognize and relish, then his reputation is fleeting; he exists by virtue of his plots only, and these the playwrights of the next generation will surely make over in accord with the changing tastes of their own time.

Yet the dramatist is strictly limited in his means of presenting his characters. He can show them only as they appear to their associates. He can put them before us only by what they say and by what they do; and he cannot explain or extenuate any word or any deed. These things must speak for themselves, since the dramatist is forced to keep himself out of his story, and since he is denied all privilege of comment. Here is perhaps the most striking difference between the play and the novel. The novelist can chat to his readers about his characters; he can tell us not only what they say and what they do, but also what they think; he can go further, if he so chooses, and let us know what he thinks of them and what he wants us to think of them.

Much of the charm of Thackeray's novels, for instance, is due to the incessant intervention of the

author and to the confidential commentary in which
the action of the story is constantly immersed. We may
like this method of Thackeray's or we may prefer
the sterner impartiality of Balzac; but to no playwright is anything of the sort permitted. In the theater, no comment is possible, no foot-notes, no sign-post
hands. On the stage, every character must stand on
his own feet and speak for himself; he must justify himself out of his own mouth and by his own deeds; and
if he is supposed to be shrewd and clever, he must
prove his shrewd cleverness in the sight of us all, for
we will not believe it unless we see it. If he is called
witty, we refuse to credit this, except on the evidence
of our own ears. If we behold him guilty of a contemptible act, the author can urge no specious argument
to make us overlook it. The characters stand before
us on the stage, and they are what they are, not what
the author might like us to believe them to be.

In spite of this limitation of his methods of representing character, — perhaps it may be, more or less
because of them, — the dramatist makes a virtue of
necessity and brings before us human beings who declare themselves clearly by what they say and by what
they do. Hamlet and Othello are as real to us as Don
Quixote; and Becky Sharp is not more alive than Lady
Teazle. The genius of Molière is great enough to de-
pict in a play a hypocrite, Tartuffe, who never drops the
mask of assumed piety, and whom we know for what
he is, even before we have heard his voice. Indeed, if
we call the roll of imaginary characters who crowd our
memories, we are likely to find that at least half of
them belong to the drama. The Œdipus of Sophocles
and the Medea of Euripides are as distinct in our re-

membrance as the Achilles of Homer and the Dido of
Vergil. The task of bodying forth these characters
may have been more difficult in the dramas than it
was in the epics; but beyond all question, it has been
as satisfactorily accomplished.

The character reveals himself to the spectators by
what he says and by what he does. He exists by his
actions; he exists first of all, for the sake of the plot of
the play, and only secondly for his own sake. And we
may go further and suggest that the dramatist often
takes little thought about those parts of the career of
any one of his characters, which are not directly connected with the special story in which they appear, and
which do not lie within the play wherein that character figures. The character is what he must be in
that drama; but how he came to be that kind of creature, the dramatist does not trouble to tell us; he may
not know, and he may not care. What the characters
are inside his play, the dramatist is intensely interested
in; but what they may have been or what they will be
outside of his play, he does not ask.

Especially is this true of Molière. Who was Tartuffe, before his sinister shadow crossed the threshold of
Orgon's happy home? What misdeeds had he been
already guilty of and what misadventures had he already met? Molière does not tell us; and very likely
he could not have told us. Probably he would have
explained that it did not matter, since Tartuffe is what
he is; he is what we see him; we have only to look
at him and to listen to him to know all we need to
know about him. And who was Célimène, the young
widow who drove the Misanthrope to despair? What
was her family? What was her education? Who was

her first husband? When did he die? These are questions Molière is not moved to answer. Célimène is alive, as Tartuffe was alive; that is enough for their creator. Molière's characters emerge into view, full-grown and full-blooded; they play their parts in the plot; and then the curtain falls and that is the last we see of them.

Here, as in so many other aspects, Shakspere is at one with Molière. We find the melancholy Jaques in the Forest of Arden, moralizing at large and bandying repartees with a chance clown; he talks and we know him at once, as we know a man we have met many times. But who is he? What is his rank? Where does he come from? What brought him so far afield and so deep into the greenwood? Shakspere leaves us in the dark as to all these things; and perhaps he was in the dark himself. Jaques is needed where we find him, in the play with the Banished Duke and his men; and there Shakspere put him, conceived all of a piece and all of a sudden, for this special purpose. And Iago, who is he? How came such an incomparable villain to be intimate with Othello? How was it that he had many friends among the foremost men of Venice? Where had he met and married Emilia? How was it that his wife was the attendant of Desdemona? These things Shakspere does not delay to explain; he takes them for granted; they are because they are; and Iago, being what he is in the play, it matters little what he was before the play began.

Before writing a novel, Turgenieff used to set down the exact and detailed biography of every character who was to appear in his story, thus deciding in advance their antecedents, their birth, their education, and their relations to each other previous to the beginning of the tale in which they were all to take part. No doubt, other novelists have found it profitable to make use of similar devices; but to a dramatist, such particularization would seem needless. His characters appear to him moving and talking; he puts them into his play alive; and there they are once for all. He asks them no questions as to the existence they must have led before they came on the stage to play their parts in his piece.

Mrs. Jameson wrote a charming and fanciful book on the "Girlhood of Shakspere's Heroines," in which she tried to reconstruct the home-life in which each of these delightful creatures had flowered into womanhood, — Portia and Rosalind, Beatrice and Ophelia. She was ingenious in amplifying what seemed to her the hints that Shakspere let fall. Her work is proof that the great poet was able to evoke characters so interesting that we want to know more about them than he has chosen to tell us. But, after all, pleasant as her labor was, it was futile. Portia and Rosalind, Beatrice and Ophelia live in the plays in which they appear; they came into being for that purpose and for that purpose only. And probably, if it could come to his knowledge, no single one of all the immense number of books which have been written about his plays would be more likely to bring a smile to Shakspere's face than this affectionate tribute of Mrs. Jameson's.

These girl-heroines of Shakspere, and all the other characters, male and female, who inhabit his plays, are self-explanatory. We accept them at first sight, without hesitation. We recognize their humanity and their vitality, although it is only a fleeting glimpse of a fragment of their lives that we are allowed. Limited though our vision may be, the opportunity is adequate for Shakspere, as it is for Sophocles and for Molière, and for all the other masters of the drama, each in his own fashion. The characters they set before us on the stage seem to us full, rounded, and complete. We feel that we are acquainted with the chief of these characters as we do not feel ourselves acquainted with our intimate friends. We know all we need to know about them, for we can guess in advance what they will do in the hour of trial. We anticipate their emotions and their acts at the moment of stress. We do not doubt that they will be true to themselves.

We feel this even when these characters are supernatural, when they are outside any possible experience that we could have had in this mortal life. Shakspere, for example, delights in ghosts and in witches and in fairies; and once, at least, in Caliban, he invites us to behold a strange, uncanny, abnormal being only half-human. And yet we never question the propriety of these weird creatures, each of whom obeys the law of its own being. They may be beyond nature, as we apprehend it, but they never strike us as unnatural. Where Shakspere seems most to recede from humanity, so Charles Lamb declared, "he will be found the nearest to it. From beyond the scope of nature if he summons possible existences, he subjugates them to the law of her consistency. He is beautifully loyal to that kind of sovereign directness even when he seems most to detest her. Caliban, the Witches, are as true to the laws of their own nature (ours with a difference) as Othello, Hamlet, Macbeth."

II

Vital as the chief characters are in the major plays of the leading dramatists, existing independently of the plot, as they seem to do when we think about them, every one of them is not only a character but also a part composed for execution by an actor, — often by some one particular actor to whose capacity it was skilfully adjusted, — Burbage or Coquelin, Mlle. de Champmeslé or Mlle. de Molière. In the plays of the inferior playwrights, there are parts only, and these parts depend for their individuality upon the histrionic power of the performers. In the plays of the superior dramatists, these parts, adjusted conscientiously to the actors, are also characters whose abiding life is detached from the performer and even from the play itself. As parts, they may have been enlarged or limited to fit themselves to the comedian or the tragedian to whom they were first intrusted when the piece was originally acted; but as characters, they so impress themselves upon us that we do not necessarily think of the stage when we consider them.

What special aspects and attributes of any character the author shall set before us, must always be decided by the situations of the piece in which that character is to figure. This is made plain when we find a dramatist presenting the same character to us in successive plays, for we cannot help discovering that the character is never quite identical in both pieces. Sophocles represents Creon in "Œdipus" and in "Antigone"; and the character is distinctly different in the later play, with a difference not to be accounted for by the lapse of time and by the strain of the passing years. The later Creon varies from the earlier Creon, because the plots of the two plays are unlike, and because he cannot be exactly the same person in all his characteristics in the one piece that he was in the other. When Shakspere showed the fat knight in love, it was a sadly shorn Falstaff which the plot of the "Merry Wives" forced him to bring before us. The action of that farce, the arbitrary sequence of its comic situations, compelled the dramatist to let us see a Falstaff who is only a shrunken copy of the superb figure that swaggered through the earlier chronicle-play. And Molière acted Sganarelle in half a dozen different pieces, in no two of which is he exactly the same being.

In their broad outlines, the two Creons, the two Falstaffs and the half-dozen Sganarelles are alike, but they differ in many minor traits, sometimes even contradicting the characteristics they had when they first appeared before the public. And it would not be difficult to show that these divergencies are the direct result of the plots of the later plays. Even if the dramatist had wanted to make these creatures of his imagination retain all their original characteristics, he could not very well have done so, since the original plot and the original character are intertwined and interwoven so inextricably that, when the characters are disentangled from this first plot to be immeshed in another series of complications, they have to adjust themselves to these new conditions. They cannot help being subdued to what they work in. On the stage, the author can show us the character only as it is involved in the action; and the action itself decides just how much of the character can be shown, and what aspects of it are to be emphasized.

In every really important play, the characters make

the plot, and the story is what it is merely because the characters are what they are. Yet after all, the characters are only and can be only what the plot permits them to be. The conjunction of character and action is no chance mechanical mixture; it is rather an intimate chemical union. Character and plot are not set side by side; they are united; each exists for the sake of the other and in combination with the other. This is perhaps the reason — or at least one of the reasons — why the dramatist knows and cares little about his characters except as they reveal themselves in the situations of his play. He cares intensely about what they are and what they do and what they say, while they are on the stage in his play. What they may be, or what they may have done or said at other times, he cares little. They have their significance for him only within the framework of his drama.

It is but a small portion of the life of any character that the dramatist can show; and if we seek to deduce the whole man from the part the author has chosen to present in action before us, we need a minute knowledge of human nature and a constructive imagination, like Cuvier's when he demonstrated his ability to reconstitute an unknown animal from a few fragmentary bones. And when we are tempted to this adventure, we shall do well to remember that Cuvier was bringing to life again a being before unknown, whereas the great characters of the great plays are already as well known to us as they are ever likely to be. We may amuse ourselves by following in the footsteps of Mrs. Jameson, but the exercise must be its own reward; and we do well to be on our guard against overestimating its importance.

Stevenson once told a friend that he knew only three ways of making a story. One might start with a group of characters and devise a plot to exhibit them; or one might begin with a plot and fit characters to this; or one might subordinate both plot and characters to a special atmosphere, which was to be realized and made impressive. In the theater, this third method is impossible, since atmosphere alone is insufficient to hold the attention of the throng. The other two methods are available for the playwright; and there is no difficulty in adducing examples of plays composed in accord with the one or the other of these methods. The "Bourgeois Gentilhomme," for example, is plainly a piece in the conception of which the author began with the character of M. Jourdain; having this central figure clearly in mind, Molière devised situations specially to set off the several facets of M. Jourdain's personality. Indeed, so intense was Molière's interest in this character, which he was elaborating for his own acting, that he was a little careless in the putting together of the plot wherein the ambitious burgher is presented; and as a result, the actual story of the play does not get under way until the third act, the two earlier acts having been taken up with the exhibiting of the foibles and personal peculiarities of M. Jourdain. In the "Bourgeois Gentilhomme," we cannot help feeling that Molière did not take trouble enough to find a plot proper for the full display of his central character; at least, we are compelled to confess that in this piece he has sacrificed plot to character.

In the great Greek tragedies, we discover the results of the other method, that of taking a story ready-made and of fitting characters to it. In fact, this method was more or less imposed on the writers of Attic tragedy by the recognized demand upon them to select their themes from one or another of the many legends which were held to be the best material for the purposes of the theatrical poet. Thus the Athenian dramatist, whatever story he might choose to handle, found his freedom circumscribed by the public expectation that he should not depart too widely from the sequence of events consecrated by tradition. The details of incident he might vary at will; but the main lines of his story were laid down for him before he began. As soon as he had announced his subject, the spectators knew in advance the successive episodes which he was at liberty to represent. He might suppress some of these episodes, and he might make others more significant than any of his predecessors had done; but he was not at liberty to contradict the legend as it had been transmitted from earlier generations.

As a result of this limitation of the themes of tragedy to a prescribed body of traditional tales, the dramatists were compelled to treat the same subjects again and again. Every poet was familiar with the plays which various of his predecessors had written on any subject he might undertake, and he was well aware that his successors would make use of the same subject, each in turn modifying it to suit his mood. The treatment of the theme was therefore all-important, since the playwright-poet could not profit by absolute novelty of story. Probably the Attic dramatists felt always that they were working in a severe competition with their predecessors and with their successors; and very likely this put them on their mettle and kept

them up to the mark. They had to take a twice-told
tale and interpret it anew; they had to revive the faded
figures of the legend and to give fresh meaning to the
old story; and this is what the greatest of them did
with unfailing felicity. Æschylus and Sophocles wrote
tragedies on these traditional themes and under these
restrictions, in which there is no suggestion of con-
straint. The "Agamemnon" and the "Œdipus" seem
to us to have been wrought with the utmost freedom;
and their plots appear to be only the logical result of
the interrelation of the several characters.

The same praise may be bestowed also upon Shakspere. If there ever was a play in which character seems
to condition plot, in which the action is what it is only
because the central figure is what he is, that play is
"Hamlet." In this tragedy, all the successive situations are the result of the special characteristics of the
hero. If we did not know better, we might well believe that Shakspere had first conceived Hamlet, and
then cast about him for a story in which that character might be revealed. But we do know better; we
are aware that this was not the case and that the plot
of "Hamlet" had been constructed by an earlier playwright, possibly Kyd, who had seen fit to make a mere
melodrama of it, a violent tragedy-of-blood, full of
broad theatricalism, certain to please the strong-nerved
playgoing public of those tumultuous days. This
tragedy-of-blood Shakspere took for his own, and made
it his own, partly by purging away some of its grosser
effects and partly by elevating the character of Hamlet
to his own loftiest level. Apparently, he did not accomplish this all at once; finding the theme congenial,
he returned to it again and again, as though it were

a labor of love. He gave "Hamlet" revision after revision until he had put himself into it amply, and until he had so ennobled it that it was the richest expression of his genius. What he found a coarse melodrama, he left the most intellectual of tragedies, — the play in which he seemed most abundantly to have voiced himself. He took over another man's invention and transfigured it by his own superb imagination.

What Æschylus and Sophocles had done with "Agamemnon" and "Œdipus," and what Shakspere did with "Hamlet," Molière did with "Don Juan." The skeleton of his great play did not differ very much from that of the Spanish piece from which he derived it more or less indirectly; but its meaning, its vitality, its final value, these qualities it owed to Molière, as indisputably as "Hamlet" was indebted to Shakspere for its enduring power. And this is evidence that it matters little where the dramatist actually begins, whether with plot or with character. What does matter is where he ends, whether the resultant play presents a story wherein the characters are merely the creatures of the plot, or a story wherein the plot seems to be subordinate to character. It is by the final result that the dramatist must be judged, and not by his original choice of a method of procedure.

The leading characters in the great plays are all good parts, forever tempting to the ambitious actor. Although they may have been devised originally for some one performer contemporary with the author, they transcend the limitation of this actor's personality. They are not mere profiles; they are rounded figures to be approached from all the points of the compass; and therefore they are open to a wide variety of interpretation by later actors. In fact, the author would often be surprised to discover that a character which he imagined for a performer of a special type, might be taken successfully by a performer of an entirely different temperament.

Perhaps the most obvious illustration of this is to be found in the stage-history of the "School for Scandal." Sheridan fitted the parts in this comedy to the company he had inherited from Garrick, and no one of them was more closely adjusted to the special performer than the character of Lady Teazle, which was intended for Mrs. Abington. Lady Teazle is a country-girl who has become a woman of fashion; and Mrs. Abington was the incomparable representative of the fine ladies of high-comedy. But when Mrs. Abington retired, Lady Teazle was undertaken by Mrs. Jordan, whose reputation had been made by the performance of romps and hoydens. Mrs. Abington had seen in Lady Teazle only the woman of fashion; and Mrs. Jordan saw in Lady Teazle rather the country-girl who was aping the airs and graces of a fine lady. This second interpretation of the character was probably not at all what Sheridan had intended; but he had builded better than he knew and the character was richer in variety than he had supposed. In its way, Mrs. Jordan's performance of the part was quite as effective as Mrs. Abington's had been. The character which can be seen from only one angle is as thin as a silhouette. It lacks the rotundity of reality.

What is true of characters in comedy, is true also of characters in tragedy. Iago, for example, was played by Edwin Booth as the steely incarnation of evil, pursuing his malignant purpose with indomitable will.

But other actors have chosen to present rather the bluff, hearty, soldierly side of "honest Iago," and thus to give greater plausibility to Othello's confidence in him. And Lewes, who saw them both, dwelt on the extraordinary differences which existed between the Othello of Salvini and the Othello of Edmund Kean. The English actor was impetuous, fiery, volcanic, where the Italian was stately, massive, and overwhelming. As wide a gulf yawned between the Hamlet of Fechter on the one hand, and the Hamlet of Booth and of Irving on the other. What Fechter saw in the play was chiefly the immensely effective series of situations; and he treated it as if it was a melodrama only. Booth and Irving made the situations subordinate to the poetry they felt in the hero; they diminished the violence of the plot as far as possible and bathed the performance in melancholy beauty.

Consider also Jaques in "As You Like It," and ask how he ought to be played. Is he a bitter cynic railing against the world and venting his venom on all mankind, the ultimate type of misanthropic pessimism? Or is he a humorist, always exaggerating his feelings and often saying far more than he means, certain in advance that his associates will not take him seriously, — certain, indeed, that they will be readier to smile at his utterances the more extravagant his speech may be? Either of these interpretations is in accord with the language which Shakspere has put into the mouth of Jaques; and it is by this language only that the character reveals himself. We have no other information about him; he must be judged by what he says; and what he says may be interpreted in these two wholly inconsistent ways.

We can know a character in a play only by what he says and by what he does. Jaques, as it happens, does nothing; his function in the comedy is merely to talk. And the remarks of the other characters in "As You Like It" throw no light on his enigmatic character. Probably Shakspere did not intend these contradictory interpretations; probably he meant Jaques to be clearly perceived for what he is. But Shakspere so projected the character that the other interpretation — whichever this may be — is quite as acceptable now as that which he did intend. In Jaques, as in Iago and Othello, as in Hamlet, Shakspere endowed his character with the complexity of a living human being, whose peculiarities of conduct and of speech we may discuss as we analyze those of one of our own intimates. The character is alive; and like all living things, it is infinitely various, taking on different aspects in the eyes of different observers.

This variety and this complexity in the representation of character may not be the result of the deliberate aim of the dramatist; but he deserves the credit for it, none the less, since he did it, even if he did not mean to do it and even if he did not know that he was doing it. Perhaps he may have supposed that he was giving to the creature of his imagination only the limited vitality demanded by the plot, and yet his imagination may have endowed this creature with a larger life and with a richer personality than the story called for. The more vigorous his imagination and the deeper his insight into human nature, the more likely is he to perform this marvel all unwittingly. The artist who always does his best often does better than the best he intended; by sheer integrity of effort, he is able to surpass himself.

IV

This guerdon is granted only to the true dramatist, and it is not bestowed upon the mere playwright. The inferior craftsman, however adroit and ingenious he may be, is not distinguished by fecundating imagination; and in his plays, the characters do not disclose themselves as more human than he had intended. In fact, the mere playwright does not create character; the most he can do is to devise effective parts for special performers; these parts derive their fleeting vitality from the actors who sustain them. In default of the creative imagination, the mere playwright is forced to rely on his plot rather than on his characters. The mechanism of the action, which is of only secondary importance in the plays of the true dramatists, is of primary importance in the pieces of the playwrights. Kotzebue, for example, and Scribe, displayed a most prolific inventiveness in devising situations; but no character from any one of their plays lingers in the memory. After beholding one of their pieces, we recall what the various personages did, but we have no definite impression as to what these personages are.

Kotzebue's characters, and Scribe's also, exist only in connection with the plots of the plays in which they appear; they were called into being for the sake of the plot; they are sufficient to carry on the action, and outside of that special story, they have no validity. This is the reason why Kotzebue and Scribe are no longer read; and their marvelous dexterity in stage-craft has not kept alive any single one out of all their scores of plays.

Even in the most flourishing periods of theatrical productivity, the true dramatists are only a few; and the immense majority of those who supply the theater are mere playwrights. These playwrights rely on their plots to please the public; and if the stories they narrate in action are interesting enough in themselves, the characters may be the stock-figures of the theater, which the public seems willing to accept generation after generation. There is the young hero, very young and very heroic, blameless and self-sacrificing. There is the lovely heroine, equally exalted in sentiment and equally addicted to self-sacrifice. There is the smiling villain, who sticks at nothing to accomplish his fell purpose and who hates everybody — except the heroine. There is the cantankerous mother-in-law, exhaling her scorn upon the unfortunate man who was unlucky enough to marry her daughter. There is the comic servant, perpetually blundering in his misunderstanding of his master's orders. There is the stern father, implacable in his determination to force his son or his daughter into the marriage he has arranged, regardless of love's young dream.

These are only a few of the traditional figures likely to reappear at any moment in a popular play. Figures equivalent to these are recognizable in the drama of every period. Latin comedy, for instance, took over from the Greek at least a dozen stock-figures which appear and reappear in play after play of Plautus and Terence. There was the greedy parasite, earning his dinner by gross flattery of his patron. There was the braggart coward, forever boasting of his exploits and yet keeping his skin whole, wherever his courage was challenged. There was the intriguing slave, who was prolific in ingenious methods for extracting money from his old master's pocket for the benefit of his young master, and who was untiring in running errands and in carrying love-letters.

These stock-figures of Greek and Latin comedy reappear again in the improvised play of the Italians, in the comedy-of-masks, which is one of the most interesting developments of the drama in all its long history. It was a development possible only among the Italians, who are facile actors and who have the faculty of improvisation. A strolling troop consisted of perhaps a dozen performers, every one of whom impersonated always the same character, a stock-figure of unchanging peculiarities. One of them might be the young lover, Lelio, the same in name and in nature, whatever the imbroglio in which he was involved. Another might be Pantaleone, an old merchant, speaking the Venetian dialect. A third might be the Doctor, an elderly pedant, speaking the Bolognese dialect. Yet another might be Pulcinella, the rascally domestic, indefatigable in ingenious roguery, and speaking the Neapolitan dialect. And a fifth might be the Captain, the self-vaunting soldier, always boasting about his marvelous feats of valor. Of the women, one might be Leonora, the young and lovely heroine; and another might be Isabella, her equally beautiful rival. A third might be Franceschina, the pert waiting-maid, as unscrupulous as the intriguing valet with whom she was likely to pair off. If the company contained a performer of old women, this would be a man, who was bold in suggesting the least attractive attributes of elderly females. Add three or four other performers to fill in the less important personages, and we have a company competent to perform any plot without the aid of a written play and often without even a rehearsal.

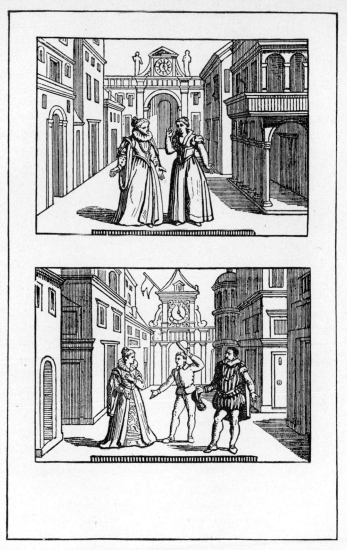

STAGE-SETS OF THE ITALIAN COMEDY-OF-MASKS IN THE SEVENTEENTH
CENTURY, AS USED BY MOLIÈRE IN MANY OF HIS PLAYS

If the manager, who was likely to be also a leading actor as well as the deviser of the plots, had happened to read the Italian story out of which Shakspere made "Romeo and Juliet," he might have " cast" it to such a company as this, discarding the tragic termination, emphasizing the romantic aspects and providing opportunities for the clowning of the comedians. Pantaleone would have had a quarrel with the Doctor. Lelio would have been the son of Pantaleone, and Leonora would be the daughter of the Doctor. The man who played the "old women" would be the nurse of Leonora; and the Captain would swagger as the cousin or brother of Leonora, whom Lelio would kill in a duel. Franceschina would be the serving-maid of Leonora, and Pulcinella would be the valet of Lelio. The manager-author would call the company together and explain to each the relation he was supposed to bear toward all the others. Then he would indicate the sequence of scenes in the several acts; and this scenario, as it was called, would be written out and pinned up behind the scenes. The play might begin with a violent altercation between Pantaleone and the Doctor; but this would be no difficult demand upon either performer, since they had often quarrelled in earlier plays. A little later might come a long love-scene for Lelio and Leonora: and this again would be no novelty, since he had been making love to her in almost every other piece since he joined the company. Lelio had in stock a dozen perfervid declarations of devotion; and Leonora had by experience a dozen different ways of receiving his declaration.

In this fashion, the story of the loves of Romeo and Juliet might be unrolled by means of these stock-figures, each of which retained his own name always and his own individuality. And in this same fashion, any other story, tragic or comic, might be represented by a similar company of Italian comedians, accustomed to one another, and realizing the advantages of conscientious "team-play." The unchanging and highly colored type, which any one of these comedians impersonated and made his own, has an obvious likeness to the bishop or knight or any other piece of a set of chessmen, whose rights and privileges are strictly limited and absolutely invariable, but who can be set in motion in varied and limitless relations with the other pieces.

That the Italians were able to interest audiences, generation after generation, with primitive plots of this kind in which character was subordinated to story, is added evidence that action is of primary importance in the theater. But the pieces these Italians improvised abundantly had only a fleeting vogue. Nothing except depth and sincerity of character-drawing can endow a play with the enduring merit which will resist the inevitable changes of theatrical fashion. The "Romeo and Juliet" of Shakspere survives to-day, as vital as when it was first acted, because its two foremost figures are eternal types of the heedless and headstrong passion of ardent youth.

CHAPTER IX

THE LOGIC OF CONSTRUCTION

You are not going to make or ruin your imagination while here. That is something that will remain if you have it in you; that you cannot acquire if you are not blessed with it. But here you may learn to handle your tools. So measure, copy, plumb. A carpenter who constantly uses a foot-rule can guess the length of a foot better than one who seldom refers to it. — AUGUSTUS SAINT-GAUDENS, *to his pupils, as reported by Homer Saint-Gaudens.*

I

THE technic of the drama is more difficult to grasp than the technic of prose-fiction, because the novelist needs to consider his readers only, whereas the dramatist has always to consider his actors, his theater, and his audience. When we contrast the constructive faculty required by the playmaker with that which we tolerate in the story-teller, we are led to the conclusion that the novel may be the product of unskilled labor, whereas the play must be the work of a craftsman who has learned his trade and acquired the mastery of his tools. Many a modern novel in the English language, more than one of Dickens's, is a sprawling invertebrate. The conduct of the story is haphazard; and we may guess that the author modified his earlier intentions more than once in the course of his writing. Scott began "Woodstock" without knowing how he was going to end it; and he recorded in his journal that when he had finished the first of the three volumes in which the story was originally published, he was at a loss to find matter for the second volume.

Now, the playwright cannot take things in this easy-going fashion. He needs a subject strong enough to carry him through, since charm of treatment and diversity of incident will avail him little, if his theme is not interesting in itself. He cannot rely on constructed decoration; he can only decorate his construction. As the shrewd Voltaire insisted, the success of a play depends very largely on the subject chosen. This subject must, as Aristotle tells us, have a certain magnitude, that is to say, it cannot be trivial or casual; and it must have a beginning, a middle, and an end. Moreover, it must be conducted from the beginning through the middle to the end, as directly as may be. The story cannot straggle into by-paths; it cannot meander into backwaters; it must move forward steadily and irresistibly, setting before the spectators the essential scenes of the essential struggle. The elder Dumas once declared that the secret of success on the stage was to make "the first act clear, the last act short, and all the acts interesting." This is no easy feat; and it can be achieved only by a scrupulous forethought akin to that employed by the architect in designing a building for a special purpose on a special plot of land. The dramatist must accept the obligations thus imposed, and he must meet them as best he can; for it is in meeting them that he fails or triumphs.

Many years ago, before he had adventured himself in playwriting, Mr. Henry James stated the case with his customary insight.

"Between a poor drama and a fine one, there is," he said, "a wider interval than anywhere else in the scale of success.

A sequence of speeches headed by proper names — a string of dialogues broken into acts and scenes — does not constitute a drama; not even when the speeches are very clever and the dialogue bristles with points. The fine thing in a real drama, generally speaking, is that more than any other work of literary art, it needs a masterly structure. It needs to be shaped and fashioned and laid together, and this process makes a demand upon an artist's rarest gifts. He must combine and arrange, interpolate and eliminate, play the joiner with the most attentive skill; and yet at the end effectually bury his tools and his sawdust, and invest his elaborate skeleton with the smoothest and most polished integument. The five-act drama — serious or humorous, poetic or prosaic — is like a box of fixed dimensions and inelastic material, into which a mass of precious things are to be packed away. It is a problem in ingenuity, and a problem of the most interesting kind. The precious things in question seem out of all proportion to the compass of the receptacle; but the artist has an assurance that with patience and skill a place may be made for each, and that nothing need be clipped or crumpled, squeezed or damaged. The false dramatist either knocks out the sides of his box, or plays the deuce with the contents; the real one gets down on his knees, disposes of his goods tentatively, this, that, and the other way, loses his temper but keeps his ideal, and at last rises up in triumph, having packed his coffer in the one way that is mathematically right. It closes perfectly, and the lock turns with a click; between one object and another you cannot insert the point of a penknife. To work successfully beneath a few grave, rigid laws, is always a strong man's highest ideal of success."

The dramatist has to choose a theme and to develop this theme into a story suitable for the stage; he has to set this story in motion so that the scenes which must be shown will follow one another easily; he has to people this story with characters, interesting in themselves and contrasting with one another; and he has to place these

characters in appropriate surroundings, devising opportunities for them to come together without unduly
straining probabilities. He has to do one thing at a time
and all things in their turn. He has to remember always
that the spectators for whose delight he is working
have only one pair of ears apiece and one pair of eyes.
The theater is not a three-ringed circus; and he must
never forget Herbert Spencer's declaration of the doctrine of Economy of Attention, quite as applicable in
the other arts as it is to rhetoric. The dramatist must
make it easy for the spectators to follow his story,
however complicated its plot may be. He must avoid
confusing them or leaving them in doubt as to the
reason for anything done on the stage. The first act
must be clear, of course; but then all the acts must be
clear, or they will not be interesting. The dramatist
has not done his duty when the spectators are puzzled
even for a moment and ask each other what it is all
about.

Yet Dumas is right in insisting that it is of prime
importance that the first act shall be clear, for if this
is obscure, the attention of the audience is distracted,
and they will not be able to follow what comes after.
Two of the most salient differences between a play
and a novel are due to two of the actual facts of performance; first, that in the theater, every minute is
counted, whereby the playwright can waste time only
at the risk of boring and of bewildering the spectators; and, second, that the spectators must seize the
thread of the story as it is unrolled before them, being
denied the privilege of turning back to the first chapter to pick up any hints they may have missed inad-
vertently.

II

Every work of literary art must have a beginning, a middle, and an end; and here is where art sharply separates itself from life, which is all middle, with an end that no man may see, and with numberless beginnings lost in the dark backward of Time. The artist has to decide just what portion and just how much he will present of this unending pattern which is a-weaving on the loom of eternity. He must have a beginning somewhere and he must make an end somehow. The epic poet of old, and his later inheritor, the novelist of to-day, have to conform to this as well as the dramatic poet; but narrative art is far freer than dramatic, far more flexible, far less restricted by the demands of a rigid form.

The strict limitation of the time allotted to him debars the dramatist from the leisurely method of approach which the novelist may adopt if he sees fit. In a story, the author can begin as far back as he likes, filling his opening pages with a detailed record of his hero's ancestry, even unto the third and fourth generation, dilating at will upon details not strictly essential, and digressing as much or as little as the spirit moves him. But in a play, the writer must select what is significant, and he must so present this that its significance is manifest at first sight. He can neither digress nor dilate; he must keep to the straight line which is the shortest distance between two points. Many things must have happened before he lifts the curtain; and out of all these, he has to make his choice, so that he can center attention on those special things which he knows the audience must have in mind for the full comprehension of his action. He suppresses rigorously all the rest, however tempting they may be in themselves. He must supply the spectators with exactly the information they will need to apprehend the movement of the plot, no more and no less.

The first desire of the audience present at the performance of a play is to understand what it is all about, and their second demand is that the action shall develop before their eyes so that it can be followed without effort. When two characters of the play meet for the first time on the stage, the spectator is glad if he already knows who they are, what their relation is the one to the other, and what they are each of them striving for. If this information has already been given to him, he can listen to their dialogue with intelligent interest. If this information has been withheld, his attention is likely to be distracted by his effort to place the two characters and to guess what they are driving at. Often the two characters can explain themselves in a word or two at the beginning of their talk; but often again their relations are more or less complicated, depending on an unusual series of antecedent events. The more intricate this complexity may be, the more obvious is the obligation of the playwright to set it forth with the utmost sharpness, so that it cannot be misunderstood. A full appreciation of the relations of the several characters to each other is a condition precedent to the playgoer's interest in the action, as it is unfolded before him.

In the vocabulary of stage-craft, this conveying to the audience of the knowledge necessary to enable them to follow the plot is known as "exposition." It is a very important part of the art of construction. It is one of the tests by which we can gage the dexterity of a dramatist, and by which we can measure his command over the resources of his craft. Some playwrights have to perfection a knack of taking the playgoer right into the middle of things in the opening scenes of the first act, with a simplicity apparently so straightforward that he has never a suspicion of the artfulness whereby he has been supplied with all sorts of information about the past history of the chief characters. Some dramatists are careless and slovenly in exposition; and some are leisurely and cumbrous.

But no dramatic author can evade the necessity of telling the audience all about that portion of his plot which took place before the curtain rises on his first act. Sooner or later this information must be supplied somehow. The dramatist can do it in a prologue which is spoken before the play begins, as Plautus does in the "Captives." He can do it inside the play in a long soliloquy which is practically a prologue, as Euripides does in "Medea." He can put it into tense dialogue supported by swift action in the opening scenes of the first act, as Shakspere does in "Othello." He can postpone it for a while and scatter it through the whole play, as Ibsen does in "Ghosts." But he must not put it off until it is too late, as Ibsen does in "Rosmersholm," where we do not learn until the final act the real motive which has been guiding Rebecca West. This we should have liked to know earlier in the play, since it would have enabled us to perceive the transformation that had been wrought in her character.

If we may deduce a principle from the practice of the most expert playwrights, we should be led to believe that the best method of exposition is to compress it into the first act, even at the risk of making the

earlier scenes a little slow and labored. When they
first take their seats in the theater, the spectators are
alert and ready to seize even the slightest hint. They
have not had time yet to be tired and they are therefore less easily bored. Besides, even if they are bored
by the first act, they have paid their money for the
evening's entertainment, and therefore they can be
relied on to stay where they are and to await patiently
the second act with the firm hope that this will turn
out to be more interesting.

This was Scribe's habit, and Scribe was a past-master
of all the mysteries of playmaking. He massed all his
explanatory matter in the earliest scenes of his piece,
making everything transparently clear, so that even
the dullest and the laziest spectators could not fail to
understand the situation. He brought his characters
into the action one by one, introducing them to the
audience carefully so that they might always thereafter
be identified. If he thought it advisable, he did not
hesitate to give up a whole act to mere exposition, well
aware that he could recapture the full attention of the
spectators by the celerity with which the action would
go forward, after these preliminary explanations and
introductions had been got rid of. Thus it is that in
"Adrienne Lecouvreur," he kept the heroine out of the
opening act, in which all the other characters appear
to lay the foundation of the plot, and he artfully reserved her first appearance to awaken fresh interest
in the second act.

Scribe's contemporary, the elder Dumas, was quite
as careful and as skilful in his introductory scenes.
He liked to begin briskly, and to combine his exposition with the action itself. He has told us that he had

invented the story of one of his most successful plays, "Mademoiselle de Belle Isle," two or three years before he was ready to write it, postponing the actual composition until he happened on an effective opening. One day he heard about a pair of lovers who had broken a coin in two, each keeping a half, with the understanding that when either tired of the other, the half-coin should be returned as a token of the end of their intrigue. He seized on this eagerly and used it as the starting-point of the play already completely plotted in his head.

The younger Dumas, the author of the perennial and pathetic piece known to American playgoers as "Camille," inherited from his father a native gift for playmaking and a subtle insight into its conditions. He declared that the art of the dramatist is an art of preparation chiefly, and that every scene should be led up to so adroitly that the spectator expects it vaguely and welcomes it warmly. And he had derived from his father also a liking for a striking beginning, which should grip the interest of the audience at the very rise of the curtain, forcing them to perceive at once and without hesitation the relations of the chief characters to one another.

But it is in one of his later and less successful pieces, the "Femme de Claude," that he provides the most ingenious specimen of his skill in opening a play with a scene which is at once explanatory and effective in itself. When the curtain rises, the stage is dark and the spectators can dimly perceive a room with its shutters closed. An old servant enters with a night lamp, which she holds up to the face of a clock; it is morning, and she is going to let in the dawn. Then she hears a tapping at the window, followed by a woman's voice, which she recognizes with regret. "Why the devil is *she* coming back?" she asks herself. "All was going well here." Then she throws wide the shutters and opens the door for the woman outside. And from the brief dialogue which follows, as sharp and as cold as the crossing of two swords in a duel, the spectators learn that the returning woman is the wandering wife of the master of the house, and in response to her questions as to what has happened during her absence, the old servant sets before us all of the facts which are necessary to interest us in the strange play.

Sardou, the contemporary of the younger Dumas, and the successor of Scribe as a dramaturgic artificer, was also ingenious in his expositions. The first act of "Fédora," for example, is a prologue which is needed to explain and to justify the play it precedes; but it is also swift in its action and pictorial in its movement; and when at last the curtain falls on it, we see that the clever playwright ended it with an interrogation mark, with a suggestion of suspense which keeps us in our seats wondering what will be the outcome of the fatal episode we have witnessed.

Often, however, Sardou adopted another method, as in his earlier social satires, "Nos Intimes" and the "Famille Benoiton," and in his later historical melodramas, "Théodora" and "Gismonda." In these plays, he used his first act, and often his second also, to paint a phase of society, modern or ancient. He brought before us a crowd of characters, entertaining in themselves and humorously contrasted with one another, making amusing remarks and revealing themselves in amusing situations. As the play goes forward, the spectator begins to have his attention drawn to a little group of more striking figures; and in the later acts, these figures take the center of the stage, the host of merely pictorial characters sinking into the background, after having served their purpose. It is by means of the talk of these subsidiary personages that we have been made aware of the relations of the really important characters. In Sardou's hands, this method was employed to advantage; but it is dangerous, since it tends to distract the attention of the audience from the core of the real drama. For its successful use, it requires the marvelous dexterity of a wizard of stage-craft, such as Sardou was; and it was Sardou's misfortune that his delight in his own skill as a contriver of artful devices led him too often to be content with a play which is only an empty mechanism, in which the spectators can see the wheels go round and by which all human feeling has been crushed out of the story.

III

One of the oldest devices, outworn now and long ago discarded by self-respecting dramatists, is to open the play with the conversation of two or three servants, dusting the room and setting the furniture to rights. These domestics are allowed to inform the spectator that it is two years or ten since master and mistress quarrelled and parted, and that now husband and wife are to meet again for the first time since their separation. Equally ancient is the obvious artifice of beginning the piece by compelling one character to tell another what that character already knows. The artificiality of this seems to us now a little too transparent. Yet Dryden did not scorn to employ it more than

once, notably in his "Spanish Friar," which begins
with the meeting of two officers at night who repeat
aloud what each of them is already familiar with.
It is no wonder that Sheridan saw the absurdity of this
threadbare convention and made fun of it in the bur-
lesque tragedy which is rehearsed in the "Critic."

And yet the audience must be told somehow, and
even the clumsiest exposition is better than leaving the
spectator in the dark. In the drama, as in all the other
arts, simplicity is the best policy; and that exposition
is most satisfactory which is at once straightforward,
and swift and clear. This is what every great dramatist has tried to attain, well aware that it cannot
be achieved without taking thought. The principles
of dramatic art are unchanging through the ages,
and Æschylus in Athens, Shakspere in London, and
Molière in Paris, had to solve the same problem that
Scribe and Sardou had to struggle with in their turn.
Each of them, in his own fashion, had to take the audience into the heart of his story, supplying the information necessary for its appreciation as best he could.

Æschylus opens his masterpiece, "Agamemnon,"
with a watchman on the roof of the palace, waiting for
the fiery beacon which shall announce the fall of Troy;
and as he waits, he delivers a long soliloquy conveying
to the spectators the needful knowledge of the state of
affairs which the returning hero will find when he
comes back to his long-deserted home. Molière opens
his masterpiece, "Tartuffe," with a piquant discussion
of the character of the hypocritical intruder, which
strikes the note of the play and which prepares us for
all that follows. Goethe said that the first scene of
"Tartuffe" is "the greatest and best example of an

introduction which shows the significance and importance of what is to come"; and he declared that Molière
was "the man from whom most about the technic of
the modern drama can be learned." And yet Molière
was sometimes bold in employing more primitive
methods of exposition, not hesitating to begin a play
by sending on a character to make a soliloquy in which
the situation is set forth boldly.

Shakspere was careful in the exposition of his earlier pieces, both comic and tragic. He plunges into the
thick of his story in the opening scene of "Othello,"
in which he shows us Iago waking Desdemona's father,
with the unwelcome news that the daughter of a Venetian patrician has married a Moor. And he follows this
with the meeting of the Senators, where Othello is called
upon to tell the story of his wooing. When the first act
of the play is over, we know all that we need to know,
and our attention has been kept keenly on the alert,
while we are eager to be told how the strange marriage
will turn out. Equally ingenious and effective is the
first act of "Romeo and Juliet," in the opening scene
of which we find the feud between the Montagues and
the Capulets so embittered that it breaks out into a street
brawl. And then, when this envenomed quarrel has
been shown unforgettably, we are allowed to be witnesses of the love-at-first-sight of the son of one house
for the daughter of the other.

It is characteristic of the incisive but often haphazard criticism of Hazlitt that he casually dismissed
the "Comedy of Errors" as a careless piece of work.
Now, it is a fact that Shakspere, who was capable of
an infinity of pains in handling his plot when his theme
had kindled his interest, was careless enough in the

construction of some of his later pieces, in "Cymbeline" especially, and in the "Winter's Tale." But
there are few evidences of this relaxing of his artistic
standard in his earlier plays, and none at all in the
"Comedy of Errors." Indeed, careless is just what
this play is not and just what it could not be, since it
depends entirely on the adjustment of its mechanism.
It is only a farce, after all, inferior, and perhaps unworthy of the hand that was to give us "Othello" and
"Macbeth." Like other farces, it has to rely not on the
humor and the veracity of its characters, but on the
adroitness of its situations. It stands revealed frankly
as farce when we examine its plot, which is patently
impossible, since it requires us to accept the existence
of two pairs of twins so alike in looks, in speech, in
manner, and even in costume that they can be constantly taken the one for the other, in spite of their
having been brought up in different places.

That the spectators may get amusement out of the
various mistaken identities which make up the plot,
it is absolutely essential that they should be told plainly,
at the very beginning, all about the two sets of twins,
and that they should have explained to them the strange
combination of circumstances which has resulted in
bringing both pairs of brothers together unexpectedly
in the same city, the one master and his servant having every reason to believe that the other master and
the other servant have been lost at sea. To tell these
things so that there shall be no doubt about them is
no easy task; and Shakspere accomplished it with absolute certainty and with perfect apprehension of dramatic effect. He opened his play with a hearing before
the Duke, who is judging the case of the father of the

two young masters.   This bereaved parent has come
to seek his missing son, and in so doing he has violated
the local law against strangers.   He pleads as his excuse his paternal love for his lost child.   Thus the whole
story of the two pairs of twins, of their birth and of
their separation, of their survival each unknown to
the other, — all this is set forth in the speech of an old
man on trial for his life, a situation which instantly
arouses the sympathy of the audience and secures their
unflagging attention.

We can see one reason for Shakspere's extreme care-
fulness in exposition when we recall the fact that more
than half of the Elizabethan playgoers were not provided with seats. The groundlings, as they were called,
had to stand all through the performance, and they
could not help being more restless and therefore less
alert to follow the explanations of the author than if
they had been comfortably seated. But even if they
were a little restless at times, the audiences for whose
delight Shakspere composed his plays were quick
enough to seize and to appreciate what the dramatist
gave them. Here Shakspere was far more fortunate
than Plautus who had to amuse the Roman populace,
made up of freedmen and of foreigners, the riffraff and
the rabble of the city, often only imperfectly acquainted
with Latin. In his "Captives," Plautus dealt with a
story the beginnings of which are rather complicated,
although not really so intricate and so difficult to explain as the antecedents of the characters in the "Comedy of Errors." The Roman playwright evidently had
no confidence in the intelligence or in the attention
of his audience; and so he took no chances. He did
not dare develop the relations of his characters in the

play itself until he had made use of a prologue, in which the whole situation is elaborately explained so that even the dullest must get hold of it. Nor did this satisfy him; he made the speaker of the prologue insist on his explanation two or three times over, until it was driven into the heads of the spectators, however stupid they might be. And no doubt this extreme emphasis of exposition was only what was absolutely necessary under the circumstances.

It is difficult always for a dramatist to gage the average intelligence of his successive audiences. What is only explanation enough for one set of spectators may be undue insistence on the obvious for another. And the wise playwright is ready to risk offending the quick-minded few to make sure of the understanding of the slow-witted many. Planché records the advice given to him early in the nineteenth century by a sagacious old stage-manager named Bartley. "If you want the British public to understand what you are doing," this shrewd observer declared, "you must tell them that you are *going* to do it; then you must tell them that you *are* doing it; and after all you must tell them that you *have* done it. And then, confound them, *perhaps* they will understand you."

IV

This is a hard saying, yet it contains much wisdom. Especially is it important for the playwright to tell the spectators what he is going to do, — or at least to evoke the interest of expectancy and to lead them vaguely to desire what he is about to set before them. In prose-fiction, it is possible to captivate readers by keeping a secret from them, disclosed only at the most impressive moment. In fact, the effect of the detective-story depends solely on this device; the author invents an enigma and he tries to keep us guessing until the last page. And even novelists of a richer endowment, possessing true imagination in addition to mere invention (which is all that the writer of mystery-tales needs), novelists like Fielding and Thackeray, may legitimately leave us in doubt for a little while, and reveal the secret of the birth of Tom Jones and of Henry Esmond only when they see fit. But this the novelists may do because their unhurried reader can take time to think. And this the dramatist cannot do. One of the first rules of the stage is not to keep a secret from the spectators. The failure of Charles Lamb's "Mr. H." was more or less due to the circumstance that the misguided author chose to conceal the real name, of which his hero was ashamed, not only from the other characters in the little farce, but also from the audience. The spectators must know the facts, even though the characters may be left groping in the dark until the last act. Indeed, the audience finds special pleasure in the perplexity of the people in the play; it wonders what will happen when Othello discovers the villainy of Iago, or when Sir Peter Teazle finds out that Joseph Surface is a hypocrite.

In Mrs. Oliphant's uninspired biography of the author of the "School for Scandal," she exhibited her total failure to grasp this principle. Herself a successful writer of prose-fiction, she had no understanding of the fundamental differences which necessarily exist between the art of the novelist and the art of the dramatist. When she came to deal with the screen-scene of the "School for Scandal," one of the most

effective episodes in the whole range of comedy, she
was guilty of a masterpiece of undramatic criticism.
Sir Peter has come to the library of Joseph and he is
told that there is a little milliner hidden behind the
screen which stands before the window; and suddenly,
when this screen is overturned, he finds himself face
to face with his own wife. And then Mrs. Oliphant
made this hopeless comment: " It would no doubt have
been higher art could the dramatist have deceived his
audience as well as the personages of the play, and
made us also parties in the surprise of the discovery."
That is to say, she would have substituted a single
shock of astonishment for the long-drawn series of an-
ticipations aroused in the spectators, from the moment
of the husband's entrance, by their knowledge that it
was Lady Teazle who was hidden behind the screen.

The playgoer likes to exercise his ingenuity and to
foresee what is about to happen on the stage. In fact,
his interest is really not so much in what is to happen
as the way in which this event is going to affect the
characters involved. He thinks it likely enough that
Sir Peter will discover that Lady Teazle is paying a
visit to Joseph Surface; but what he is really anxious
to learn is the way the husband will take it. What
will Lady Teazle have to say when she is discovered
where she has no business to be? How will Sir Peter
receive her excuses? What will the effect be on the
future conduct of both husband and wife? These are
the questions which the spectators are eager to have
answered. The dramatist may excite curiosity by all
sorts of ingenious devices, but he must never deceive
the spectators. He may keep them in suspense or in
doubt, but he must not absolutely mislead them.

INTERIOR OF DRURY LANE THEATER, LONDON (1808)

For the earlier house on the same site, Sheridan wrote the "School for Scandal"

Even in prose-fiction, the impression made by a startling surprise is only fleeting. When we have once been granted an explanation of the mysterious deeds, our curiosity is satisfied; and the book is rarely taken up a second time. Few of us ever care to peruse a tale of Wilkie Collins after we have once found out the key of the puzzle, although we may return again and again to Tom Jones and to Henry Esmond, following the career of either with renewed interest, in spite of the fact that we are in possession of the secret of his birth. Poe was very shrewd when he asserted that "Barnaby Rudge" would have been more interesting if Dickens had eschewed all mystery-mongering. In the drama, our knowledge of the end of a play in no wise interferes with our enjoyment. We go to see the "School for Scandal" and "Othello," whenever they are properly presented, regardless of the fact that the end is familiar in advance. We are glad to have new dramatists handle again the old themes, "Francesca da Rimini," and "Faust," curious to observe the variations which the younger generations can play on the old tune we have known from our own youth. In this, we are like the Greeks of old, the Athenians who, in spite of their longing to hear some new thing, contented themselves in the theater with the traditional stories which every dramatist took over in turn, transforming them to suit his own genius.

Here, as in all matters of art, the Greeks displayed their good sense. Novelty of plot is possible only within narrow limits; and every dramatist has to borrow again the situations which were the common property of his predecessors. Gozzi, the Italian playwright, once declared that there were only thirty-six possible situations; and when Goethe and Schiller tried to catalogue them, they could not find even thirty-six. There was truth of a kind in the schoolboy's definition of a plagiarist as " a writer of plays." The dramatist must be forever working over old material, since there is nothing new under the sun. But if the situations he can use are very few, the characters he may create are without number. Human nature is infinitely various, and the playwright has unlimited credit when he is drawing a draft on our common humanity. His plot may be as old as the hills, if he can only people it with lovers as young as the springtime, with men and women eternally fresh because they are true to life. Brisk young fellows had wooed coy maids in many a comedy before Orlando and Rosalind met again in the Forest of Arden, and Orestes had set out to avenge his murdered father centuries ere the same burden was too heavily laid on Hamlet.

The plot is only the frame in which the portrait is suspended, even though plotting is more essential than character-drawing. The ultimate value of the situations is that they enable the dramatist to reveal human nature. And this is one reason why dramatists of high distinction have sometimes seemed careless in winding up their plays. Of course, every playwright must work out the end of his piece before he writes his first line. Until he knows just where he is going, he cannot set out on his journey, since he has no leisure for a false start. And yet this goal to which he is journeying may be arbitrarily chosen, and when it arrives it may seem illogical or even contradictory.

It is difficult to exaggerate the necessity of an exposition so clear that no misunderstanding is possible even on the part of a preoccupied spectator. The beginning of a play is really more important than the end, although in strict logic the proper untying of the knot would seem to be the more necessary. But if an audience has sat for three hours, following with keen enjoyment the successive episodes of a conflict between forces evenly balanced, it does not insist upon logic; it is often better pleased to have the knot cut arbitrarily than to be delayed by the process of untying. It has had its pleasure, pressed down and running over; and it is not churlish in denying to the author the privilege of finishing off the play as he thinks fit. The play itself is what counts, not the way the story is made to end. The picture of life is what the spectators have enjoyed; and they do not — or at least the most of them do not — care what moral may be tagged to the fable by which they have been entertained. Perhaps this is one reason why Shakspere and Molière are sometimes so casual in the winding up of their plots, as though they were admitting that since in real life nothing ever comes to an end, so on the stage, even if an end of some sort is asked for, one end is about as good as another.

The modern playgoer prefers a happy ending. He has a fondness for the old-fashioned fairy-tale finish, "and so they lived happily ever after." It is only in opera that he is willing to tolerate the sadness of death. He is not like the playgoer of Athens who seems to have expected always to see the doom fulfilled and fate accomplished. And this is not a recent trait of the playgoer's temperament; we can find an earlier yielding to this in the marrying off in the last acts of "Measure for Measure," for example, when that gloomy play demanded a more serious conclusion. And Molière not only brought Tartuffe to justice, but also took the trouble to restore the fortune of Orgon, which is in the nature of a concession to this predilection of the public for a pleasing solution. So Mr. Gillette, in his "Secret Service," an admirable play in its veracity as well as in its ingenuity, carried us straight to the tragic end which is the only logical issue of the circumstances and the characters, — and then, at the culmination, when the prompter's hand was on the bell to ring down the curtain, the author suddenly reprieved his hero and married him off in the twinkling of an eye. The effect is as though the dramatist was saying to the audience, "Of course, this play is a tragedy, and it cannot really be anything else, but, if most of you insist on a happy ending, you may have it your own way!" It is true that there had been so much comedy here and there in "Secret Service" that the spectators were not ready to take the play as a tragedy.

Such a violation of logic would have been very offensive to the younger Dumas, who was stern in his insistence that the plot of a play ought to be like a mathematical demonstration. The conclusion must be the sum total, the working out, of all the other scenes. This principle is sound enough when it is applied to Dumas's own pieces in which he was defending a thesis or expounding his own opinions. It is sound when applied to the social-drama of Ibsen, sustained by a moral proposition. In the social-drama, the playwright is bound to be honest with himself and with the audience. He has then no right to be illogical, for logic is of the essence of the contract, as the lawyers say. He must keep faith with the spectators, since he is presenting

to us a sociological problem and inviting us to accept
his solution of it. But in the comedy-of-character and
in the comedy-of-manners, no such obligation is really
imposed on the playwright. In the plays of these allied
types, the dramatist has no thesis to sustain, no private
opinion to parade; and he is content to set before us a
group of human beings whom he puts through their
paces, whom he turns inside out before us. And when
he has done this, he has accomplished his purpose, and
the play can be wound up summarily by the customary
wedding bells.

V

This license allowed him at the termination of his
work, the playwright sometimes asks for in the middle
also; and here he is on dangerous ground, where he
must move circumspectly, picking his way cautiously.
It must be ever his chief aim to make his work appear
as "natural" as may be; and his art is held in the highest esteem only when he is able to avoid not only the
extravagant and the arbitrary, but even the accidental.
It should be his constant endeavor so to present the result of his loving labor that it can be apprehended and
appreciated with as little effort as possible. This is a
quality of sculpture and of painting, when these arts
are at their best. It is a characteristic more especially
of those literary arts in which the poet undertakes to
tell a story either in drama or in prose-fiction. Whether
the story-teller is setting his tale in action on the stage,
or presenting it in narrative in verse or in prose, he is
bound to do his best to give the utmost verisimilitude
to the series of events to which he is inviting the attention of the spectator or the reader. In planning his plot,
he must endeavor to make these events coherent and

clear and complete in themselves. He can do this only
by isolating them from all the other events which have
been taking place at the same time. From out of the
tumultuous turmoil of existence, he must select a sequence of happenings to which he has to give a semblance of unity; and he chooses this particular chain
of events, and not any other, because he can see in it
a significance worthy of artistic presentation.

These actions of certain characters plucked out from
the tangled web of real life he has to set by themselves;
he has to condense them and to relate them logically;
he has to keep out all extraneous and casual circumstances not bearing directly upon them. Only by this
process of exclusion is he able to focus attention upon
the group he has determined to show us. He is compelled to neglect and deliberately to leave out of account all the other persons then going about their business anywhere in the world at large. It is his duty so
to deal with this group of picked men and women that
their deeds shall seem to be determined by themselves
and by themselves only, unaffected by what might be
done by outsiders.

Here, of course, the artist has to depart from the
mere facts of life as we all see them; and by tacit agreement, the spectators authorize him to make this departure. In life, there are no groups of human beings
detached from their fellows, sufficient unto themselves
and uninfluenced by the rest of humanity. We cannot
help knowing that every man and every woman is eternally immeshed in the intricate complexity of existence,
and that we are all of us affected by the myriad movements of our fellow-creatures. And yet when we are
spectators at a play, or readers of a novel, we not only

permit this departure from the circumstances of actual life, we demand it absolutely. We are eager to have the artist profit by the convention proper to his art.

What we desire from the artist is not the exact fact, but the underlying truth, of which the several facts are only the external accompaniment. We want him to choose his little knot of characters and to segregate them from out the mass of their fellow-beings, that we may the more easily follow the story he is ready to set before us. It is this isolated action of an isolated group of characters that we want to see. And we are swift to praise the artist for the skill with which he can depart from the actual to give us what we are glad to accept as the real. As Victor Hugo insisted in the preface of "Cromwell," the "domain of art and the domain of nature are absolutely distinct," since a reality in art is and must be different from a reality in nature.

The dramatist and the novelist demand from the public the permission to select what they prefer, to arrange this as they may see fit, and to leave out all that they have no immediate use for; and they do this so that the public shall be called upon to give its attention only to a single group of characters taking part in a single sequence of events, logically related the one to the other, and moving forward without any interruption from the outside world and without any obtrusion of chance. And this the public gladly allows, hoping to see in the story, whether it is on the stage or in a book, the working out of a single notion, taken by itself, naked of non-essentials, and uncontaminated by external accidents such as occur commonly enough in actual life.

In childhood, we can be amused easily by tales of the Impossible and of the Improbable; and most of us never outgrow this childishness. But as we advance in years and in wisdom and in knowledge of the world, many of us become more exacting; and we insist that the author who wants our regard shall not stray too widely from the Probable. A few of us will go so far as to bestow our warmest welcome on the writer who seeks to deal only with the Inevitable, and who tries resolutely to tell the truth about his characters and to let them obey the law of their being, doing only what they must do and eschewing everything that they would not do if they were left to themselves.

We hold those plays and those novels to be the finest and the most enduring in which we are made to feel that nothing has happened by accident or because the author himself intervened at the critical moment, and in which every action of every character is what it is because it could not be otherwise, if the conditions are what they have been represented. This ultimate truth, this abiding veracity, this inexorable inevitability, is what we are delighted to proclaim in most of the mightier masterpieces of literature — in the "Œdipus" of Sophocles, in the "Macbeth" of Shakspere, in the "Tartuffe" of Molière, — and also in the "Heart of Midlothian" of Scott, in the "Scarlet Letter" of Hawthorne, in the "Smoke" of Turgenieff, and in the "Anna Karénina" of Tolstoy.

While both the novelist and the dramatist are held strictly accountable to this ethical standard and are both of them bound to tell the truth as they see it, the playwright has a more difficult task esthetically than the story-teller. His explanations have to be summary,

and the deeds of his characters must speak for themselves. It is always difficult for the dramatist, and indeed it is not always possible for him, to make his plot
as clear and as swift as it ought to be, without a single
intervention of chance or a single deed which is not the
spontaneous result of the individual will of the character who performs it. While we have a right to demand
from the leisurely novelist a strict obedience to the
letter of the law, we are inclined to relax the code now
and again for the benefit of the dramatist. And the evidence that we are not so severe with the playwright as
with the story-teller is to be found in the fact that we
tolerantly overlook in more than one of the great plays
the intervention of chance or the obtrusion of the arbitrary, which we should be much less likely to pardon
in a story claiming equal rank.

For example, "Romeo and Juliet" is a tragedy, and
in a tragedy nothing ought to be left to chance and
everything ought to be the result of the volition of the
various characters. And yet we cannot help seeing
that the fatal termination of the story, seemingly inherent in the deadly feud of the rival houses, is brought
about at last by what is only an accident. If Friar Laurence had but thought of the device of the potion two
minutes earlier, before Romeo parted from Juliet in
the cell, or if only the letter Friar Laurence sent after
Romeo to Mantua had not miscarried, then Romeo
would have known that Juliet was not dead but sleep-
ing; he would not have taken poison; and Juliet would
not have been glad to die on his dead body. A recent
commentator has made bold to defend this as a subtle
touch of Shakspere's art, in that it serves to remind
us of the large part which chance plays in all human

affairs. Ingenious as this defence may be, it is radically unsound, since it confuses the reality of nature with the reality of art.

The reason why this obtrusion of accident into this tragedy of Shakspere's does not shock us, or even annoy us, is twofold. In the first place, we cannot help feeling that doom is ever impending over the ill-starred lovers, and that even if Romeo had known about the potion, something else would assuredly have brought about the unavoidable end. And in the second place, Shakspere very adroitly wastes little time on explaining why the letter failed to reach Romeo. Indeed, the letter is something we do not see; it is something that we are merely told about. Now, in the theater nothing grips our attention except what is actually shown to us. What is talked about makes little or no impression; the empty words go in one ear and out the other. And nobody knew this better than Shakspere.

In "Romeo and Juliet," the plot ends as it does because of an accident, which is indisputably arbitrary. In certain other of Shakspere's plays, the action is what it is, because one or another of the characters acts arbitrarily, not of his own accord, but solely because the poet compels him to this deed that the plot can be carried on. If this arbitrary character is one of the important personages of the play, then this act of his focuses our attention and we cannot help noticing it. But if this arbitrary character is unimportant in himself, we pay little heed to him, and we may even not note his departure from truth. In the first case, the falsity of his conduct is so paraded that the interest of the play suffers, whereas in the second case, we are so taken up in following the fortunes of the vital figures, that we pay no heed to the misdeeds of the minor characters, who exist merely to work the plot.

In "As You Like It," for instance, the conduct of the usurping Duke and of Oliver, the elder brother of Orlando, is not logical, or at least it is not so presented as to make us believe in its strict relation to their characteristics. The Duke and Oliver fulfil their purpose, when their ill-founded jealousies bring about the union of Rosalind and Orlando in the Forest of Arden. And their sudden and absurd repentance at the end of the play, their reformation in the twinkling of an eye, does not vex us because we really do not care what they may do or how completely they may contradict themselves. So also in "Much Ado about Nothing," the malignant machinations of Don John and Borachio are almost motiveless, — at least their willing wickedness is taken for granted by the playwright and accepted by the playgoers. The cause of their villainous intrigue against the gentle Hero is suggested summarily, with no serious effort to buttress it into plausibility. We can discover this weakness, if we care to look curiously at the construction of the plot; but this is just what we are not tempted to inquire into. We are so busy following the wit-battle of Benedick and Beatrice that we have no leisure to peer into the motives which move two minor but necessary persons to bring about the startling climax of the comedy.

On the other hand, if the character who acts arbitrarily is in the thick of the story and holds the center of the stage, then with all our good will we cannot help noticing what he is doing, and it irritates us to be forced to observe his inadequately motived actions. Necessarily our interest flags, when we hear the machinery creak a little too loudly. In the "Winter's Tale," for instance, the swift jealousy and violent rage of Leontes seems to us in the twentieth century merely wilful, and almost without justification. It is quite possible that this unexpected transformation of character was pleasing to the Elizabethan audiences, for whom the play was originally prepared and who relished surprises of all kinds, even if these contradicted the strict logic of the character. But nowadays we like to see every character obeying its own logic ; and when it renounces this continuity, we are vexed that the author had not taken more pains to attain plausibility. So in the "Two Gentlemen of Verona," a chief personage of the piece, Proteus, is shown to us as a perfect gentleman at one moment, and at the next as an unspeakable cad; and the plot turns on this unexplained and inexplicable change in him. And in this arbitrariness of Proteus and of Leontes, set in the forefront of these dramas, we may find one reason why the "Winter's Tale" and the "Two Gentlemen of Verona" are not so popular in the theater to-day as are "As You Like It" and "Much Ado about Nothing," in both of which the arbitrary characters are subordinate and unimportant.

VI

These illustrations have been taken from Shakspere, but they might have been chosen from almost any modern playwright. Sardou, for example, never wrote a more ambitious drama than his "Patrie," a historical play having for its background the manly resistance of the Netherlands to Spain. The piece abounds in pathetic situations and in adroit inventions; but it has always proved disappointing in the theater, because the heroine, whose shoulders bear the burden of the plot, acts more than once not as she would have acted, but as the author forced her to act so that the play may be what he had plotted. The ordinary spectator may not be able to give this as the reason why he has not enjoyed the performance, but he feels dumbly that something is wrong.

A central character who acts arbitrarily before the eyes of the spectators, so that they are forced to witness his self-contradiction, is certain to alienate the sympathy of the audience and to imperil the success of the play, unless this central character happens to be either of two distinct things. He may be enigmatic, and then the spectators will tolerate what they do not clearly understand; or else he must be openly the villain of the play, and then they are ready enough to accept any dark scheme, however obscure its motive.

Hamlet is the best possible example of the character who is both arbitrary and enigmatic; but Hedda Gabler is almost as significant. Hamlet is subtle and moody and changeable; and we never know what he will do next. Hedda is queer and abnormal and freakish; and we accept her for what she seems to be at the moment, tolerating in her many things which would be intolerable in another woman. It is only when we study this play of Ibsen's in the library and endeavor to dissect its mechanism, that we perceive that more than one of the heroine's actions, which appeared sufficiently spontaneous in the theater, was really the result of the adroit author's desire to bring about the fatal termination he had resolved on.

Iago is the best possible example of a very important character who acts arbitrarily without interfering with our interest in the play. Iago's hatred of Othello is the mainspring of the plot; and this Shakspere calmly takes for granted. It is true that the author feels the need of explaining it, and of justifying it. He gives three or four different reasons for it; but none are convincing. Indeed, one of them is almost absurd, — Iago's jealousy of Othello because he suspects his chief of an intrigue with Emilia. All of them taken together fail to account adequately for the fiendish malignity of Iago's revenge. But we are not moved to protest, since we see in Iago a figure of incarnate evil, capable of any wickedness and working destruction without restraint and almost without cause, simply because of his blackness of soul. From a creature morally so hideous nothing astonishes us.

But it is only a villain or an enigmatic character whom we are willing to pardon for acting arbitrarily. The hero and the heroine of a play must conform to our idea of the natural. They must act as we think they would act in real life, or else they lose our sympathy. If the hero and the heroine continually do before our eyes what seems to us unreasonable, our interest in their story slackens and is soon dispersed. This is a chief reason why Browning's "Blot in the 'Scutcheon," powerful as it is, has never been able to establish itself in the theater. Nor is Browning the only poet who has fallen into this error. The plays of Beaumont and Fletcher, for example, abound in scenes of infinite pathos and of striking theatrical effectiveness; but these authors were careless of probability and reckless in the conjunction of incoherent episodes. In any one of their pieces, any character may do anything at any moment wholly regardless of consistency.

This liking for the unusual and for the violent is not uncommon among the tragic dramatists, many of whom seem to have felt that ordinary life is so commonplace that nothing is really dramatic unless it is strange and unheard of. Corneille, for example, deliberately sought for the most unlikely combinations, and searched history to find them, not unsuccessfully, since fact is often stranger than fiction. Again, Schiller allowed Karl Moor, in the "Robbers," to believe the worst on a mere hint from his villainous brother, although the hero is well aware that no dependence ought to be placed on anything from such a source; and yet such is the sweeping force of Schiller's story as it surges swiftly along that the spectators have scarcely time to notice this inconsistency. Victor Hugo also constantly made use of very improbable coincidences. In his "Ruy Blas," almost every character is more or less arbitrary, and hardly a single incident occurs except by the more or less obvious intervention of the author; and yet such is the charm of the resonant verse with which these prearranged happenings are presented, that the play still pleases in spite of its inherent artificiality.

Ibsen, on the other hand, sought to express the inner significance of the commonplace and to disclose the tragedy which may lie latent in the humdrum. The arbitrariness of incident and the frequency of coincidence, which are raised to the maximum in Hugo's romanticist pieces, are reduced to the minimum in Ibsen's realistic social-dramas. But even Ibsen is sometimes a little disconcerting; and the startling transformation of Nora in the final act of the "Doll's House" has seemed to some critics, if not actually in contradiction to her character, at least not satisfactorily prepared for.

Perhaps also the confession and self-abasement of Consul Bernick, in the " Pillars of Society," is not what the author had led us to expect from a character so self-seeking and so smugly self-complacent. In both of these plays of Ibsen's, however, this element of the arbitrary is to be found only in the last act, after our interest has been aroused and sustained by the veracity of all that has gone before.

If an author cannot work out his plot absolutely without the intervention of the arbitrary, then he will do well to follow Aristotle's advice and keep it out of that part of the story which he is going to present, and to throw it back before the beginning of the play. This is what Sir Arthur Pinero did in " His House in Order," which turns on the discovery by a downtrodden second wife that her predecessor had been unfaithful. Here the arbitrary character is the first wife; and she is dead long before the play begins. This again is what Sophocles did two thousand years earlier in " Œdipus the King." An oracle had predicted that Œdipus would kill his father and marry his mother; and when the play opens, the prediction has been fulfilled. If Œdipus had ever inquired into the circumstances of the death of Iocasta's first husband, he would have been able to avoid the predicted incest. But if he had made this inquiry, we could not have had the play. As we look back over the whole story, we cannot help perceiving the overwhelming improbability that after the warning of the oracle, Iocasta should ever have dared to marry a man young enough to be her son. The Greek poet was not bound to supply any explanation for this inexplicable procedure of hers, because he was only dramatizing a legend long familiar to the immense

majority of the Athenian audience. The improbability
being in the legend, it had to be in the drama dealing
with the legend; and Sophocles very wisely wasted no
time in any effort to explain it away. Here he was
shrewder than the modern poets who have handled
the same myth, and who fatigued themselves in a vain
attempt to make the improbable a little less improbable,
with the sole result of forcing the spectators to notice
something they might otherwise have taken for granted.

These two arbitrary situations, the failure of Œdipus
to pursue the slayer of Laius, and the marriage of Iocasta with a man many years her junior, — this is the
foundation of the story. The two things may be impossible to accept, but if we refuse to accept them, then
we reject the play which is based on them. It was an
interesting discovery of Sarcey's that an audience is
never unduly exacting about the assumption on which
a play is founded. It will listen to the exposition of a
most unlikely state of affairs; it will give its attention
to the author while he sets forth the existence of two
pairs of twins so alike that their own wives cannot
tell them apart (as in the "Comedy of Errors"); or
while he explains that a wandering Englishman is
the very image of the sovereign on the throne (as in
the "Prisoner of Zenda"). It will sit back calmly and
wait to see what will happen next, giving the author
all the rope he asks for, but whether to hang himself
or to pull himself on deck is as the event turns out.
If the play which the author builds on an arbitrary
supposition of this sort catches the interest of the spectators and holds them enthralled as the story unrolls
itself, then they forget all about its artificial basis and
they have no leisure to cavil. If, on the other hand, the

play is dull and fatiguing to witness, their attention strays away from it and they have time to go back to its arbitrary foundation. And then they rise up in their wrath and denounce the foolishness of the author who dared to suppose that they could ever be interested in anything built upon an absurdity so flagrant.

CHAPTER X

THE ANALYSIS OF A PLAY

Back of every art product there is a conception, vaguely or definitely present in the artist's mind. Upon the character of this conception or content depends the significance of the work of art; its formal beauty depends upon the artist's skill to express his thought or feeling in the particular medium he has chosen. Content and form are therefore most intimately related in the artist's personality. He can express nothing through the concrete medium of his particular art — whether it be a pigment or clay or a harmony of musical sounds or a succession of words — unless it has first passed through the lens of his own nature. It is always difficult, and in a certain sense unnatural, to make a sharp separation between the elements of content and form. The artist himself rarely attempts it. He "thinks in color" or feels in terms of musical sound. The finer the work of art, the more indissolubly are the elements fused through the personality of the artist. And yet it is often of the greatest value to the student to attempt this separate analysis, — to distinguish what has gone into the work of art from the external form in which it is clothed. — BLISS PERRY, *A Study of Prose Fiction.*

I

WHEN we have witnessed the performance of a play in the theater, or when we have read it in the library, making the imaginative effort needful to visualize its action, we find ourselves either liking it or disliking it. We have an opinion as to its merits and its demerits; but we may not be able to formulate this opinion to our satisfaction or to bring forward the several reasons which have led us to it. We may wish to analyze the emotions we have experienced and to find justification for the faith that is in us. If the play pleased us, we want to know why it pleased us. We may even go further and desire also to know whether our pleasure was legitimate or not. What was the source of it? Is the play really as good as it seemed to us? We may have felt that here was a drama that we ought to like, and yet that it did not interest us; and in that case, was the fault in the play or in us? On the other hand, we may have enjoyed it, having all the while a sneaking suspicion that it was not really worthy of our approval. In short, what are the proper tests to apply that we may each of us be assured of our own judgment?

The beginning of wisdom is honesty with ourselves. Our own impressions must always be the basis of our opinions, or we are certain to be insincere and to weaken our grasp on reality. First of all, did this play interest us? If so, why? If it did not, why did it not? Interest is something that can easily be gaged. If the play was actually seen in the theater, when did our attention begin to flag? If it was only read in the library, when did we fail to visualize the action and begin to skip as though in haste to be done with it? Just here, use can be made of a device which may seem a little pedantic at first sight, but which is in fact practical and helpful. We can make a diagram of the interest aroused in us as the play progressed, drawing a single line which shall rise with our increased attention, which shall run on a level when our attention slackens, and which shall droop when we admit ourselves to be bored.

This diagram of interest will mark and measure the path we have traveled. It is a visible record of our impressions, and it gives us a tangible foundation for further inquiry. It is wholly distinct from the artificial pyramid which Freytag exploited in his "Technic of the Drama"; and it has no relation to the needlessly complicated figures which have been devised to elucidate (or to obscure) Shakspere's plot-making. It is simplicity itself, and yet it serves to bring before us graphically the immediate effect of the play upon ourselves.

As the dramatist has carefully to attend to his exposition in the first act, to introduce his several characters, to inform us as to their past lives and as to their present desires, and, in a word, to get his machinery started, we need not be surprised if the line of interest is almost level in the earlier scenes. But it ought to begin to rise before the end of the first act. And it ought not to droop again until toward the end of the last act, flattening a little perhaps when the spectators are at last able to foresee just how the story is going to turn out. In a well-made modern play in three acts, the line of interest, broken into three pieces, is not likely to vary greatly from this : —

DIAGRAM A.

This diagram would represent exactly the increasing interest the average spectator would take in such a play, if he had kept his finger on his pulse, so to speak. A similar but unbroken line would serve to indicate the interest taken by the audience at the performance of a great Greek tragedy, except that it would rise more sharply and that it might fall off more emphatically

toward the end, since the delicate artistic perception of
the Greeks led them to relax the tension after the culminating moment. Here is the diagram of interest of
the "Œdipus the King" of Sophocles: —

DIAGRAM B.

"Whether it can be artistic," so Professor Bradley has
declared, "to end any serious scene whatever at the point
of greatest tension seems doubtful, but surely it is little short
of barbarous to drop the curtain on the last dying words,
or, it may be, the last convulsion, of a tragic hero. In tragedy,
the Elizabethan practice, like the Greek, was to lower the
pitch of emotion from this point by a few quiet words . . .
and so to restore the audience to common life, 'in calm of
mind, all passion spent.'"

There is a modern play, akin to this masterpiece of
the Greek drama, in its somber gloom and in its inexorable inevitability. This is Ibsen's "Ghosts"; but the
Scandinavian playwright refused to relax the tension
at the end. He even prolonged it beyond the limits of
the play, leaving us wondering what happened after the
final curtain fell. So we may represent its line of interest thus: —

DIAGRAM C.

In "Hamlet," the interest is constantly ascending from the very beginning, that admirably effective opening scene on the battlements of Elsinore, which carries us at once into an atmosphere of impending doom; but it wavers a little in the fourth act and it flattens off almost in the Greek fashion after the death of Hamlet himself. This then would be the diagram: —

DIAGRAM D.

In "Othello," the exposition is also swift and gripping; and the attention is held all through the first act. But in the second act, the story shifts to Cyprus; and several scenes elapse before the dramatist can key up the action to the same pitch of intensity. When he does achieve this at last, he is able to intensify our interest by every succeeding episode almost to the final word. And this is made clear in the diagram: —

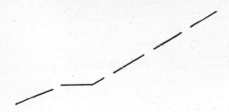

DIAGRAM E.

Victor Hugo, in two of his plays, "Hernani" and "Ruy Blas," was so far negligent of cumulative effect that his fourth acts were filled with matter not closely knit into the central theme. And it is therefore not unfair to disclose this defect in the diagram of "Hernani," thus:—

DIAGRAM F.

and in that of "Ruy Blas," thus:—

DIAGRAM G.

This diagram makes clear the reason why the English adaptation, acted by Fechter and Edwin Booth, was in four acts only,—the uninteresting act being boldly omitted.

In the "Weavers" of Hauptmann, one of the most striking of social-dramas, there is unity of impression but no concentration of story. The several acts have each of them an interest of their own; but, as a whole, the plot is not coherent or cumulative. And this is disclosed at once in the diagram:—

DIAGRAM H.

Now and again we happen upon a play which is frankly disappointing and which is quite unable to hold our interest whether on the stage or in the study. And then we might be forced to a discouraging diagram like this: —

—— —— —— —— ——

DIAGRAM I.

or even to another, still more condemnatory: —

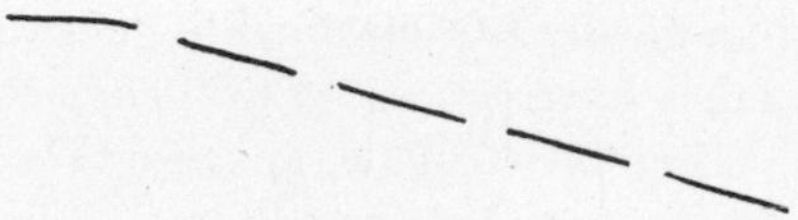

DIAGRAM J.

This translation into a diagram of our fluctuating interest in a play is a test primarily only of the skill of the playmaker. It is a test of the form of the piece and not of its content; for every work of art is to be judged by its form as well as by its content. The great plays are great only because a worthy content is presented in a worthy form. The dramatist must do his best to arouse and to hold the interest of the spectators before whom his play is performed. And the merit of any message he may have to deliver does not excuse him for any failure to master the technic of the dramaturgic art. If he prefers to express himself dramatically, then he must abide by the decision of the theater. From that there is for him no appeal, since an audience of his own contemporaries is the tribunal he has himself chosen. He may have a message of high importance, he may have his own vision of human life, he may have his own philosophy; but these things he can present in a play only after he has acquired the craft of the playwright. And the value of his subject-matter will not excuse him for any technical deficiencies. He must master the methods of the stage of his own time, adjusting his story to the actor and to the theater, and keeping in mind always the opinions and the prejudices of the audience for whose pleasure he is working.

II

The dominant peculiarity of a body of spectators assembled in a theater is their unwillingness to be interested unless they have presented to them a story which discloses an essential struggle, an assertion of human volition, a clash of contending desires. This essential struggle, whether comic or tragic, must be the core of the play; it must be sharply visible; or else the attention of the audience will wander. If we are moved by any performance to make diagram I or diagram J, we shall probably find that the play thus disparaged lacked an essential struggle, that the characters did not know their own minds, and that things seemed merely to happen and not to be brought about by the logic of character and circumstance. If we find ourselves led to make diagram H, we may be assured that the play had no dominating figure, and that the struggle was fragmentary and not concentrated and coördinated. If we consider carefully the plays for which diagrams E, F, and G were made, we can easily discover that the level or dropping lines were due to a straying away from the essential struggle, to a momentary wandering into a by-path, after the dramatist had indicated to us the main road along which he promised to travel.

Yet diagrams not unlike E and F and G would have to be made for the plays of many of the Elizabethan dramatists, especially for certain of those credited to

Beaumont and Fletcher, — because these authors were able to obtain their startlingly effective situations only by an arbitrary change in one or more of their characters. It is disconcerting to us nowadays — whatever it may have been to Elizabethan playgoers — to see an important character do or say something which we feel he never would have done or said. We cannot help applying the standard of common sense, of normal human conduct. And when a character fails to attain this standard, when we see him doing something which he would not naturally do, something which is in contradiction with all we know about his motives, then we have our attention violently distracted. We are forced for the moment to consider this deed; and thus we lose contact with the play as it is going on before us.

Our interest may fall for yet another reason not quite so simple to grasp. The author may have avoided the arbitrary and he may have stuck to his main story, but without presenting in action all the special scenes which he had led us to expect, the *scènes à faire*, as Sarcey called them. If he has suppressed these or shirked them, then we find ourselves disconcerted, as though deprived of a promised pleasure. We do not always know exactly what it is that we have been defrauded of, but we are vaguely conscious that all is not as it should be. Thus our attention is again distracted, although it is only by taking thought that we can discover the special scene which we had hoped for and did not get. Here a diagram reveals its utility. It tells us just where it was that the interest fell off and it points out the precise spot where we must seek the explanation. A supreme test of dramaturgic instinct lies in the choice of those parts of the plot which shall be shown in action and those which shall be merely narrated. Goethe revealed his deficiency in the native gift of playmaking in his version of "Romeo and Juliet," wherein he omitted the actual quarrel between the Montagues and the Capulets and contented himself with telling about it instead of putting it visibly before the spectators.

Another cause of relaxing interest is the use of outworn traditions, of temporary conventions no longer acceptable to us, even if they were satisfactory enough to an earlier generation of playgoers. The permanent conventions we are glad to allow always, since by denying them we should be depriving ourselves. But there are temporary conventions, which correspond to temporary theatrical conditions and which begin to strike us as absurd as soon as these theatrical conditions have changed. For example, a device, now so outworn that it is likely to raise a smile and thus to break the current of sympathy, is eavesdropping. When we see a gentleman concealing himself deliberately behind a curtain, to overhear the conversation of two ladies, we feel that this is an act of which he ought not to be guilty. He loses our regard and the play suffers immediately. It was the duty of the dramatist to invent some less obvious method of putting this gentleman in possession of the information thus improperly obtained. The audience is ever applying the standard of good manners as well as the standard of common sense.

III

Another source of distracted attention is to be sought in the uneasiness which spectators sometimes feel when they find that the play they are witnessing does not belong to the type which they had been led to expect. A good farce affords amusement to many; and farce itself is a perfectly legitimate type. But when we are invited to a comedy-of-manners, or when a play begins as though it was a comedy-of-manners, and then degenerates into farce and turns out to be quite different from what it had at first declared itself to be, then we are likely to be disconcerted. Naturally, we are tempted to apply to this farce the standards proper enough to the comedy-of-manners and not to those of the farce itself; and the result is unsatisfactory. Sooner or later, we may make a mental readjustment, and take the farce for what it is and not for what we had supposed it to be; but in the meanwhile, we have felt a certain confusion.

So it is that when we go to see a poetic play, a tragedy, whether in prose or verse, we apply the standards proper to tragedy, and we expect to be thrilled by the deeds of men and women governed by the stern logic of their own characters. The sadness of tragedy is due to the pity of it, to our feeling that it had to be what it is, and that the catastrophe was all foredoomed by fate. Our pleasure may be austere, but it is noble, and it depends upon the artistic honesty of the poet. It is his duty to make us sympathize with the characters who are battling with destiny, who are doing their best, and who are waging a losing fight. And we are swift to perceive and to resent any arbitrary intervention of the author, whereby his tragic figures lose their large humanity and sink into mere puppets pulled here and there by the visible hand of the playwright.

Here we find an explanation for the doubt which often obsesses us after we have witnessed the performance of a poetic play. We recognize the poetry; we cannot deny the fine quality of the writing; and yet we wonder why it is that the play has left us cold. Our modesty may even make us believe that the fault is in us and that we ourselves may be incapable of appreciating a work of art at once delicate and noble. We know what we like, after all, and we are aware that this drama did not give us the pleasure proper to the theater. Of course, the fault may be in us; but in the case of Browning's " Blot in the 'Scutcheon," for example, the fault is in the author. If we have failed to enjoy his play, the blame must lie at his door, because he has not been able to sustain his tragedy on the lofty tragic level. The discredit for the failure of a play of high aspiration is very rarely to be borne by the audiences. It must be assumed, more often than not, by the dramatist himself, because he has not really given us what he thought he was giving us.

As the French painter put it pithily to his American colleague: "True art is a method of expression, done by a man who has something to say in poetry or prose, paint or clay." It is not sufficient that he have something to say; he must also master the method of expression which he has chosen. He must say what he has to say in such fashion that we cannot choose but hear. He must deliver his message so appealingly that we are glad to listen to it, even if we may be unwilling to accept it. He must remember always that the content of his work will avail him little or nothing if the form of it is not also satisfying to the main body of his contemporaries.

IV

Closely akin to this necessary veracity of character-delineation is the larger truth of the play as a whole.

Is this portrayal of our common humanity in accord, not only with the logic of the several characters introduced, but also with the manners and customs of the time? Is it true to life as we all know life? We are disappointed if we fail to find the accent of verity in what purports to be a picture of existence as it is. If this accent of verity is lacking in a serious drama or in a high-comedy, the principle of Economy of Attention is violated at once. We cease following the story on the stage while we look at each other with dumb inquiry. We find ourselves asking who these strange creatures are that behave in this curious fashion, refusing to play the game of human intercourse according to the established rules.

Mr. Henry James once suggested as a test of the rank of a novel that we ask ourselves whether it aroused in us the emotions of surprise or the emotions of recognition. If it amuses us only by the ingenuity of its story and by the startling effect of its unexpected incidents, it stands on a lower plane than if it please us by revealing unsuspected recesses of the human soul, which we accept as veracious although we had never before perceived them. The same test is as valid in the theater as in the library; and in a serious drama, as well as in a high-comedy, mere surprise must always be subordinate to the subtler recognition. We expect the dramatist to explain us to ourselves and to turn his lantern on the hidden corners of character, whether tragic or comic. When we see a personage in a play do this, or when we hear him say that, we ought to feel instantly that however unforeseen the deed or the saying may be, it was precisely what that personage would have done or said at that particular moment of his life.

Of course, we are not justified in applying this test to the humbler forms of the drama, perfectly legitimate as they are, but dwelling on a lower level. We have no more right to expect the emotions of recognition in a melodrama or in a farce than we have in a detective-story or in a tale of adventure. In these humbler forms of prose-fiction and of the drama, the story itself, the successive situations, the plot, are of primary importance: and they awaken chiefly the emotions of surprise. The characters exist for the sake of the story ; the story is not created by the characters moved by their own volition. When we go to a farce or a melodrama, we cannot justly expect to discover in them the essential qualities of serious drama or light comedy. We ought to be satisfied if the author has given us the essential qualities of farce or of melodrama.

v

The playgoer is disconcerted when the story represented before his eyes on the stage is peopled by characters who seem to him unreal and untrue to themselves. But he is willing enough to accept any frank departure from the actual; he is not insistent on the mere facts of life. If he can get the deeper truth, he has no objections to make believe if he is invited to do so; he is willing enough to accept the supernatural, for example, and to follow with unflagging interest the actions and the words of ghosts, of witches, and of fairies, although he refuses to credit the actual existence of any such beings. All he demands is that these non-existent creatures shall be represented as obeying the law of their own being. He knows well enough that the story of the "Midsummer Night's Dream" never happened and that it is not in accord with the facts of life. But he accepts it as artistically true, since the fairies in that delightful fantasy are seen to do precisely what he imagines fairies would do if there were any fairies. So he does not cavil at the Ghost in "Hamlet" or at the Witches in "Macbeth," because their words and their deeds are just what might be expected from such creatures. The spectator accepts them for what they are in the play, so long as they comport themselves as he conceives such weird embodiments would comport themselves. He is glad to adventure himself in a realm of fantasy; but he expects its inhabitants to be bound by its own legal code. In other words, essential veracity has no relation to the mere actuality of every-day existence. It is the permanent truth that the audience expects, not the accidental fact.

And this leads us to a consideration of the question of the moral influence of a work of art. Morality enters into art only when art deals with human conduct, when it sets before us that which may have an influence upon our own acts. Music, architecture, pure decoration, landscape and marine painting, and also the poetry which is only music or decoration, — these forms of art have no moral quality. They lie wholly outside of the domain of ethics. But the lyric of human feeling, epic poetry, prose-fiction, the drama, — these are forms of art which deal directly with human passions; and therefore they cannot evade moral responsibility. Whenever an artist is dealing with human beings, he is subject to the moral law; and he must be judged by the ultimate effect of his portrayal of life. In man, and in man only, is morality bound up.

This is why we do not protest against the customary

puppet-play of "Punch and Judy," which we allow our children to laugh at. Considered by any human standard of conduct, this little drama is hideously immoral, for it sets before us a career of triumphant and self-satisfied crime. We behold Punch rejoicing in a series of atrocious assassinations; he kills his baby; he murders his wife; he slays the policeman; he hangs the hangman; and finally he beats the life out of the Devil himself. And throughout the long succession of evil deeds, Punch remains smilingly cheerful, wholly unconscious of his own total depravity. And this is the reason why the little play is not really immoral. It has no possible relation to mankind; and we never dream of applying to Punch, only a little figure animated by the hand of the concealed performer, the strict code of human conduct. Punch stands outside the circle of our common humanity; we do not accept him as one of ourselves; and his example carries no weight.

If the lamentable tragedy of Punch is morally innocuous, can the same plea be made for other plays, such as the British pantomimes at Christmas, and the American musical-shows, peopled with beings of a fantastic unreality? Probably there is a certain validity in this plea. These pantomimes and these musical-shows are absurdly remote from life as we all know it; and they contain a very large element of fantasy. And yet they are performed by men and women, after all, not by puppets; and it is impossible for them wholly to escape from the jurisdiction of the moral law. It was this plea that Charles Lamb put forward in behalf of the English comedy of the Restoration. He admitted that it was immoral, if tried by the ordinary code of human conduct; but he insisted that the characters of

Congreve and Wycherley were so far removed from
reality, they showed so contorted a vision of life, that
they were no more human than Punch. "The whole is
a passing pageant, where we should sit as unconcerned
at the issues of life or death, as at the battle of frogs
and mice," so Lamb asserted, after having declared
that he confessed himself "glad for a reason to take
an airing beyond the diocese of the strict conscience."
Lamb presented his paradox with all his frolicsome
humor; but none the less it is a paradox, as Macaulay
had no difficulty in proving. Perhaps Lamb himself
could sit as unconcerned before the unlovely intrigues
of Congreve's gallants and fine ladies as at the battle
of frogs and mice; but the rest of us cannot attain to
this fanciful detachment. After all, these gallants and
these fine ladies are human beings, going about their
affairs, and differing only in the callousness of their arid
souls. They cannot subtract themselves from the jurisdiction of the moral law, by renouncing "any preten-
sions of goodness or good feelings whatsoever." We
feel them to be flesh and blood with us; and we apply
to them properly enough the standard of morals.

VI

To say that the English comic dramatists of the
Restoration are immoral, because their plays convey
a totally misleading impression of life, is a very different thing from saying that they are blameworthy because their comic pieces are not explicitly moral. The
playwright is never called upon to be a preacher. The
direct inculcation of morality in the drama or in prose-
fiction is bad art. Charles Lamb justly complained
of the writers who insisted on tagging a moral to their

tales, "like the *God send the good ship safe into harbor* of the old bills of lading." We have cast aside the antiquated theory of poetic-justice, so-called, which practically required a playwright to endeavor to prove that vice always comes to a bad end. This doctrine obtained generally in the eighteenth century; and we can find it declared emphatically in the English translation of d'Aubignac, in 1684: —

"One of the chiefest, and indeed the most indispensable Rule of Drammatick Poems, is, that in them Virtues ought always to be rewarded or at least commended, in spight of all the Injuries of Fortune; and that likewise Vices be always punished, or at least detested with Horrour, though they triumph upon the stage for that time."

The doctrine of poetic-justice demanded that the drama should be overtly didactic, even at the cost of departing from the truth of life. We all know that vice does not always come to a bad end in this world, whatever may happen to it in the next. We all know, also, that if the author persists in blackening his evil characters, he may end by arousing our sympathy for them as victims of persecution; and it seems as though Thackeray had not quite escaped this blunder in his insistent unfairness to Becky Sharp. Bret Harte told us of a Californian who contemplated Hogarth's series of engravings contrasting the careers of the Idle and Industrious Apprentices, and who was moved with an irresistible feeling in favor of the one whom the moralist had condemned. It seemed to him, he said, that "the cards had been stacked against that fellow from the start." And in a work of art, this is ever the danger of a paraded moral purpose, external rather than internal, not inherent in the theme but applied to it from the outside. Stevenson spoke of the morality which is thrust into many an English novel "like a carpet thrown over a railing."

We have outgrown the demand for this sign-post preaching. The artist cannot evade his moral responsibility, if he chooses to handle human life; but he is no longer required to get up into the pulpit. It is not the artist's business to prove a thesis, but to picture life as he sees it and feels it and knows it. His attitude has been stated admirably by Shelley in the preface to the "Cenci" : —

"The highest moral purpose aimed at in the highest species of the drama is the teaching of the human heart, through its sympathies and antipathies, the knowledge of itself; in proportion to the possession of which knowledge, every human being is wise, just, sincere, tolerant and kind."

To teach the human heart the knowledge of itself — this is a lofty aim; and it can be attained only by resolute honesty in dealing with the problems of conduct. The artist must ever be sincere with himself. He must tell the truth as it is given to him to see the truth, to tell nothing but the truth, — even if he is not bound always to tell the whole truth, because it is not given to any man to grasp the whole truth. That he is privileged and empowered to do this is the supreme happiness of the artist. "The conscious moralist often seems rather stupid and arbitrary," so Professor Gilbert Murray remarks; "the poet has the immense advantage that he is not trying to say what he believes to be good for other people, or what he believes they believe to be good for them, but is simply expressing what he himself loves most."

Although the dramatist need not put morality into

his plays, he cannot leave it out, since it is an essential constituent element of any truthful portrayal of life. But he need not take thought about it. His work will have ethical validity in proportion as his own vision of life is truthful. While the dramatic author can never appear on the stage in his own person, and while he cannot speak for himself, commenting on his characters as the novelist may if he chooses, there is no literary form in which the author expresses himself more completely than he does in the drama. Shakspere does not intervene in the action, as Thackeray does, to hold confidential colloquy with us; and yet Shakspere's philosophy is quite as clear to us as Thackeray's. Molière the man, with his abhorrence of affectation, with his hatred of hypocrisy, with his gentle and alluring humanity, stands revealed in his plays, although we have not a single letter of his to take us into his confidence; and his correspondence, if we had it, would not substitute another portrait for that which rises before us after a study of his plays. As George Sand once wrote to Flaubert: "Real painting is full of the soul which impels the brush." And a truthful painter of human life cannot hope to hide his own soul, however adroitly he may think that he has concealed it.

Here is another reason for a sudden diminution of interest as we follow a play. The author may have begun veraciously enough, only to yield at last to the temptation of contaminating truth and of contorting it for the sake of quick effect. If we perceive this, we resent it; and the stronger our feeling the more certainly is our sympathetic attention diminished. We expected the bread of life; and we find ourselves put off with a stone. It needs to be noted also that even veracity may momentarily disconcert us, if it pierces deeper than we relish. The author may have a wider knowledge and a deeper vision; and he may go searchingly below the surface, disclosing things ugly and abhorrent. This may shock us, but what shocks us is not necessarily immoral. Very often, indeed, it is profoundly moral, with the particular morality which we happen most to need. Morality is not in the choice of subject-matter, else would "Œdipus" and "Othello," the "Scarlet Letter" and "Anna Karénina" be immoral. It is in treatment, in the stern firmness which braces the soul for combat with evil, or in the looseness of tone which tends to relax the fiber. It is not in the avoidance of dangerous topics that morality lies, but in the temper with which they are treated.

So it is that in a real work of art, there is no one obvious moral; there are as many separate morals as there are spectators of that work. Every man finds his own moral for himself, as he gages the total effect on himself, whether he is ethically strengthened or weakened by that work of art. Sarcey declared that, after seeing a certain play by the younger Dumas, — a piece which most English-speaking spectators would not be likely to find ethically stimulating, — "it is difficult not to take home with you a wish to examine your conscience and a certain disquieting wonder as to the result; this is the sign by which we can know a truly moral work."

CHAPTER XI

Forty poets, amongst them ten of superior rank, as well as one, the greatest of all artists who have represented the soul in words; many hundreds of pieces, and nearly fifty masterpieces; the drama extended over all the provinces of history, imagination, and fancy, — expanded so as to embrace comedy, tragedy, pastoral and fanciful literature, — to represent all degrees of human condition, and all the caprices of human invention, — to express all the perceptible details of actual truth, and all the philosophic grandeur of general reflection; the stage disencumbered of all precept and freed from all imitation, given up and appropriated in the minutest particulars to the reigning taste and public intelligence: all this was a vast and manifold work, capable by its flexibility, its greatness, and its form, of receiving and preserving the exact imprint of the age and of the nation. — H. TAINE, *History of English Literature.*

I

THERE have been four or five periods in history when the drama has risen to a supreme height. The first of these was in Greece when Æschylus, Sophocles and Euripides, Aristophanes and Menander, followed one another in swift succession. The second and the third were almost simultaneous in England and in Spain, when Marlowe, Shakspere, and Ben Jonson led the way in the one language, while Lope de Vega and Calderon revealed the lyrical richness of the other. The fourth was in France, when Molière followed Corneille and preceded Racine. And we may perhaps add a fifth period, in France again, in the middle of the nineteenth century, when Victor Hugo and the elder Dumas were followed by Augier and the younger Dumas.

Each of these epochs of superb playmaking has its own characteristics; and each of them will amply reward lifelong study. Yet for us who have English as our mother-tongue, there is no doubt which is the most interesting of the five. It is that splendid expression of the poetic power of our race, which took place in the spacious days of Elizabeth, and which died down in the leaner years of James. In any study of the drama among us, the plays of Shakspere and of his gifted contemporaries must always be the center of our interest.

There is no denying that the dominant characteristic of the English-speaking race is energy, and that this energy never expressed itself in literature more completely than it did in the later years of Elizabeth's reign. There was then the most abundant revelation of the power and passion of this sturdy people, the most magnificent luxuriance of its essential imagination, and a sudden outflowering of the vigor of a hardy and prolific stock. And above all the turmoil of those glorious days, there towered aloft the genius of Shakspere. Small wonder is it that many lovers of literature have been blinded by the effulgence of all this genius, and have closed their eyes to all except its glory, unable to perceive anything but absolute perfection. So long have we made a habit of using a megaphone to proclaim its manifest and manifold beauties, that a microphone would suffice for our infrequent and unwilling admissions that all was not equally faultless in this splendid era. Some of us still recall the shock of surprise with which we first happened upon a passage in one of Matthew Arnold's essays, seeming to suggest that there might be weak places in Shakspere's works, and that even his genius did not always maintain him at the topmost pinnacle of transcendent achievement.

But to adopt an attitude of insistent admiration is to renounce the privilege and the duty of criticism, as Gautier did when he declared that, if ever he found a single line of Hugo's to fall short in any way, he would not confess it to himself alone, in a cellar, on a dark night. We deny ourselves the pleasure of knowing wherein the Elizabethan poets are truly mighty, if we give them all credit for all possible excellence, or if we carelessly fail to see clearly that even the mightiest of them does not always sustain himself at his highest level. The work of the great Elizabethans is what it is; and for that we love it. But also it is not what it is not; and we ought to be honest enough not to claim for it the qualities which it lacks, and which it could not have because they are inconsistent with those it actually has. Largeness of vision it has, and depth of insight, and the gift of life itself, and many another manifestation of the energy of the race. These possessions are beyond question; and yet, because it possesses these qualities, because it has sweep, and penetration, youthful daring, and robust vitality, it is often violent, often trivial, often grotesque. Reckless and ill-restrained, it is likely to be wanting in taste and lacking in logic. Energy it has above all things else, and a compelling imaginative fire; but balance and proportion it rarely reveals. Infrequently do we find symmetry and harmony, — qualities somewhat incompatible with the wastefulness of effort always characteristic of this masterful people.

More than any other group of the Elizabethans, have the dramatists suffered from this practice of indiscrim-

inate praise and from the absence of measured appreciation. Sometimes it seems as though the commentators
have chosen wilfully to shut their eyes to everything
they would wish away. They have made no effort to
free themselves from the spell of Lamb's contagious en-
thusiasm; and they have not resisted the evil influence of
the extravagant eulogy habitual with Swinburne, whose
overpowering rhetoric once bade fair to have as perni-
cious an effect on literary criticism as Ruskin's overpowering rhetoric had for a while upon criticism of
painting. As Ruskin misled many and discouraged
more, who, under wiser guidance, might have learned
in time to take keen pleasure in the painter's art, so
Swinburne by his indiscriminate overpraise must have
repelled many a reader who might have been lured into
a liking for the real value of the Elizabethan dramatic
poets, if this had been set forth modestly.

Many commentators and critics yield themselves up
to be hypnotized by the dramatic poet they are dealing
with, crediting him with a host of merits and refusing to
counterbalance their commendation by allowing weight
even to such demerits as they are compelled to record.
An amusing instance of this abdication of the critical
function can be found in the introduction to a recent
edition of "Old Fortunatus," in which the editor is
permitted to say that this comedy of Dekker's, "though
containing numberless faults in construction, in weak
and ineffective character-drawing, and in improbable
psychological deduction, is nevertheless one of the
greatest of Elizabethan dramas." Surely, this is the
very negation of criticism, to call a piece containing
"numberless faults" one of the "greatest of dramas."
Such writing is disheartening, not to term it dishonest.

The truth is that " Old Fortunatus " is only a narrative in dialogue; it has little dramaturgic merit; its character-drawing is mere prentice-work; and it pleases because of its primitive unpretentiousness and its fleeting glimpses of poetry. It has none of the broad humor or of the hearty veracity of character which lends charm to its author's "Shoemaker's Holiday," a brisk comedy of the contemporary life of London, which the sturdy author knew so well and relished so keenly.

II

In considering the lack of playmaking skill, abundantly evident in the works of the Elizabethan poets, two points must ever be borne in mind. The first of these is that the literary form which happens to be popular and therefore profitable, in any period, attracts to it many who have little or no native gift for that special art. In the nineteenth century, for example, the vogue of the novel was overwhelming; and many a man of letters who had but a small share of the narrative faculty undertook to express himself in fiction. So, at the end of the sixteenth century, the drama was the one field in which an aspiring genius might hope to make money; and it is not surprising, therefore, to find only a few among all the mass of Elizabethan dramatic poets who either were born playwrights, or willingly took the trouble, by dint of hard work, to master the secrets of the craft. Chapman, for one, had no natural bent toward the theater; and Webster, for another, for all his striving after the horrible, does not prove his possession of the native endowment of the instinctive playmaker. Chapman and Webster were poets, beyond all question; but they were not born playwrights.

The second point to be kept in memory is that the dramatic art was not highly esteemed in Elizabeth's time. The theater was a means whereby a poet might earn his living; but plays were scarcely held to be literature; they were devised only to satisfy the two hours'traffic of the stage; they were looked down upon by men of letters, much as journalism is looked down upon to-day. Accustomed as we are to consider the drama as the chief glory of Elizabethan literature, we do not always remember that the Elizabethans themselves scarcely held it to be literature at all. Nothing is more significant of this contemporary opinion than the fact that Shakspere corrected the proof of his two narrative poems carefully, while he gave no thought to the printing of his plays, carelessly abandoning the manuscripts to his comrades of the theater. One result of this contemptuous attitude toward the drama was that the poet was not held to any high standard, and that what was good enough for the rude playgoing public of those turbulent times was often good enough for the playwright himself.

Perhaps it is well also to note a third point, the recalling of which will help us to understand certain of the dramaturgic deficiencies of those days; and this is that the drama had not yet come into its own. It was still imperfectly differentiated; it had not disengaged itself from elements wholly undramatic. Just as the Greek drama in the time of Æschylus retained a lyrical element which often delayed the movement of the play itself, so the English drama in the time of Shakspere had not freed itself from elements which had nothing to do with the setting of a story on the stage. It needs to be remembered that, in those early days, the theater was not only the theater; it was also, to a certain extent, the newspaper, the lecture-hall, and even the pulpit. So it is that we find the dramatic poet sometimes halting his plot to deliver a lecture or a sermon, which his audience received gladly, but which clogged the movement of his action, and which is seen now to be a hindrance to the artistic shaping of his plot.

Here we touch the connection between the drama as it was under Elizabeth and the drama as it had been under Henry VIII and his predecessors. An Elizabethan playhouse was open to the air; it got its light from the sky; its stage, encumbered with spectators, had no drop-curtain and no scenery; its methods were those of the mystery performed in the market-place and the churchyard. There is really very little difference in structure between the miracle-play of the later Middle Ages and the chronicle-play of Elizabeth's youth. If the method of the elder is medieval, the method of the younger is semi-medieval, to say the least. It could not be anything else until the roofed and lighted theater came into being, with its separating drop-curtain and its realistic scenery. There was no modern theater in London until after the Restoration; and so it is that the Elizabethan drama could not be modern; it had to remain at least semi-medieval even in its loftiest efforts. It was not the fault of the Elizabethan drama that it had not the severe simplicity of the ancients or the neat dexterity of the moderns; but there is no denying that it had neither, and that it could not have them.

And when we consider what were the actual circumstances of performance in the Globe Theater, our wonder is not that the structure of Shakspere's plays is often straggling and slovenly, but rather that the great dramatist was ever able to attain to a more orderly

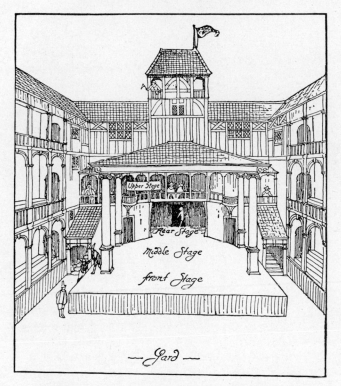

Upper Stage

Rear Stage

Middle Stage

front Stage

— Yard —

INTERIOR OF THE FORTUNE THEATER, LONDON (1599)

From the restoration by Walter H. Godfrey, Esq., after the builder's contract

conduct of his plot, such as he did achieve in "Othello" and in "Macbeth." Perhaps, indeed, there is no better proof of the might of Shakspere's genius than this, — that now and again he was able to overcome conditions which seem to be unconquerable, and to produce a play which endures for all time even though it was originally adjusted adroitly to the circumstances of performance upon a semi-medieval stage.

Furthermore, the Elizabethan dramatist not only put his plays together in conformity with the customary methods of representation that obtained in the Elizabethan theater, he also kept in mind always the audience before which they were to be produced. It was for the playgoer of the present that he exerted himself; it was not for the reader of the future. The absence of critical standards and the contempt of the acted drama, account for many of the defects of the plays of that renowned period; but the chief cause is ever to be sought in the necessity of pleasing a special public, probably far more brutal in its longings than any other to which a great dramatist has had to appeal. The Athenians, for whom Sophocles built his massive and austere tragedies, and the Parisians, for whom Molière painted the humorous portrait of his fellow-burghers, — these were quite other than the mob before whom Shakspere had to set his studies from life, a mob stout of stomach for sheer horrors, and shrinking from no atrocity. It is the Elizabethan public which is mainly responsible for the fact that the Elizabethan drama, glorious as it is with splendid episodes, taken separately, has only a few masterpieces, only a few plays the conduct of which does not continually disappoint even a cordial reader. As M. Jusserand has pointed out, with the calm sanity which is characteristic of French criticism, it is not difficult to select many "luminous parts, scenes brilliant or tragic, moving passages, characters solidly set on their feet," but it is very rare indeed to find complete wholes sustained as a lofty level of art, "plays entirely satisfactory, strongly conceived, firmly knit together, carried to an inevitable conclusion."

III

Why take the trouble to knit a story strongly and to deduce its inevitable conclusion, when the public the play had to please cared nothing for this artistic victory? Not only did the playgoers of those days find no fault with the lack of plausibility in the conduct of the story, with sudden and impossibly quick changes in character, with coincidences heaped up and with arbitrary artificialities accumulated; but these, indeed, were the very qualities they most enjoyed. They preferred the unusual, the unexpected, the illogical; and it was to behold startling turns of fortune and to get the utmost of surprise that they went to the theater. We are now annoyed by the huddling of two and three stories into a single play, wholly unconnected, the joyous and the gruesome side by side, and in no wise tied together; but to them, this was entirely satisfactory, for it gave them variety, and this was what they were seeking. We must always be ready to "make believe," when we surrender ourselves to the charm of these semi-medieval poet playwrights.

No doubt, there were gallants sitting on the stage who had a tincture of cultivation; and there must have been other men of education in the rooms of the gallery. But the most of those who stood in the yard below were unable to write or to read. Among them were discharged soldiers home from the wars, sailors from the ships of Frobisher and Drake, runaway apprentices, and all the riffraff and rabble of a seaport town which happened also to be the capital of an expanding nation. They were violent in their likings, with a constant longing for horse-play and ribaldry, and with a persistent hankering after scenes of lust and gore. They were used to cock-fighting and bear-baiting and bull-baiting; and these brutal sports were shown sometimes within the very building where on other occasions there were performances of those raw tragedies-of-blood, the plays which could best stir the nerves of so tumultuous a public. These supporters of the stage were used to battle, murder, and sudden death, not only in the theater, but in daily life, for there were scores of public executions every year; and in those spectacular times, the headsman of the Tower was a busy man, with his ghastly trophies frequently renewed on the spikes above the gate.

The pressure of the main body of playgoers upon the playwrights was not unwholesome then, as it is not unwholesome now, in so far as it led the dramatic poets to avoid preciosity and to eschew style-mongering, — in so far as it forced them to deal directly with life, and to handle passion boldly and amply. But the playgoers of those days had cruder likings also; they craved constant excitement, both for the eye and for the ear; and the aspiring playwright gave them good measure, pressed down and running over. For the pleasure of the eye, he lavished processions, coronations, funerals, encampments, single combats and serried battles. For the pleasure of the ear, he was prolific of songs.

melancholy or smutty; and he never stinted such other sounds as he could command, — the roll of the drum, the staccato call of the trumpet, the clangor of loud bells, the rattle of musketry, and the long reverberation of thunder. Sheeted ghosts and bloody specters were sure of their welcome in advance; and the playwright was prompt to produce them whenever he had an excuse. He knew also that these ignorant playgoers had a rough sense of fun and liked to laugh heartily; and so he sprinkled throughout his pieces a variety of ingenious retorts and of obvious repartees, even descending now and again to get his laugh by the more mechanical humor of a practical joke. Furthermore, he was aware that, gross as was the taste of the yardlings, they could enjoy pretty sentiment, sometimes presented with simple truth, and sometimes surcharged with the utmost of lyric exaggeration.

When we consider how rank was the quality of those who stood in the yard of the Globe in those days, how deficient their education, how harsh their experience of life, how rude their likings, the wonder is not that the play prepared for their pleasure was often violent and arbitrary and coarse, but rather that any play devised to delight them was ever logical and elevated, shapely and refined. If the best of Shakspere is for eternity, the worst of him was frankly for the groundlings who were his contemporaries, and whose interest he had to arouse and to retain as best he could. It is evidence of the intense practicality which ever directed his conduct that he was in the habit of taking over old plays which had already proved their power to attract paying audiences. It is evidence of his strict adaptation of his plays to his semi-medieval audiences that he had a total disregard of chronological, historic, or geographic accuracy, giving clocks and cannons to the Romans and having the Italians going from Verona to Milan to take ship when the tide served, because this was the mode of travel most familiar to the Londoner then. It is evidence of his understanding of his public that he is open in having his villains proclaim their own wickedness, so that the spectator might never be in doubt as to their motives.

In nothing else is the superiority of Shakspere over his contemporaries more obvious than in the adroit dexterity with which he played upon the prejudices of his audience and made profit out of them. He sought always to give the spectators of his own time what he knew they wanted; and yet, now and again, perhaps a dozen times in the score of years of his playmaking, uplifted by his genius and by his love of his craft, he looked above the spectators and beyond them, and he took a trouble they did not require of him. On these occasions, all too few, he made a play, pleasing to them indeed, but also pleasing to himself, and to his own intense artistic enjoyment of technical mastery. So it happens that we have the compact and logical "Othello," as well as the sprawling and incoherent "Cymbeline," which came a few years afterward.

The most of his contemporaries, brilliant and highly gifted as they were, were incapable of this, and they were unable to profit by the example Shakspere had set them in those of his plays in which he was himself interested enough to do his best and to put forth his full strength. It is because he is at his best only on occasion, and when the spirit of perfection moved him, that he founded no school. He was not a master to

follow unhesitatingly, partly because the mark at which
he aimed was not always the best target for others,
since he was willing often to let the incomparable felicity of the poet cover up and cloak the careless planning of the playwright; and partly, also, because no
weaker arm could bend the bow of Ulysses. His chief
gift was incommunicable; it was the power of endow-
ing all his creatures with independent life. This power
is the test of his work; and it never leaves him. We discover it abundantly even in his most recklessly arbitrary plots, and even in those of his episodes which are
based on a childish make-believe. It is not to the credit
of critics like Brandes, that they gloss over the absurdities that abound in Shakspere's plays, because Shakspere was ready enough to give the spectators of his
own time the puerile devices they delighted in, — the
pound of flesh and the trial of the caskets in the " Merchant of Venice," for example, and the test of the affec-
tion of Lear's daughters, when that fatherly monarch,
unless he was already imbecile, ought to have learned
the characters of his children in the long years of their
family life. If a critic does not see these absurdities, if
he is blind to the arbitrary and muddled plot of "Cymbeline" and to the shocking callousness of the last act
of " Much Ado about Nothing," then we may well doubt
whether he is really able to appreciate the masterly
simplicity of "Othello" and the orderly richness of
"Romeo and Juliet."

IV

The significant fact is that Shakspere was, after all,
an Elizabethan; and that, like the others, he had to
accept the conditions of a semi-medieval theater and

to please a full-blooded public. The others cannot climb with him; but not infrequently he sinks with them. They were ready enough to be satisfied themselves when they had satisfied the playgoers of their own day. They had no hesitation in sacrificing consistency of character to immediate effect on the mass of spectators, — very much as their fellow playwrights in Spain were doing at the same time and for the same reason. Climbing to impossible heights of honor or sinking to impossible depths of dishonor, abounding in the most romantic reversals of fortune and in the most inexplicable transformations of character, caring little for reality or even for plausibility, disregarding the delicacy of art no less than the veracity of nature, they were fertile in inventing striking episodes; and they failed, as a rule, to combine the several parts into a coherent whole, sustaining itself throughout and gathering power as it proceeded. Capable on occasion of the finest shadings of a subtle psychology, they were content, for the most part, with a bald daubing of character in the primary colors. In other words, they often proved themselves true poets, but far less frequently did they reveal themselves as real playwrights.

This is the reason why the flamboyant and iridescent eulogy of Swinburne is doing them an ill service to-day, while they gained greatly by the apt selection of Lamb, who artfully singled out the perfect passages. Only too often the parts are far finer than the whole; and Lamb presented the best bits so enticingly that he must have lured to disappointment many readers who went straight from his " Specimens " to the complete works of the several dramatic poets. Here, also, we may find an excuse for Hazlitt and for Lowell, who have praised these poets more especially as poets to be read in a library, while almost wholly neglecting to consider their plays as plays intended to be performed by actors in a theater and before an audience. To Hazlitt and Lowell, these dramatic poets appealed primarily as poets; and that the poets were also dramatists rarely arrested the attention of either of these acute critics.

Of a certainty, there must be many other readers who are willing enough to follow the example of Hazlitt and of Lowell, and to accept the pure poetry which is abundant in the works of the Elizabethan dramatists, without caring to consider whether or not the plays enriched by this poetry are all that they ought to be, merely as plays. Some of them may even be inclined to resent any attempt to call attention to the dramaturgic defects of plays possessing a host of splendid passages, wherein poetry combines with psychology to give the keenest pleasure. Others there are who are willing to admit the existence of the defects themselves, but who deny the justice of a criticism which gages the semi-medieval playwrights by tests properly applicable only to the modern drama. This protest was voiced most persuasively not long ago by a devout admirer of the old dramatists, who insisted on the impropriety of judging Massinger and Greene by the standards proper enough in judging Scribe and Ibsen.

There is a certain speciousness in this claim; but analysis shows that it is not valid. It may be unfair to weigh the semi-medieval Greene and Massinger on the same scales as Scribe and Ibsen, who are moderns; but it is not unfair to measure them by the standards we can derive from the comparison of the greatest dramatists, both ancient and modern. If we find certain principles of the art of playmaking exemplified in the best dramas of Æschylus and of Sophocles, of Shakspere and of Molière, of Calderon and of Racine, of Beaumarchais and of Scribe, of Ibsen, of Sudermann and of Pinero, it is not unfair to consider these principles as the eternal verities of dramaturgy, and to point out that Massinger and Greene fail to achieve an excellence of which we find frequent examples all through the long history of the drama, some of them a score of centuries before Scribe and Ibsen were born.

At its best, the dramatist's art reveals itself as akin to the architect's; and a really good play ought to have a solid framework and a bold simplicity of planning, with a foundation broad enough to sustain the superstructure, however massive or however lofty this may prove to be. It ought to have unity of theme, freedom from all extraneous matter, veracity of motive, contrast of character, clearness of exposition, probability of incident, logical coherence, swift movement, and culminating intensity of interest. These qualities can be found in " Agamemnon." and " Œdipus the King," as well as in " Othello " and in " Tartuffe," in the " Alcalde of Zalamea " and in " Phèdre," in the " Barber of Seville " and in the " Ladies' Battle," in " Ghosts," in " Magda," and in the " Second Mrs. Tanqueray." But these qualities are not to be found in any large degree in " Doctor Faustus " or in the " Roman Actor "; and they are not often to be found in the plays of any of the Elizabethan dramatists, — far more often in Shakspere than in any of the others.

And if these deficiencies exist, surely it is unwise to

close our eyes to the fact; surely it is unjust to pretend that the Elizabethan drama, as a whole, possesses that which it has not; surely it is safer and honester to admit frankly that the art of building plays solidly and symmetrically was little cultivated by the Elizabethan dramatists, just as it was little considered by the Elizabethan critics. Surely, again, it is wisest to try to see things as they really are and to tell the truth about them, the whole truth, and nothing but the truth. Even in criticism, honesty is the best policy; and the Elizabethan poets are indisputably great enough to make it worth while for us to assure ourselves wherein their true greatness lies. They are none the less great as poets when we have seen clearly that — excepting Shakspere — they are great as playwrights only occasionally, and almost, as it were, by accident.

CHAPTER XII

THE POETIC DRAMA AND THE DRAMATIC POEM

The attempt to write tragedy for the closet rather than for the stage has resulted either in adopting the supposed conditions of the Greek or some other foreign theater, or in breaking away from the strict limits defined by the stage and writing lyrical medleys or dramatic monologues or imaginary conversations. . . . Object as tragedy rightly may at times to the limitations and trivialities of the theater, it cannot safely leave its precincts without losing its own identity.

In the past nearly all tragedies of any effect on the drama's development have not only been planned for the stage but have succeeded when acted. This seems likely to be the case in the future. For the reader of a play is confronted by difficulties not found in other fiction; and, in general, only a play suited to presentation on the stage is likely to secure for a reader the visualization, the impersonations, the illusion of actuality, similar to those experienced in the theater. — ASHLEY H. THORNDIKE, *Tragedy*.

I

THE divorce between poetry and the drama, visible in English literature in the nineteenth century, is acknowledged to be most unfortunate for both parties to the matrimonial contract; and those of us who have a warm regard for either of them cannot help hoping that they may be persuaded soon to make up their quarrel and get married again. The theater is flourishing more abundantly than ever before; and the prose-drama of modern life, dealing soberly and sincerely with the present problems of existence, has at last got its roots into the soil, and is certain soon to yield a richer fruitage. Perhaps it is even not too much to foresee the possibility of a speedy outflowering of the drama in the next half-century, in the English language, as well as in the other tongues. In all the earlier epochs of dramatic expansion, the masterpieces of the art have been truly poetic, in theme and in treatment. Have we any reason to suppose that our coming drama will also be poetic, both in essentials and in externals?

If the law of supply and demand were as potent in the arts as it is in commerce, we should be justified in expecting that return of the poetic drama, which is eagerly awaited by all who cherish the muses. But when we station Sister Ann on the watch-tower, and when we keep on asking if she sees any one coming, we ought to have in our own minds a clear vision of the rescuer we are looking for. When we cry aloud for the poetic drama, what is it that we stand ready to welcome? Of course, we do not mean that bastard hybrid, the so-called closet-drama, the play that is not intended to be played. A mere poem in dialogue not destined for performance by actors, in a theater, and before an audience, may have interest of its own to the chosen few who can persuade themselves that they like that sort of thing; but it is not what the rest of us want. The poetic drama, in its most splendid periods, has always been adjusted to the playhouse of its own time. It has always been dramatic, first of all; and its poetry has been ancillary to its action. It is in the theater, and not only in the library, that we desire now to greet the noble muse of tragedy with her singing robes about her. Brunetière insisted that " it cannot be repeated too often that a dramatic work does not begin to exist as such except before the footlights by virtue of the collaboration and complicity of the public, without which I assert that it never has been and never can be more than mere rhetoric." In other words, we must ever distinguish sharply between the poetic play and the dramatic poem, between the compositions in dialogue which were intended to be spoken on the stage itself, and the compositions in dialogue which were intended only to be read in the study. So long as these latter make no pretence to be other than they are, dramatic poems and not genuine plays, they are legitimate enough. It is only when their authors and their admirers claim for them the praise due to the true drama that we must make a swift protest. The true poetic drama designed for the actual theater and the dramatic poem intended only for the library are distinct things; they are essentially unlike; and there is danger in any attempt to confuse them. The dramatic poem becomes illegitimate only when it claims to be judged as a poetic drama; then it stands exposed as a mere pretender to a crown belonging to another.

Yet, like other pretenders, it does not lack advocates. One of these has boldly asserted that the so-called closet-drama "is a quite legitimate product of literary art," since "the playhouse has no monopoly of the dramatic form." This assertion reveals a misunderstanding of the essential principles of the drama, as all students of its history will instinctively feel. They cannot help believing that the playhouse has now, has had in the past, and must always have, a monopoly of the dramatic form. And they can see clearly enough that the closet-drama is generally the offspring of the unwillingness or the inability of certain poets to acquire the craft of the theater, — the special craft which makes the dramatist what he is.

Probably no one of its admirers would dispute a definition to the effect that a closet-drama is a play not intended to be played. It is a poem in dialogue, conceived with no thought of the actual stage, not contaminated by any subservience to the playhouse, the players, or the playgoers. It is wrought solely for the reader in the library, without any regard for the demands of possible spectators in the auditorium. If we accept this definition, we find ourselves able to subtract from any catalogue of the so-called closet-drama two important groups, one containing poetic plays and the other dramatic poems. First of all, there is the group represented by Tennyson's "Becket." If a closet-drama is a dramatic poem not intended to be played, then "Becket" is not a closet-drama, for Tennyson did intend it to be played. And Tennyson was not the author of a single closet-drama, since he meant all his plays to be acted, and was even intensely anxious that they should be seen in the theater, revealing his readiness to make whatsoever modifications, suppressions, or additions the managers might suggest to him. That these plays met with little success on the stage itself can be accounted for either by asserting that the laureate was without the dramaturgic faculty, or by admitting that he did not take the trouble to master the necessary technic of the theater. Browning's "Strafford" and "A Blot in the 'Scutcheon" were written not only to be acted, but to be acted by one particular actor. And as Browning had Macready in view, so Shelley had Miss O'Neill in view when he wrote the "Cenci." Coleridge composed "Remorse" and Johnson wrote "Irene" to be performed, and they were performed.

If these poetic plays failed in the theater, this is partly because their authors did not keep an eye single on the stage. They may have had the impatient spectator in mind, but they had also the leisurely reader; and as a result they fell between two stools. They laid themselves open to the reproach which Stendhal brought against Manzoni's dramatic poems, that the "characters seem to be held back by the pleasure of finding fine words." And they failed to take to heart the warning which Goethe expressed to Eckermann in 1826: "When a play makes a deep impression on us in reading, we think it will do the same on the stage, and that we could obtain such a result with little trouble. But a piece that is not originally, by the intent and skill of the poet, written for the boards, will not succeed. Whatever is done to it, it will always remain unmanageable." And then he added out of his own experience: "What trouble have I taken with ' Götz,' — and yet it will not go right as an acting-play."

The dramatic poems of another class can be considered as closet-dramas only by stretching the definition, since they are frankly dramatic poems, not copying the outward form of the modern play. This second group includes Arnold's "Empedocles on Etna" and Swinburne's "Atalanta in Calydon," and all the other attempted resuscitations of Greek tragedy. The most obvious characteristic of these attempts to resuscitate a departed form is to be found in the fact that they are deliberate imitations. They are exercises in poetry to be ranked with the anatomies of the old painters. They are *pastiches*, as the French call them; and the poet has found his chief interest in recalling the flavor of a day that has gone forever. They may reveal the range of the metrical artist's accomplishment and his ingenuity in grappling with the endless difficulties of a revival which can never be really successful, since it is frankly impossible for a modern poet to put himself back into the skin of a Greek of old and to strip himself of all the accretions of thought and feeling that he has inherited from the long centuries separating him from the Athenians. "Atalanta in Calydon" may be the most Greek of all English imitations of Attic tragedy; but it is intensely modern and intensely English, none the less. It is not by imitations, however adroit and however skilful, that a poet can establish his fame, even though an imitation or two may serve to broaden our appreciation of his craftsmanship. Lowell was considering Swinburne's "Atalanta in Calydon" when he declared that "every attempt at reproducing a bygone excellence by external imitation of it, or even by applying the rules which analytic criticism has formulated from the study of it, has resulted in producing the artificial, not the artistic." And in the same essay, there is another passage which also demands quotation here: "The higher kinds of literature, the only kinds that live on, because they had life at the start, are not the fabric of scholarship, of criticism, diligently studying and as diligently copying the best models, but are much rather born of some genetic principle in the character of the people and the age that produce them."

II

The real reason why the closet-drama fails to justify itself is that it is too easy. Nothing is more stimulating to the artist than the necessity of grappling with difficulty. Then and then only is he forced to put forth his whole strength. To make his work easier in any way, to relax the bonds, to let down the bars, — this is not to help the artist; it is to hinder him from lofty achievement. As Huxley once said, it is when a man can do as he pleases that his troubles begin. A strong nature is ever anxious for a wrestle with an opposing force; and he knows very well how the strain braces his muscles. This is what is forgotten by the admirers of the closet-drama, one of whom once ventured to set up this claim for it : —

"As the closet-dramatist is not bound to consider the practical exigencies of the theater, to consult the prejudices of the manager or the spectators, fill the pockets of the company, or provide a *rôle* for a star performer, he has, in many ways, a freer hand than the professional playwright. He need not sacrifice truth of character and probability of plot to the need of highly accentuated situations. He does not have to consider whether a speech is too long, too ornate in diction, too deeply thoughtful for recitation by an actor. If the action lags at certain points, let it lag. In short, as the aim of the closet-dramatist is other than the playwright's, so his methods may be independent."

Now, almost every advantage which is here claimed for the writer of the closet-drama is in reality a disadvantage. The more willingly a poet avails himself of these licenses, the more remote must the result be from the true drama, as Shakspere and Molière conceived it, with their careful adjustment of their characters to the actors of their own companies and with their keen interest in the takings at the door. The poet stands revealed as a shrinking weakling when he wants to cast off the shackles that all the supreme dramatists have worn lightly. If the aim of the closet-dramatist is other than that of the playwright, and if his methods are

independent, then in all fairness the conclusion ought
to follow that his achievement is not drama. There is a
taint of unreality about it. A closet-drama of this sort
irresistibly recalls a summer cottage with its shingled
turret and with a parapet carefully machiolated so that
the residents can the more readily pour molten lead on
the besiegers. " When you build a portcullis to let in
cows, not to exclude marauders, it is apt to become
rather ludicrously unreal; if you know that your play
is to be read and not to be seen, the whole dramatic
arrangement is on the way to become a mere sham,"
said Sir Leslie Stephen, who then asked: "Why bother
yourself to make the actors tell a story, when it is
simpler and easier to tell it yourself?"

In the dedicatory epistle to his collected poems,
Swinburne asserted that when he wrote plays, it was
"with a view to their being acted at the Globe, the Red
Bull, or the Blackfriars," — the semi-medieval playhouses with which the Elizabethan playwrights had to
be content, since they knew no other, and to the conditions of which they carefully conformed their plays.
And in discussing his own "Marino Faliero," Swinburne declared that this dramatic poem, "hopelessly
impossible as it is from the point of view of modern
stagecraft, could hardly have been found too untheatri-
cal, too utterly given over to thought without action,
by the audience which endured and applauded Chapman's eloquence — the fervid and inexhaustible declamation which was offered and accepted as a substitute for study of character and interest of action,
when his two finest plays, if plays they can be called,
found favor with an incredibly intelligent and an in-
conceivably tolerant audience."

The first comment to be made upon this characteristic vaunting is that we do not know whether Chapman's plays did or did not find favor with Elizabethan
playgoers; and the second is that these playgoers may
have tolerated the eloquence and the declamation for
the sake of the violently melodramatic plots which held
the plays together. A third comment would be to deny
incredible intelligence to the audiences of Chapman's
time and place. And a fourth would point out that
eloquence belongs to the oration and not to the drama,
and that the proper place for declamation is the platform and not the stage, which expects — and has a
right to expect — the "interest of action" and the
"study of character."

But there is really little need of comment, since
Swinburne revealed a total inability to understand the
drama as that has been understood by all the really
dramatic poets from Sophocles to Ibsen, and by all the
real dramatic critics from Aristotle to Lessing. It is
true that Sidney, who had been infected by the sterile
theoretic criticism of the Italian Renascence, believed
that the English dramatists ought to model themselves
on the great Greeks; and yet Swinburne himself has
never found fault with Shakspere for rejecting this
advice and for adjusting his plays to the actual theater
of his own time. It is curious that Swinburne, whose
adoration for Hugo is almost as perfervid as his admiration for Shakspere, did not follow their example.
Shakspere was satisfied with the stage as he found it,
semi-medieval and unworthy of his genius as it may
seem to us. Hugo, who had perhaps little more of the
native dramaturgic gift than Swinburne himself, went
to school to the professional playwrights whose melo-

dramas were popular in his youth, and absorbed their processes. The poet of "Hernani" was no closet-dramatist; his aim was that of the professional play-wrights, and he took over the skeleton of melodramatic action which they had devised to please the multitude, flinging over it the splendor of his lyric verse, with the result of evoking from Swinburne the assertion that he was a dramatist of "the race and lineage of Shakspere."

III

It is curious also that Swinburne, in his study of French literature, had not observed that the foremost critics of France have never a good word for the closet-drama, — perhaps because the closet-drama has rarely tempted the French poets, who have generally con-tented themselves with the theater as it happened to exist when they took up the art of the dramatist. Ros-tand has found his profit in writing for the stage as it is; and even Musset, who turned his back on it for a season, composed his poetic fantasies so closely in accord with its conditions that they needed very little modification when they were transferred from the library to the theater.

In Great Britain and in the United States, in the nineteenth century, while these closet-dramas were being published, there was no scarcity of actors capable of performing characters loftily conceived; and these actors were many of them eager for new parts worthy of their histrionic ability. And the continued popu-larity of Shakspere's plays in the theater proves also that there was no lack of audiences ready to welcome new poetic dramas, if only these novelties resembled the plays of Shakspere in being dramatic as well as poetic. There is no reason to suppose that the poets of the English language would have failed in the play-house any more than the poets of the French language failed, if these English poets had followed the example of Hugo and of Rostand, and had taken the time and the trouble needful to master the methods of the contemporary theater. But this is what they were not willing to do; they shrank from the toil; and therefore they cannot now claim the guerdon due only to that successful conquest of difficulty which sustains the masterpieces of every art. They chose the easier path and they wrote poems in dialogue, devoid of the essential qualities of the drama, even if rich in the essential qualities of poetry. What right have they now to the same laurel we bestow on Hugo and on Rostand? It is almost as though they had composed music with no understanding of the several instruments which make up the modern orchestra, and with no intention that the composition should ever be heard.

It is a significant fact in the history of literature that the closet-drama has appeared only when there is a divorce between literature and the theater. It is first seen in Rome under Nero, when the stage was given over to vulgar and violent spectacle; and so Seneca seems to have polished his plays solely for recitation by an elocutionist. It is visible again in Italy, when men of letters, enamored of the noble severity of Greek tragedy and of the artistic propriety of Latin comedy, despised the ruder miracle-plays and the lively but acrobatic comedy-of-masks, which were the only types of drama then popular on the stage; and they therefore attempted empty imitations of the classic dramatists with no regard to the conditions of the contempo⌐

rary theater. It emerged once more in England early in the nineteenth century, when adaptations of Kotzebue, and later of Scribe and his cloud of collaborators, were the chief staple of the stage, and when the overwhelming vogue of the "Waverley" novels drew the attention of authors away from the drama to the novel, which was easier to write, easier to bring before the public, and more likely to bring in an adequate reward. Behind every appearance of the closet-drama, we can discover a latent contempt for the actual theater, and a desire to claim its rewards without the trouble of mastering its methods or the risk of facing its perils. This is why the closet-drama has never appeared in any period of affluent dramatic productivity, for then the poets who happen also to be dramatists are glad to study out the secrets of theatrical technic and to brave the dangers of actual performance.

Even if there were some slight excuse for the appearance of the closet-drama in Rome under Nero and in Italy during the Renascence, there was none for its revival in England in the nineteenth century, when actors and audiences were alike waiting to recognize and to reward a new dramatic poet. For its continued existence in the twentieth century there is still less excuse, since Ibsen has shown us how the austerest themes may be treated in the modern theater. The poet of our time has no right now to despise the stage, where Shakspere and Ibsen are accepted; he has no right lazily to refuse to comply with its conditions, if he wishes to win its rewards. The drama is not for the library, but for the theater; and it is not for the joy of the little group of dilettants, but for the stimulation of the public as a whole. It was the wise Boileau who once said that "even when a work is approved by a small number of connoisseurs, if it is not filled with a certain pleasure for the general taste of men, it will never pass for good, and at the end the connoisseurs themselves will admit that they were at fault in giving it their approbation."

IV

The closet-drama is like poverty in that it is always with us; and it is far removed from the poetic drama which we hoped to see revived in our language. But what is the exact nature of this poetic drama that we long for? It is not, or at least it ought not to be, a sort of dramatized historical novel, full of high deeds and pretty words, a costume-play in blank verse, as empty of true poetic inspiration as the "Virginius" of Sheridan Knowles or the "Richelieu" of Bulwer Lytton. In the illuminating address on "Literature and the Modern Drama," which Mr. Henry Arthur Jones delivered at Yale in the fall of 1906, he asserted that playgoers on both sides of the Atlantic have a notion that a costume-play, with its scenes laid anywhere except in the last half-century and with its personages talking "a patchwork diction, compounded of every literary style from Chaucer to a Whitechapel costermonger," seems to have a literary distinction and a profound significance "which rank it immeasurably above the mere prose play of modern every-day life," and which give to the ravished spectator an elevation of mind and "a vague but gratifying sense of superiority."

Probably this notion is to be found in the heads of not a few playgoers, pleased with the belief that they are revealing themselves possessed of fine literary discrimination when they pay their money to behold a costume-play in blank verse. But the clothes of long ago and the lines of ten syllables have no power in themselves to confer literary merit, even when they are united. These are but the trappings of the muse, often laid aside when she warms to her singing. They may deck a play wholly artificial, unreal, false to life, — and therefore wholly devoid of literary merit. It ought to be evident to us all that an unpretending farce which has happened to catch and to fix a few of the foibles of the moment is really more worthy of serious critical consideration than a tawdry melodrama, bombasted with swelling sonorities and peopled by heroes strutting in the toga or stiff in chain-armor. It ought to be evident also that this farce, in so far as it has its roots in reality, is a better augury for the future of the drama, and may have even more genuine literary quality, than the pretentious costume-play in blank verse, illumined by no gleam of true poetry.

Poetry, essential poetry, is not a matter of versifying only. Many a play in verse is prosy, whether written in French alexandrines or in English pentameters. Many a play in humble prose is shot through and through with the radiance of poesy. Perhaps the most truly poetic dramas of the end of the nineteenth century are the little pieces of M. Maeterlinck; and neither the "Intruder" nor "Pelléas and Mélisande" is in verse. Certainly the most poetic plays of the middle of the nineteenth century are the delicious fantasies of Alfred de Musset; and "On ne badine pas avec l'amour," and its fellows, did not need the aid of verse. And it would be easy to give many another example. Aldrich's "Judith," for instance, which is in verse, is not only less dramatic, it is actually less poetic than his "Mercedes," which is in prose. More significant still is the fact that the most charmingly lyric of all the comedies of Shakspere, "As You Like It," filled with the fragrance of young love and of perennial springtime, is very largely in prose. So is the sleep-walking scene of Lady Macbeth, tense with tragic emotion and lifted to the loftier altitudes of poetry.

It may not be too bold to suggest that Shakspere knew what he was about. He had the right instinctive feeling; and he varied his instrument as the spirit moved him. Nothing will better repay study than the skill with which Shakspere, in "Julius Cæsar," for example, commingled blank verse and rhythmic prose and the plainer speech of every day, giving the verse to his nobler characters, Brutus and Cassius and Antony, letting the cadence of balanced sentences fall from the lips of those less important, and bestowing the simplest words on the mob of under citizens. A modern dramatic poet could scarcely have refrained from sustaining the whole of "As You Like It" and "Macbeth" and "Julius Cæsar" at the higher level of blank verse. And even Shakspere's contemporaries had not his instinctive art. Massinger, for one, often used verse in plays of contemporary life, such as the "New Way to pay Old Debts," which demanded rather the realistic directness of prose. This has led astray many of the later imitators of the Elizabethans, — Sheridan Knowles, for example, whose "Hunch-back" is in the blankest of verse.

The dramatic poets of the other modern languages have sometimes fallen into the same error. Augier's "Paul Forestier" deals with a highly emotional situation in modern life; but it loses more than it gains from its verse. Ibsen eschewed verse after he had written "Love's Comedy," which is the least significant of all his modern plays; and he declared that prose was not only more appropriate to plays of contemporary character, but "incomparably more difficult." We ought to be able to see that "When We Dead Awaken" and the "Intruder" and "On ne badine pas" are truly poetic, although in prose, whereas "Richelieu" and "Virginius" are emphatically prose, although in verse. It is not the cowl that makes the monk, said the medieval proverb. Perhaps it may seem like bad manners to look Pegasus in the mouth; but it is good sense to see that he is entered for the right race before we bestride him.

Although the dramatic poets of other modern languages have also made the mistake of employing verse when prose would have served their purpose better, it is the dramatic poets of the English language who have most often been guilty of the blunder. And this is due, no doubt, to the weight of the example set by the Elizabethan dramatists. What these earlier poets did spontaneously, the later bards have striven to do by main strength. Most of the Elizabethans used blank verse indiscriminately, whether their theme was poetic or not. Even Shakspere employed it in handling subjects essentially unpoetic, as in "All's Well" and "Measure for Measure." It is a question whether the overwhelming influence of the Elizabethans has not hampered the true development of a later English poetic drama. They set a standard; and they have been copied in their defects no less than in their virtues; indeed, their defects have proved far easier of imitation than their finer qualities.

Our modern theaters impose on the modern play-wright very different conditions from those which the semi-medieval Elizabethan playhouse imposed on the Elizabethan playwright. This may be a gain or it may be a loss; beyond all question, it is a fact. Just as the drama of the Athenians would have been a bad model for the Elizabethans, so the drama of the Elizabethans is a bad model for the poets of to-day. This is not only because the earlier English plays were conditioned by the earlier English theater, but also because certain medieval traditions survived with the result that much that was not truly dramatic was tolerated in a play and even expected. The absence of scenery tempted the poet to passages of pure description, just as the presence of actors who had been choir-boys tempted him to lyrics introduced often for their own sake. Nowadays the drama has shed these extraneous elements and is sufficient unto itself. The actors of our own time have rarely had a training as singers also; and the scenery of our time renders it needless for a poet to indulge in description.

v

The drama has cast out all that is undramatic; and it has now no room for anything but the action and the characters. It is compacter than ever before; and it rejects not only description but also narrative. Its duty is to show what was done and the consequences of the deed; and it has neither time nor space for narrative for its own sake, however beautiful in itself. Here is one weakness of the modern poets who write plays, Mr. Stephen Phillips, for one. His verse is often epic or lyric or idyllic rather than dramatic. He is felicitous in polished narrative and in suggestive description, but he more rarely achieves the stark boldness of vital drama, when the speaker has no time and no temper for fanciful comparisons or adroit alliterations, and when his phrase ought to flash out suddenly like a sword from its scabbard. His lines have often a beauty of their own, but it is a conscious and elaborate beauty out of place when the action tightens and a human soul must be bared by a word. They lack that unforced simplicity, that colloquial ease, that inevitable naturalness which grip us in the great moments of Shakspere.

How unadorned are the words of Viola and how full of meaning and of melody also, when she has told the Duke of her alleged sister's unspoken love. He asks: —

"But died thy sister of her love, my boy?"

And she answers: —

"I am all the daughters of my father's house,
    And all the brothers, too; and yet I know not.
    Sir, shall I to this lady?"

Consider also how free from fine language and phrase-making, how completely devoid of simile and metaphor, and yet how vitally poetic, is the parting of Romeo from Juliet: —

Juliet. I have forgot why I did call thee back.
Romeo. Let me stand here till thou remember it.
Juliet. I shall forget, to have thee still stand here,
    Remembering how I love thy company.
Romeo. And I'll still stay, to have thee still forget,
    Forgetting any other home but this.

The true poetic drama is not the closet-drama; it is not the mere costume-play in blank verse; it is not the empty imitation of the Elizabethan formula. It is a play composed in accordance with the conditions of the modern theater, whether in verse or in prose matters little, but poetic in theme and poetic in treatment, as well as dramatic in theme and dramatic in treatment. It is a play at once truly poetic and truly dramatic, — only this and nothing more. It is not a play with a commonplace subject decked with fine phrases and stuccoed with hand-made verses. It must be lifted up into poetry by the haunting beauty of its story, since it cannot be made truly poetic by any merely lyrical decoration. The story need not be strange or exotic or unusual; it may even be a tale of to-day and of every day, one of the old, old tales that are forever renewing their youth. Dramatic art has a right to follow the practice of pictorial art, when, in Whistler's sincere words, it was "seeking and finding the beautiful in all conditions and all times, as did her high priest Rembrandt when he saw the picturesque grandeur in the Jew's quarter of Amsterdam, and lamented not that its inhabitants were not Greeks."

The poetic drama must be truly dramatic and truly poetic; but it must not plead its poetry as an excuse for mere foolishness, and it must not give us characters who are not governed by common sense at the crucial moments of the action. The principle is laid down by Professor Lounsbury in his incisive analysis of a "Blot in the 'Scutcheon'": "The plot may be what you please. The story upon which it is based may be so far from probable that it verges on the impossible. But this, while objectionable, can be pardoned. What is without excuse is to find the characters acting without adequate motive; or, if the motive be adequate, to find them acting in the most incomprehensible way for rational beings." The keen critic then pointed out that Shakspere is almost always unerring in his observance of this dramatic propriety. "The plot of his play may rest upon a story which is simply incredible, as is notably the case in the 'Merchant of Venice.' All that Shakspere asks is that the story shall be one which his hearers are willing to accept as likely to happen, whether in itself likely or not. This granted, there is no further demand upon our trust in him as opposed to our judgment. We say of every situation: This is the natural way for the characters as here portrayed to think and feel and act. The motives are sufficient; the conduct that follows is what we have a right to expect."

When this test is applied to Browning's play we are told that "the characters throughout scrupulously avoid doing what they might reasonably be expected to do; while the things they might naturally be expected to avoid are the very things which they do not seem to conceive the idea of refraining from doing. The play consequently violates every motive which is supposed to influence human conduct; it outrages every probability which is supposed to characterize human action." In other words, Browning, in a "Blot in the 'Scutcheon," has a perfectly possible story, which he has chosen to people with characters arbitrarily unnatural in their conduct, whereas Shakspere in the "Merchant of Venice" has an almost impossible story, carried on by characters unfailingly natural. In Browning's play, "we are in a world of unreal beings, powerfully portrayed; for the situations are exciting, and the pathos of the piece is harrowing. But the action lies out of the realm of the reality it purports to represent, and therefore out of the realm of the highest art," — that realm of the highest art which easily includes Shakspere's play in spite of the incredibility of certain of its episodes.

Abundance of poetry, of power, of pathos will not excuse paucity of common sense in the conduct of the personages of the play. No bravura fervor of phrase will palliate sheer foolishness of deed. This defect may be more or less hidden from us when we read the play in the library, but it stands out undisguised and naked when we see the story bodied forth on the stage. There is then no excuse for any effort to apologize for it or to gloss it over. It is fatal, for the massed spectators in the theater have sharp eyes and plain tongues; and they resent every effort to make them admire a play which they find revolting to their every-day knowledge of human nature.

VI

Nothing is more unfortunate for the future of the poetic drama than the frequent attempts of superior persons to dragoon the ordinary playgoer into the theater to behold a play which he is certain not to enjoy. He resents being berated for not admiring that which has annoyed him by its artificiality or bored him by its clumsiness. The attitude taken by many merely literary critics after a performance of "Pippa Passes" or of the "Sunken Bell" is distinctly harmful to the cause they have at heart. If these performances wearied the average spectator, as they indisputably did, and if he is scolded because he has failed to appreciate these alleged poetic dramas, he is very likely to stay away the next time these merely literary critics seek to browbeat him into the theater to see another poetic drama. Per-

haps it is just as well for us all to remember that the
playgoer not only knows what he likes, but also that he
knows very definitely what he does not like. When he
goes to the playhouse, he wants to see a play peopled
with recognizable human beings and affording him the
kind of pleasure he expects in the theater. He has no
objection to poetry, if poetry is added to the play. He
rejects poetry unhesitatingly, when he finds it proffered
as a substitute for a play. He is in the present very
much what he was in the past; the playgoers of Shakspere's time did not have to be coerced into paying to
see "As You Like It" and "Hamlet"; they went
gladly, for they had been told that they would get their
money's worth. The playgoers of Mr. Barrie's time
have flocked to see "Peter Pan," a truly poetic play,
compounded of fantasy and reality.

The example of Mr. Barrie is suggestive : he has succeeded on the stage because he has mastered its mysteries. We cannot expect a rebirth of the poetic drama
until our poets turn playwrights or our playwrights
develop into poets. The poets must go to school in the
theater and learn the craft of the playmaker in his own
workshop, as Mr. Barrie has done, and as Victor Hugo
did when he set himself to spy out the secret of the success attained by the melodramatists of the unliterary
theaters. For a poet to compose a poem in dialogue,
and then expect that some adroit stage-manager can
lick it into shape and make an actable play out of it, —
this is very much as if he should ask the monthly nurse
to put a backbone into the baby after it is born. A
poetic play must be dramatic in its conception, or it
will never be a play at all. The fundamental principles
of dramaturgy are not really difficult to acquire; and if

a poet has it in him to be a playwright, he ought to be able to get hold of the essentials of the new art without a prolonged apprenticeship. But he needs to feel, first of all, that it is an art, a very special art, closely connected with the actual theater. If he begins by assuming an attitude of haughty disdain, he is not likely to find profit in his venture.

While some poets will choose to master the craft of the playwright, some playwrights will prove themselves possessed of the faculty divine. We are accustomed to consider the great dramatists primarily as poets, and we do not often look closely enough into their careers to observe that some of them began as playmakers, pure and simple. Shakspere, for one, and Molière, for another, were at first merely professional playwrights, composing their earliest pieces to please contemporary playgoers and revealing in these earliest pieces scarcely a foretaste of the abundant poetry which enriches their later and greater plays. No examination of the firstlings of their muse would have warranted any prediction of their extraordinary development in their riper years. And perhaps some of the professional playwrights of the twentieth century will rise to loftier heights as they grow in power and in ambition. They may bourgeon into verse when the fascination of a truly poetic theme some day seizes them. They, at least, will not need to be reminded that whenever and wherever the poetic drama has existed, it has been primarily dramatic in its intent and only secondarily poetic.

CHAPTER XIII

THE THREE UNITIES

And here the *Reader* may please take notice that the Design of these Rules is to conceal the Fiction of the *Stage*, to make the *Play* appear Natural, and to give it an air of Reality and *Conversation*.

The largest compass of the first *Unity* is Twenty-Four Hours: But a lesser proportion is more regular. To be exact, the Time of the History, or *Fable*, should not exceed that of the *Representation:* Or in other words, the whole Business of the Play should not be much longer than the Time it takes up in *Playing*.

The Second *Unity* is that of Place. To observe it, the *Scene* must not wander from one Town or Country to another. It must continue in the same House, Street, or at farthest in the same City, where it was first laid. The reason of this Rule depends upon the First. Now, the Compass of *Time* being strait, that of *Space* must bear a correspondent Proportion. Long journeys in *Plays* are impracticable. The distances of *Place* must be suited to Leisure and Possibility; otherwise the supposition will appear unnatural and absurd.

The Third *Unity* is that of Action. It consists in contriving the chief Business of the *Play* single, and making the concerns of one Person distinguishable great above the rest. — JEREMY COLLIER, *Remarks upon the Relapse.*

The truth is that the spectators are always in their senses, and know, from the first act to the last, that the stage is only a stage and that the players are only players. They came to hear a certain number of lines recited with just gesture and elegant modulation. The lines relate to some action, and an action must be in some place; but the different actions that complete a story may be in places very remote from each other; and where is the absurdity of allowing that space to represent first Athens and then Sicily, which was always known to be neither Sicily nor Athens but a modern theater?

. . . Time is, of all modes of existence, the most obsequious to the imagination; a lapse of years is as easily conceived as a passage of hours. In contemplation we easily contract the time of real actions, and therefore willingly permit it to be contracted when we only see their imitation. — SAMUEL JOHNSON, *Preface to Shakspere.*

I

IN the ever-delightful pages in which Dickens describes the unexpected characters with whom Nicholas Nickleby is brought in contact during the days of his association with the strolling players under the management of Mr. Crummles, we are made acquainted with a worthy country gentleman, Mr. Curdle, who poses as a patron of the drama. When Mr. Curdle is informed that Nicholas Nickleby is the author of the new play in which the Infant Phenomenon is to appear, he expresses the hope that the young dramatist has "preserved the unities." He insists that incident, dialogue, and characters are "all unavailing without a strict observance of the unities."

" ' Might I ask you,' said the hesitating Nicholas, 'what the unities are?'

" Mr. Curdle coughed and considered. 'The unities, sir,' he said, 'are a completeness — a kind of universal dovetailedness with regard to time and place — a sort of general oneness, if I may be allowed to use so strong an expression. I take those to be the dramatic unities, so far as I have been enabled to bestow attention upon them, and I have read much upon the subject, and thought much.' "

Very likely the creator of Mr. Curdle and of Mr. Crummles would have found it difficult to give any better definition of the unities than this which he put in the mouth of one of his comic characters. But then Dickens did not pretend to have read much upon the subject and thought much. Probably many a playgoer who has heard about the dramatic unities and

about the duty of preserving them, has no more exact
idea as to what they really are than Mr. Curdle. Indeed, we may find the term used by some dramatic
critics of to-day with a haziness of meaning recalling
the vagueness of Mr. Curdle's definition. Yet the term
has a precise content, known to those who have really
read much upon the subject and thought much; and
the theory of the dramatic unities has a history which
has been made clear comparatively recently.

It is not uncommon to read references to the "unities of Aristotle"; and yet Aristotle knew them not
and did not discuss them at all. It has happened of
late that they have been termed the "unities of Scaliger"; and yet they were not completely declared by
Scaliger. They are to be found formulated with the
utmost sharpness in Boileau's "Art of Poetry"; but
they were familiar to Sidney when he penned his "Defense of Poesy." Jonson tried to preserve them; but
Shakspere refused to let them shackle him. Lope de
Vega admitted their validity and yet evaded their rule,
as he regretfully confessed. Corneille had never heard
of them when he wrote his fieriest play; and they were
at the bottom of the famous "Quarrel of the Cid,"
in which Richelieu involved the French Academy he
had recently established. Lessing analyzed them un-
favorably in the eighteenth century; and in the nineteenth, Victor Hugo derided them in his flamboyant
preface to "Cromwell," wherein he raised the red flag
of the romanticist revolt. And yet the dramatic unities are preserved once more in the "Francillon" of
the younger Dumas, son of Hugo's early rival, and
in the "Ghosts" of Ibsen, the austere Norwegian
realist, — although in all probability neither of these

latter-day dramatists had paid any attention to the theory which insisted that the unities must be preserved.

What are then these unities which some dramatic poets believe in, but reject, and which others preserve without taking thought? What are they, and where do they come from? Why should anybody want to preserve them? How could anybody achieve this preservation without effort? To find the answer to these queries, we must be willing to go on a loitering excursion through literature after literature, straying from French into Italian and then wandering back into Greek before strolling forward again into English, — an excursion which will force us to fellowship with Boileau and Aristotle, with Shakspere and Ben Jonson, as well as with the ingenious critics of the Italian Renascence and with the ardent playwrights of French romanticism.

The clearest and most succinct declaration of the dramatic unities was made by Boileau when he laid down the law that a tragedy must show "one action in one day and in one place." It must deal with only a single story; and this obligation is the Unity of Action. It must never change the scene, massing its episodes in a single locality; and this is the Unity of Place. And it must compress its successive situations into the space of twenty-four hours, into a single day; and this is the Unity of Time. When a tragedy presents a simple and straightforward story without change of scenery and without any longer lapse of time than a single revolution of the sun, then and only then are the three unities preserved, as Boileau understood them. And in thus laying down the law which must bind the tragic poet, the French critic believed that he was only echoing the regulations promulgated by

Aristotle, the great Greek, whose authority then over-
awed critics and poets alike. Yet Boileau would have
held with the Abbé d'Aubignac, his predecessor as a
critic, and with Corneille, his contemporary as a poet,
that the strict observation of the three unities is demanded not only by authority but by reason also.
Two and three hundred years ago, all men of letters
seem to have agreed that even if the ancients had not
prescribed these limitations, they would have been
evolved by the moderns independently, as a result of the
strenuous search for the perfect form of the ideal play.

It was lucky for the theory of the three unities that
its advocates sought to prop it up by this appeal to reason, since it was not actually supported by the authority of Aristotle. Although they were long called the
Aristotelian Unities, only one of the three is formally
set forth by the Greek philosopher, even if a second
has been implied from one of his statements. Boileau
and his contemporaries, like their Italian predecessors,
made the natural mistake of thinking of Aristotle as
a theorist, like unto themselves, as engaged in working out an ideal system for the drama. But this was
just what Aristotle was not. Whether he was considering the constitution of Athens or the construction of
the Attic drama, the Greek inquirer was unfailingly
practical. He dealt with the thing as he saw it before
his eyes, taking it as he found it, relishing the concrete
and eschewing the abstract.

Aristotle's attitude is the same as Lessing's in the
eighteenth century and Sarcey's in the nineteenth.
He did not retire within himself and weave theories
out of thin air. He was no closet-critic of a closet-drama.
He sat himself down in the theater itself to see plays

performed by actors before an audience, and the principles he lays down are the logical deduction from his observation of the effect produced on him by the actual performance of the particular kind of tragic drama he is analyzing. He is no spinner of theories in a vacuum; and he kept himself in close contact with the realities of the theater. He came early in the development of the drama; and the plays of the Greeks were all that he knew. With his marvelous acuteness of insight, he mastered the mechanism of Attic tragedy; he discovered the principles which had governed its makers and according to which they had worked, — more or less unconsciously, as is the wont of artists. If Aristotle had known any other type of drama than that of the Greeks, he would have had standards of comparison; and his deductions would have been different. As it was, he handled the matter before him with incomparable certainty. Even though he was acquainted with only one form of tragedy, he pierced to the center and said many things which are applicable to every form of tragedy, ancient and modern. It is true that he also said many things which are applicable only to the tragic drama of the Athenians.

II

Of the three unities, only one is to be found formally stated in Aristotle's treatise. This is the Unity of Action; and it is as valid in the modern drama as in the ancient. The Greek critic declared that a tragedy ought to have a single subject, whole and complete in itself, with a beginning, a middle, and an end. This is true of every work of art, tragic or epic, pictorial or plastic. Every work of art ought to leave a direct and simple impression, which it cannot make without a concentration upon its theme and without a rigorous exclusion of all non-essentials. It is true that there are great works of literary art, in which we perceive two stories intertwined and demanding equal attention, — the "Merchant of Venice," for example, and "Vanity Fair" and "Anna Karénina." But they are great in spite of this bifurcation of interest; and they number very few among the masterpieces of literature. In most of these masterpieces, we find only a single theme, as in the "Œdipus" of Sophocles and in the "Tartuffe" of Molière; in the "Scarlet Letter" of Hawthorne and in the "Smoke" of Turgenieff.

Shakspere is often careless in the construction of the plots of his romantic-comedies and of his dramatic-romances, "Much Ado about Nothing," for example, and the "Winter's Tale"; but he is very careful to give essential unity to the loftier tragedies in which he put forth his full strength, in "Othello," and "Hamlet," and "Macbeth." In these supreme efforts of his tragic power, he achieves not only the needful unity of plot, but also the subtler unity of tone, of color, of sentiment. With his customary acuteness, Coleridge dwelt on the "unity of feeling" which Shakspere observes.

"Read 'Romeo and Juliet,'" he declared; — "all is youth and spring; youth with all its follies, its virtues, its precipitancies; — spring with its odors, its flowers, and its transiency; it is one and the same feeling that commences, goes through, and ends the play. The old men, the Capulets and the Montagues, are not common old men; they have an eagerness, a heartiness, a vehemence, the effect of spring; with Romeo, his change of passion, his sudden marriage, and his rash death, are all the effects of youth; — whilst in Juliet, love has all that is tender and voluptuous in the rose, with whatever is sweet in the freshness of spring; but it ends with a long deep sigh like the last breeze of the Italian evening."

In asserting the necessity of the Unity of Action, the only unity which is to be found plainly set forth in his fragmentary treatise, Aristotle was anticipating the demand of Mr. Curdle that the dramatist should give to his work " a completeness, — a kind of universal dovetailedness, a sort of general oneness." Apparently, the Unity of Action was the only one of the three unities that Mr. Curdle knew anything about, even though he had read much upon the subject and thought much. And it is the only one which has imposed itself upon all the greater dramatists, whether Greek or English, French or Scandinavian. It is the only one of the three which is now accepted as imperative beyond all question; and it is the only one the acceptance of which by the dramatic poet is everywhere to his abiding advantage.

Thus we see that Boileau was justified in demanding that tragic poets should deal only with a single theme. Was he right also in insisting that they should limit the action to a single day and to a single place? And what was his warrant for believing that they should impose these limitations on their freedom? His justification was twofold, the appeal to reason and the appeal to authority, — to what had been read into Aristotle's treatise although it had not been explicitly expressed therein. Yet there is possibly some slight foundation for the belief that Aristotle had declared the Unity of Time, as well as the Unity of Action. The Greek drama was acted outdoors in the level orchestra of the theater; and the single story of the play was unrolled before the audience without any such intermissions as our modern interacts. The Greek playwright was therefore under strong pressure to relate his successive episodes as closely as he could, to avoid distracting the attention of the spectators from his plot to the mere lapse of time. Therefore he tended to avoid all mention of time and to present his situations as following swiftly one after the other.

"Tragedy endeavors," so Aristotle tells us, "so far as possible, to confine itself to a single revolution of the sun, or but slightly to exceed this limit." But the great critic is not here laying down the law; he is merely declaring the habitual practice of the playwrights whose works he was studying, to spy out their secrets. He is not asserting that this must be done; he is only informing us that it was done as far as possible. He could not help knowing that it was not always possible, and that when it was not possible, the Greek dramatists did not hesitate to extend their plot over as long a period as they might think necessary. For example, the "Agamemnon" of Æschylus begins with the Watchman on the tower looking for the flaming signal which was to announce the fall of Troy, flashing from beacon to beacon, from hilltop to hilltop across leagues of land and sea. At last the Watchman catches sight of the blaze, and he descends to tell Clytemnestra that her husband is that day set free to depart on his long voyage homeward. It would be many more days before the hero could be expected to arrive; and yet in the middle of the play, Agamemnon appears and enters the palace to meet his death. Here is a long lapse of time, foreshortened by the dramatist, because it was not possible otherwise to deal advantageously with the story.

It may be admitted that the "Agamemnon" is the only extant Greek play which covers so protracted a period. But that Æschylus should have ventured to do this is evidence that the Greeks themselves had accepted no hard-and-fast rule compelling them to limit the duration of the story to twenty-four hours. Now, if the Unity of Time was not always observed by the Greek dramatic poets and if it was not formally prescribed by Aristotle, how did it come into being? And thanks to Professor Spingarn's illuminating investigation into Italian criticism during the Renascence, this question is now easy to answer. Giraldi Cinthio, — from one of whose tales Shakspere was to derive the suggestion for his "Othello," — wrote a "Discourse on Comedy and Tragedy," in which he limited the time of a play to a single day, thus converting Aristotle's statement of a historical fact into a dramatic law, and changing Aristotle's "single revolution of the sun" into a "single day." A little later, another Italian critic, Robortello, cut down the time to twelve hours, "for as tragedy can contain only one single and continuous action, and as people are accustomed to sleep in the night, it follows that the tragic action cannot be continued beyond one artificial day." And a little later, still yet another Italian, Trissino, declared that the Unity of Time is imperative on all playwrights, though it is disobeyed "even to-day by ignorant poets."

This final sneer is very significant. In the Italian Renascence, all literature — and criticism more especially — was frankly aristocratic. It made its appeal not to the many, but to the few; it was not for the plain people, but only for the cultivated, who were alone capable of understanding the artist. This attitude is not dead in America to-day; it was universal in Italy four centuries ago. The educated classes had come into the splendid heritage of the classics; and they felt themselves more than ever elevated above the common herd. What the common herd could enjoy was by that very fact discredited. The men of letters kept aloof from the vulgar throng; they were artists working for the appreciation of their fellow dilettants. To take this attitude is ever dangerous even for the lyric poet; for the dramatist it is fatal. The drama is of necessity the most democratic of the arts, making its appeal to the people as a whole, educated and uneducated alike. But the Italian critics despised the popular acted drama of their own day; and they deemed it wholly unworthy of consideration. However much they as individuals might enjoy the rollicking comedy-of-masks or the more primitive miracle-plays, they as a class despised this unpretending folk-drama. So Sidney, who had been nurtured on Italian criticism, despised the popular drama which was the connecting link between the rude medieval mystery and the noble Elizabethan tragedy.

Here, indeed, is the difference between Aristotle and his Italian commentators. He was a regular playgoer; and the principles he sets forth are only the results of his study of a great dramatic literature, as this was vividly revealed in the actual theater. They had never seen a good play well acted. What they had beheld on the stage was not good, according to their standards; and what they esteemed good they could not behold on any stage. This explains their academic theorizing, their pedantry, their insistence upon conformity with arbitrary limitations. While Aristotle,

with the hard-headed common sense of the Greek, had
his eye fixed on the concrete as he saw it, they, with
the super-ingenious subtlety of the Italian, bent their
gaze on the abstract. They longed for a noble dramatic literature and they tried to make it out of hand
by servile imitation of Latin tragedy and Latin comedy.
They did not guess that the folk-plays enjoyed by the
vulgar throng needed only to be improved, to supply
a foundation for a living drama at once poetic and
popular. Their aristocratic contempt for the common
herd prevented the Italians from developing out of
their own folk-drama a type of play dignified and
national, such as the English, the Spanish, and the
French were to develop. The sacred-representations,
medieval as they might be, had in them the germ of
lofty tragedy; and the comedy-of-masks might have
been purged of its grossness and lifted into literature
(and this is exactly what Molière was to do more than
a century later). Because they scorned the acted
drama of their own day, meager as it might be and
barren of art, the clever Italians deprived themselves
of a living dramatic literature. In its stead, they had
only a code of laws, arbitrarily declaring what a dramatic literature ought to be.

The Unity of Action was proclaimed by Aristotle;
the Unity of Time was elaborated into a rule from one
of Aristotle's casual statements of fact; and the Unity
of Place was deduced by the Italian critics from the
Unity of Time, as Professor Spingarn has made plain.
Almost suggested by Scaliger, it was actually formulated first by Castelvetro, who differed from his contemporaries in that he took account of the desires
of a possible audience. It is true that Castelvetro, in

spite of his talk about the actual stage, knew quite as
little about it as any of his contemporaries. Yet he
declared it to be the duty of the dramatist to please the
spectators, of whatever sort, and to consult always
their capabilities. He had no high opinion of the intelligence of these spectators, believing that they could
not imagine a lapse of time or a change of scene. At
least, he suggested that they would be annoyed if the
action was not confined to one day and contained in
one place.

The fallacy underlying Castelvetro's theory is the
result of his assumption that the spectators, while sitting in their seats, suppose themselves to be witnessing
reality. He fails wholly to appreciate the willingness
of an audience to "make believe" almost to any extent.
And his own logic breaks down when he convinces himself that the spectators cannot imagine two or three
places in turn, just as well as one at a time, and that
they are not ready to let the author pack into the two
hours' traffic of the stage the events, not of twenty-four
hours only, but of twelve months or more. He does not
grasp the conventions which must underlie every art
and which alone make an art possible. Every artist
must be allowed to depart frankly from the merely
actual, if he is to please us by his representation of life
as he apprehends it.

Probably the Unity of Place would not have taken
its position by the side of the Unity of Time and the
Unity of Action, if it had not seemed to be supported
by the practice of the Greek dramatic poets. In the
surviving specimens of Attic drama, there are a few
instances where the action is apparently transported
from one spot to another; but in the immense majority

of the Athenian plays which have come down to us, we
note that the story begins and ends in the same place.
And the reason for this is not far to seek. The Greek
drama had been evolved out of the lyrics of the chorus;
and to the end of the Athenian period, the chorus continued to be a most important element of a tragic performance. When the chorus had once circled into the
orchestra, it generally remained there until the end of
the tragedy. Now, this presence of the chorus before
the eyes of the spectators prevented the dramatist from
shifting the location of his action even if he had desired
to do so. He could ask his audience to imagine a change
of place only when the orchestra was empty, which
was very rarely the case. Furthermore, we must keep
in mind the fact that the theater at Athens was in all
probability devoid of scenery, and that therefore there
was no way of visibly indicating a change of place.

III

This, then, is the theory of the three unities, long
credited to the great Greek critic, but now seen to have
been worked out by the supersubtle Italian critics of
the Renascence. Indeed, there is little exaggeration
in saying that they evolved it from their inner consciousness. From Cinthio and Scaliger, Castelvetro
and Minturno, the theory passed to Sidney and Ben
Jonson in England, to Juan de la Cueva and Lope de
Vega in Spain, to the Abbé d'Aubignac and Boileau
in France. For two centuries and more, this law of
the three unities, with the other rules elaborated at the
same time by the same Italians, were accepted throughout Europe by almost every critic of the drama. There
was an established standard of "regularity" and "cor-

rectness," which imposed on all playwrights a strict obedience to the critical code. This body of laws was supposed to be supported by the inexpugnable authority of Aristotle; but it was also believed to have its basis in reason. It dominated the drama of France until early in the nineteenth century; and even if Corneille now and again chafed under it, Voltaire was insistent in supporting it. Dr. Johnson suggested that if "Othello" had opened in Cyprus and the preceding incidents been occasionally stated, "there had been little wanting to a drama of the most exact and scrupulous regularity." Yet this theory was not obeyed by the popular playwrights of Spain, not even by Lope, who was frank in declaring that he knew better than he practised; and it was rejected by the Elizabethan dramatists in England, excepting only Ben Jonson.

And this raises two interesting questions. If the code of correctness, including the rule calling for the preservation of the three unities, was accepted by all those who discussed the art of the drama, why did the practical playwrights of England and of Spain refuse to be bound by its behests? And why did the practical playwrights of France submit to be cribbed, cabined, and confined by its restrictions? The most obvious explanation is to be found in the fact that the great expansion of the drama arrived in France at least half a century later than it had in Spain and in England. A really literary drama, rich in poetry and vigorous in character, had been developed out of the popular medieval folk-play far earlier in Spain and in England than it had in France; and the Spanish and the English playwrights, having succeeded in pleasing the playgoing public with a large, bold, and free drama, saw no good reason why they should surrender their liberties and risk their popularity by conforming to a standard of correctness which might gratify the cultivated few, but which would deprive the uneducated many of the variety the main body of spectators had been accustomed to expect in the theater. Indeed, this is the excuse which Lope de Vega makes for himself in his significant address on the "New Art of Making Plays."

While this may have been the main motive of the chief of the Spanish playwrights, there is no difficulty in surmising that the chief of the English dramatic poets had a better reason for rejecting the law of the three unities and for refusing to submit himself to its chains. Shakspere was preëminently a practical man, with a keen eye to the main chance. He could find no profit in foregoing any part of the freedom which had enabled him to catch the favor of the playgoers who welcomed his "native wood-notes wild." And he could not help fearing an obvious and immediate loss if he should choose to let himself be governed by the Unity of Time. No small part of Shakspere's incomparable power as a dramatist is due to his understanding of the forces which modify character, transforming it under pressure, or disintegrating it under stress of recurring temptation. Now, character is not modified in the twinkling of an eye, nor can it disintegrate in twenty-four hours. If Shakspere had chosen to preserve the Unity of Time, he would have been compelled to suppress all the earlier episodes of "Julius Cæsar," for example, which are so significant and which revive in our memories when we are witnesses of the later quarrel of Brutus and Cassius; and he would have had to present Macbeth only in the final stage of his moral deliquescence, without showing us the manly soldier before the virus of mean ambition had poisoned his nobler nature.

This concentration of action into the culminating moments of the story was not a disadvantage to the Greek dramatic poets, since they were expected to present a trilogy, three separate plays acted in swift succession on the same day to the same audience, whereby they were enabled to show the tragic hero at three different moments of his career. But the obligation to preserve the Unity of Time was a sad restriction upon the French dramatic poets, who had not the privilege of the trilogy and who were compelled always to present characters fixed and unchanging. By his compulsory obedience to this rule, Corneille was robbed of not a little of his possible range and sweep, even if Racine, with his subtlety of psychologic analysis, may even have gained by an enforced compacting of his story and by a limitation to its culminating moments.

Shakspere did not care to discuss the principles of his craft, as Ben Jonson was wont to do. He digresses in "Hamlet" into a disquisition on the art of acting; but he nowhere expresses his personal opinions on the art of playwriting. He was no more a theatrical reformer than he was a dramatic theorist. He was content to take the stage as he found it and to utilize all its conventions and all its contemporary traditions. If he declined to listen to the precepts of the critics, and if he refused to preserve the unities, he had his own reasons; and we can see that they were sufficient. But it is unimaginable that he did not know what he was doing or that he was ignorant of these theories.

It is very improbable that he had not in his youth read Sidney's "Defense," in which the rule of the three unities is stated for the first time in English. It is most unlikely that in his maturity, and when he and Ben Jonson were engaging in their wit-combats at the Mermaid, he had not had occasion to hear the whole code of the drama proclaimed again and again by his robust and scholarly friend.

We have seen that an Italian critic dismissed the playwrights who failed to preserve the unities as "ignorant poets." Probably the reproach of ignorance of the rules was one that Shakspere would bear with perfect equanimity. Yet, although he himself drew no attention to it, and, for all we know, may not even have bidden Jonson to remark it, he was moved once, in the later years of his labors in London, to preserve the unities, as if to show that it was not ignorance, but a wise choice, which had led him to reject them in all his other plays, tragic and comic. The "Tempest" is in all likelihood the last play which Shakspere wrote without collaboration, and in the "Tempest," he chose to preserve the unities, — as they were then understood in England and as they had been preserved by Jonson in several comedies. The Unity of Place required that the action should be confined to a single place, but place was interpreted liberally. A single place meant one palace or one town, not necessarily a specific room in this palace or a specific house in this town. It meant a single locality, but not a single spot. The action of "Every Man in his Humor" passes in London, which is a single locality, but it is not restricted to a single room or even to a single house in that city.

The "Tempest" sets before us, as Professor Lounsbury has pointed out, a single story, direct and swift
and uncomplicated; and therefore it preserves the
Unity of Action. It is compact within a single revolution of the sun, as the author takes care to tell us
more than once, — and therefore it preserves the Unity
of Time; indeed, its story is compressed within three
hours, not exceeding the limit of the performance itself.
It has for its locality an island with the water immediately surrounding that island; and therefore it preserves the Unity of Place (as that was then liberally
interpreted). As we study the "Tempest," it is as
though we could hear its author saying that he could
play the game as well as any one else when he chose,
and if he had not played it before, this was simply
because he did not deem it worth the candle.

IV

That Shakspere wrote the "Tempest" is pretty
plain evidence that he knew the "rules of the
drama" quite as well as Lope de Vega did. That
both the English and the Spanish dramatic poets refused to abide by them is equally evident. And this
brings up again the question why the doctrine of the
unities should have been accepted willingly by the
professional playwrights of France after it had been
rejected by the professional playwrights of England
and of Spain. One answer to this query has already
been suggested — that the outflowering of dramatic
poetry was later in France than in England or in Spain,
and therefore after the doctrine of the three unities
had hardened into a dogma. Another answer might
be that the French are the inheritors of the Latin

tradition, that they like to do things decently and in order, and that they relish restraint more than the English or the Spaniards. We might go further and say that the French are naturally the most artistic of the three races and that, to an artist, there is always a keen joy in working under bonds and in grappling with self-imposed obligations. But there is a third explanation of the apparent anomaly which comes nearest to being adequate.

The drama of every modern literature is the outgrowth of the drama of the Middle Ages, — of the passion-play and of the popular farce. But the development from this unliterary folk-drama into true tragedy and true comedy is different in the different countries, and it is only by tracing back this evolution in France that we can lay hold of the chief reason why the Unity of Place was accepted in France, even though it had been rejected in England, where the theater had followed a slightly different line of development.

The full-grown passion-play was the result of putting together the several episodes of the gospel-story, which had been shown in action in the church on different days, more especially Christmas and Easter, as an accompaniment of the service. Each of these episodes had been set forth in the most appropriate part of the edifice, — the Holy Child in the manger, on the chancel-steps, the Raising of Lazarus, near the crypt, the Crucifixion, near the altar. These scattered places where the separate parts of the sacred story were represented in action and in dialogue were known as " stations," and when the overgrown religious drama was finally thrust out of the church and confined to laymen, the useful device of the stations was taken

over by the new performers. In France, the passion-
play was presented on a long and shallow platform,
with the successive stations ranged side by side at the
back; and they were known as "mansions." In fact, all
the important places in the play were set on the stage
at once, each coming into use in its turn and as often
as need be, while the most of the acting was done in
the neutral ground further forward on the platform.

After the performance of the mysteries in Paris had
been confided to the Brotherhood of the Passion, this
body established itself in the Hotel de Bourgogne, the
stage of which was prepared to accommodate as many
mansions as the story might demand. In time, dramatizations of the lives of the saints followed the dramatization of the life of Christ; and, after a while, these were
succeeded by dramatizations of the lives of heroes,
at first of history and afterwards of romance. Thus
the sacred drama gave way to the profane, which had
been slowly developed out of it. Yet the lay playwrights, though they might borrow their plots from
modern legends, retained the medieval device of the
mansions, finding it very convenient, since it enabled
them to show on the stage all the many places where
their hero met with his manifold adventures. However incongruous this simultaneous set may seem to
us, accustomed as we are nowadays to a succession
of sets, it was familiar to French audiences and acceptable to them well into the seventeenth century. But
in time, its disadvantages became more and more
obvious. The spectators who had not found it hard
to follow the well-known Bible story and to identify
the Temple at Jerusalem, the House of the High-
Priest, and the other mansions it demanded, began to

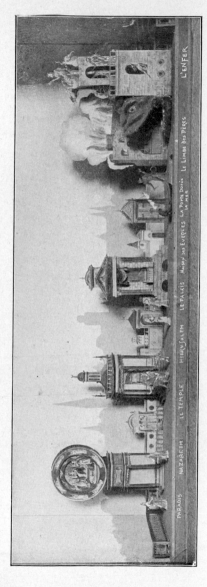

RESTORATION OF THE STAGE ON WHICH A PASSION-PLAY WAS ACTED AT VALENCIENNES (1547)

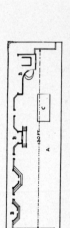

PLAN OF THE PASSION-PLAY STAGE AT VALENCIENNES

A, stage ; B, B, B, the mansions ; C, the sea

be a little confused when Hardy put before them unknown stories acted amid mansions only summarily
indicated by the carpenter and the decorator. Hardy
cluttered the stage with all sorts of strange places,
bringing together in one play, a ship, a palace, a bed-
room and a cave on a mountain; and the audience had
to strain its ingenuity to recognize all these localities.

It was for a stage thus fitted up that Corneille composed the "Cid," the action of which takes place in a
neutral ground, backed by the residences of the chief
characters. When he wrote this play, he had never
even heard of the doctrine of the unities, which had
been ignored by the Spanish dramatist from whom
he borrowed his plot. He soon found himself severely
criticised for his ignorance of the rules of the drama;
and, although his play was overwhelmingly successful, he confessed his error. In all his following plays,
he preserved the Unity of Place, discarding the medley
of mansions that he had employed freely in his earlier
pieces; and we cannot doubt that this simplification
of the scenery on the stage was most welcome to the
spectators, who were no longer forced to guess at the
significance of accumulated bits of scenery. And so
powerful was the prestige of Corneille, that his contemporaries and his successors followed his example
and showed one action in one place in one day.

Corneille himself often found it rather irksome to
conform to the rules; and Molière, in his adaptation
of the laxly constructed Spanish piece, "Don Juan,"
was forced for once to disregard them. But they imposed no painful bonds on Racine, who was satisfied to deal only with the tense culmination of a tragic
complication. What Corneille and Racine had done,

Voltaire was glad to do, although he and his contemporaries might be reduced to the absurdity of making conspirators hold their meetings in the palace of the monarch they were leagued against. For two centuries, the serious drama of the French was chained in the triple-barred cage of the unities; and it was not released until Victor Hugo brought out "Hernani," long after freedom had been won in other countries.

After "Hernani" had blown his trumpet and the hollow walls of classicism had fallen with a crash, the doctrine of the three unities was finally disestablished; and Mr. Curdle is easily excusable for not knowing exactly what it was. Perhaps its evil effect even upon the drama of France has been overestimated; at least we may doubt whether Molière and Racine, Marivaux and Beaumarchais really lost anything by accepting it. On the other hand, we have reason to rejoice that it was rejected by the dramatic poets of England and of Spain. In our own time, no playwright ever gives a thought to the preservation of the unities. And yet even to-day, when a dramatist is dealing with the result of a long series of events, and when he seeks to set this forth as simply and as strongly as he can, we are likely to find him compacting his single action into a single day and setting it in a single place. This is what the younger Dumas did in " Francillon," and what Ibsen did in " Ghosts "; probably either of them would have been not a little surprised if he had been told that in these plays he had preserved the unities.

This unconscious compliance of two practical playwrights of the nineteenth century with the theoretical precepts of the dogmatic critics of the sixteenth and seventeenth centuries, suggests that there is, after all, something to be urged in behalf of the three unities. They represent an effort toward simplicity of plot and toward logic of structure, two qualities greatly needed by the drama in its semi-medieval condition. That the effort was unfortunately misdirected is not to be denied; yet it had a worthy motive.

APPENDIX

APPENDIX

I

It may be well to suggest a series of questions which the student can put to himself when he begins to study any play, ancient or modern.

A. Has this play a single plot? — or is the story double or even treble? If there is more than one story, which is the main-plot? Is the under-plot worked into the structure of the play, or is it independent, being merely juxtaposed? Does the existence of more than one plot divide the interest of the play, or scatter it, or does the under-plot sustain the main story by adroit contrast? Does the play contain any non-dramatic elements, epic or lyric, oratorical or descriptive? If so, to what extent do these interfere with the dramatic interest?

B. Has the play an essential struggle sustaining it from beginning to end? If so, what is this struggle? By what characters is this struggle maintained on the one side and on the other? Are both opponents justified in their own minds? Or is one of them absolutely right and the other absolutely wrong? With which character do you find yourself sympathizing? Why? Does the outcome of the struggle satisfy you? If not, why not? Has the author played fair with his characters? Or has he obviously intervened to make them do what they would not do? And, if so, has this interfered with your interest in the play?

C. What happened before the play began? At what point in the story does the author choose to begin and at what point to end? Why did he choose between these points of beginning and ending? Was he well advised in both choices? How has he conveyed to you what you need to know about the past to enable you to follow the play from the beginning? What is his method of exposition? Has he massed his necessary explanations in the earlier scenes? or has he reserved some interesting disclosures for later acts? If so, was he right in so doing? Has he failed to tell you, early in the play, anything that you would have liked to know then to appreciate better what was being done on the stage? Does he at any time violate the principle of Economy of Attention?

D. What is the main theme? Is this held to unswervingly? Or does the story digress into by-paths? Does the play contain any scene which could be omitted? If so, why was it inserted? Does the author fail to present any scene which he ought to have shown in action? If so, can you discover any sound reason for this omission? Has he led you to expect any scene which he has not given you?

E. Does the interest of the play rise steadily from the beginning to the end? If not, where does it droop? And what is the cause of this flagging in each case? Draw the diagram of interest and use it to aid you in your analysis.

F. What dramatic conventions does the author avail himself of? Which of these are permanent and necessary? Which of them are temporary and peculiar to the theater of his day? Has he a chorus? If so, what is the function of this chorus? Does he employ the soliloquy? If so, is it for constructive purposes, to tell you facts? Or is it only to reveal the thoughts of a character alone on the stage? Does he use asides addressed directly to the audience? Does he employ the device of eavesdropping? And in these things is he merely accepting the traditions of his immediate predecessors? In other words, how far is his method of construction influenced by the conditions of the actual theater of his own time?

G. Do you discover or suspect any evidence that the author had any special actors in mind in composing his play? Is there anything said or done by any character which is the result of the fitting of that part to the original performer?

And if so, does this help you to understand better the author's intent?

H. What evidence do you discover that the author had in mind the opinions or even the prejudices of his contemporaries, of the audiences of his own time? Is there any overt appeal to the playgoers of that period and of that time? Is there any frank claptrap? What light does the contents of this play cast on the manners, the customs, and the beliefs of the people for whom it was originally written? Is it local and temporary in its appeal, or permanent and universal?

I. Is the play really a picture of life? Are the characters veracious? Could they have existed? If so, would they have acted as they do in the play? Is the conduct of the plot coherent and logical? Is the end inevitable or is it arbitrary? Is the story warped by the obvious effort of the author? Does casual accident affect the plot? If so, could this have been avoided? Ought it to have been avoided? Is there any arbitrary character? If so, does this interfere with your interest? And if it does not, why? Are there carefully contrived coincidences? If so, are they so brought about as to seem natural in the play? And how is this accomplished?

J. What was the author's aim in writing the play? Did he set out merely to present the several facets of a single character to whom all the others are subordinate? Did he intend to present primarily a picture of life, as it is or as it might be? Did he have an ulterior object, a thesis to sustain? Does the play prove anything? If so, was this the author's deliberate intent? Or was this merely incidental to his picture of life? Has the play a moral value? What effect had it on you? Did it uplift or depress you?

K. Does this play conform to the Unity of Action? To the Unity of Place? To the Unity of Time? If it does conform to any one of these, why? And was the conformation advisable? Did the play gain or lose thereby? Does it conform to the theory of poetic justice? If not, ought it to have done so? Does the author unduly sympathize with any one of the characters? Does he dislike any one of them? If so, does this help or hurt the play as a whole?

L. Can you classify the play easily? — that is to say, is it
a tragedy or a melodrama, a comedy or a farce, a chronicle-
play or a dramatic-romance, a romantic-comedy or a comedy-
of-manners? Or is it commingled of two or more types? If
so, what are these types? And does this departure from the
strict type interfere with your pleasure? Does the author
indulge in *mots d'esprit?* Does he reveal character by *mots
de caractère?* Is he happy in finding *mots de situation?*

II

BIBLIOGRAPHICAL SUGGESTIONS

IN the preceding pages, stress has been laid upon the fact
that the art of the drama has essential principles which are the
same throughout the ages. The conditions of performance
may change and the desires of different audiences may differ
wholly, but the dramatist has ever to conform to the same
code. This being the case, there is profit in considering the
drama as a whole, and in comparing the plays produced
in different periods and by different people. The following
list of plays has been drawn up to facilitate this comparison,
and to help the student to attain a perspective of the development of the drama. The historical evolution of the art of
the playwright, with incidental criticism of the successive
masters of dramaturgy, has been outlined in my own volume
of lectures on the *Development of the Drama* (Scribners,
1903).

For an understanding of the theatrical performances in
Greece, see Barnett's *Greek Drama* (Dent, 1900); Haigh's
Attic Theater (Macmillan, 3d ed., 1908); and also Haigh's
Tragic Drama of the Greeks (Macmillan, 1899). There are
many translations of the surviving plays of the Greek dramatists, some of them published in cheap editions. The *Sup-
pliants* of Æschylus, although not one of his best plays, is
interesting as illustrating the growth of an actual drama out
of the earlier chorus. His two most important plays are the
Prometheus Bound and the *Agamemnon.* The *Œdipus the*

King of Sophocles was held by Aristotle to be the most masterly of all the Attic tragedies; and second to it is the *Antigone*. Of Euripides, the *Medea* and the *Alcestis* are the most characteristic. Perhaps the *Frogs* is the easiest understood of all the lyrical burlesques of Aristophanes, since its theme is literary rather than political. The best translation of the masterpiece of Greek criticism is in Butcher's *Aristotle's Theory of Poetry and Fine Art* (Macmillan, 2d ed., 1898).

Unfortunately no complete play of Menander's has survived. In M. Collins's volume on Plautus and Terence in the Ancient Classics for English Readers, there are abstracts of all their plays with abundant quotation. Perhaps the *Captives*, although not characteristic, is the play of Plautus most likely to amuse modern readers. The *Aulularia* might also be read, as well as the *Andria* of Terence.

Horace's "Art of Poetry" is to be found in any translation of his poems; but it is accessible also with the poems of Vida and Boileau in Cook's *Art of Poetry* (Ginn & Co., 1892).

The most accessible translation of Seneca's plays is that by Professor Miller (University of Chicago Press, 1908), with a preface by Professor Manly. See also Cunliffe's *Influence of Seneca on the English Drama* (1893). There is no single book describing the organization of the Roman theater corresponding to Haigh's *Attic Theater*.

But Chambers's *Medieval Stage* (Clarendon Press, 1903) traces admirably the successive steps by which the modern drama was evolved out of the ritual of the church. And the actual text of the earliest dramatic attempts are collected in two volumes of Manly's *Specimens of Pre-Shaksperean Drama* (Ginn, 1900). A briefer selection, with a useful introduction, is Pollard's *English Miracle Plays* (Clarendon Press, 5th ed., 1909).

The most important plays of the Elizabethan dramatists can be found in Gollancz's Temple Dramatists, Baker's Belles Lettres Series, and the Mermaid Series; and the one-volume selection by Professor Neilson, *Chief Elizabethan Dramatists, excluding Shakspere* (Houghton Mifflin Company, 1910), will be sufficient for most readers. Neilson's one-volume edition of Shakspere (Houghton Mifflin Company, 1906) can also be highly recommended, especially because of its indication that the customary division into acts and scenes is unwarranted. Perhaps the most useful edition of Shakspere in separate volumes is Clark and Porter's First Folio Edition (Crowell). Sufficient abstracts from the Restoration Playwrights can be found in Crawfurd's *English Comic Dramatists* (Appleton, 1884) in connection with which attention must be called to Lamb's essay on "Artificial Comedy" and to Macaulay's answer, the "Comic Dramatists of the Restoration." The later dramatic authors of the English language are accessible in the Mermaid Series and in the Belles Lettres Series.

The plays of the contemporary dramatists are now generally published, although not always in satisfactory editions. Unfortunately Mr. Barrie has so far refused to put his comedies into print. Perhaps the most significant of these modern plays are Pinero's *Second Mrs. Tanqueray* and the *Benefit of the Doubt*, Jones's *Liars* and *Mrs. Dane's Defence*, Shaw's *Candida* and *You Never can Tell*, Bronson Howard's *Kate*, Clyde Fitch's *Climbers*, and Augustus Thomas's *Arizona*.

The masterpiece of French farce is *Master Pierre Patelin*, translated by Holbrook (Houghton Mifflin Company, 1903). There are several complete translations of Molière, but Professor Page's two volumes containing the more important plays (Putnam's, 1908) surpass all their predecessors. Of Corneille and of Racine, there are no complete translations in English, but separate pieces can be found in *Great Plays : French and German* (Appleton, 1901). Translators have also failed to provide adequate English versions of the comedies of Beaumarchais, of Scribe, of Augier, and of the two Dumas. The lyrical melodramas of Victor Hugo are included in the more or less complete translations of his works. And there are several versions of Rostand's *Cyrano de Bergerac*.

Lope de Vega has tempted few translators, but one of his comedies can be found in the *Drama*, edited by Alfred Bates

(1903). FitzGerald made free renderings of *Six Dramas of Calderon;* and there are translations of other of Calderon's plays by Denis Florence MacCarthy. *Life is a Dream* and the *Alcalde of Zalamea* are characteristic examples of Calderon's method. Of the contemporary Spanish dramatists, only Echegaray is represented in English; his *Gran Galeotto* is most noteworthy. There is an account of the Italian comedy-of-masks in the introduction to Symonds's translation of the memoirs of Carlo Gozzi. Several of D'Annunzio's plays are available in English, especially the *Gioconda* and *Jorio's Daughter.*

There are translations of the works of Goethe and Schiller, which include their chief plays. Perhaps the most noteworthy are Goethe's *Götz von Berlichingen* and Schiller's *Robbers* and *Don Carlos.* Of the contemporary German playwrights, Sudermann and Hauptmann are the most important. There are English translations of Sudermann's *Magda* and the *Joy of Living* and of Hauptmann's *Weavers* and *Hannele.*

Archer's edition of Ibsen now includes nearly all the plays, both in prose and in verse; the characteristics of Ibsen's method are revealed in the *Doll's House,* in *Hedda Gabler,* and in *Ghosts.* Björnson's *Beyond Human Power* and *Glove* also exist in English translations.

Spingarn's *Literary Criticism in the Renaissance* (Columbia University Press, 2d ed., 1908) discusses the dramatic theories which resulted in the establishment of the classicist formula in France. The English translation of d'Aubignac, entitled the *Whole Art of the Stage,* is scarce; but it is often to be found in the larger libraries. Lessing's *Hamburg Dramaturgy* is included in the Bohn Series; it prepared the way for Schlegel's lectures on *Dramatic Literature* (also in the Bohn Series), which is still useful, although unduly polemic in its hostility to the French. There is an inadequate English version of Freytag's *Technic of the Drama* (McClurg, 1895). Later books dealing with dramatic theory are Jerome's *Playwriting* (reprinted from the *Stage,* 1888); Hennequin's *Art of Playwriting* (Houghton Mifflin Company, 1890);

Calmour's *Practical Playwriting* (Arrowsmith, 1891); Price's *Technique of the Drama* (Brentano, 1892) ; F. Archer's *How to write a Good Play* (Sampson Low, 1892); Woodbridge's *Drama; its Law and Technique* (Allyn & Bacon, 1898); Price's *Analysis of Play Construction and Dramatic Principle* (published by the author, 1908); Caffin's *Appreciation of the Drama* (Baker & Taylor, 1908); and Clayton Hamilton's *Theory of the Theater* (Holt, 1910).

For an insight into the principles of the art of acting, which is so closely allied to the art of playwriting, the student may be referred to Lewes's *Actors and the Art of Acting* (Smith, Elder, 1875, now accessible also in the Tauchnitz collection); and Colley Cibber's *Apology* and Joseph Jefferson's *Autobiography*. See also Archer's *Masks or Faces* (Longmans, 1888).

For a longer discussion of the non-literary qualities of the drama, the reader may be referred to my papers on the "Relation of the Drama to Literature" in the *Historical Novel and other Essays* (Scribners, 1901), and to that on the "Importance of the Folk-Theater" in the third edition of *Aspects of Fiction* (Scribners, 1902). The earlier periods of dramatic evolution are considered from the anthropological point of view in Hirn's *Origins of Art* (Macmillan, 1901), and in Grosse's *Beginnings of Art* (Appleton, 1897).

A more elaborate analysis of the conventions of the drama will be found in a paper included in my *Historical Novel and other Essays*.

Professor Schelling has traced the career of the *English Chronicle-Play* (Macmillan, 1902); and in his *History of the Elizabethan Drama*, he has outlined the development of other dramatic species. To Professor Neilson's Types of English Literature, Professor Thorndike has contributed an illuminating study of *Tragedy;* and for the same series Professor Fletcher is preparing an account of the *Pastoral*.

In the opening paper of A. B. Walkley's *Drama and Life* (Methuen, 1907), there is a consideration of the effect produced on the drama by the change from the platform-stage to the picture-frame stage. To the Stratford Town Edition of

Shakspere, Mr. Robert Bridges contributed a paper discussing the influence of the Elizabethan audience on Shakspere; and in Mr. A. C. Bradley's *Oxford Lectures on Poetry* (Macmillan, 1909), there is a lecture on "Shakspere's Theater and Audience."

To be mentioned, also, is Karl Mantzius's *History of Theatrical Art*, five volumes of which have appeared in English (Lippincott, 1904–1909).

INDEX

Abington, Mrs., 167.

Academy of Music, the, 77.

Accident, ruled out by Aristotle and Coleridge, 101; by the best art, 197, 200; in *Romeo and Juliet*, 201–202.

Acropolis, the, 49, 70.

Action, placed by Jefferson above literary merit, 21; is the expression of will, 95; declared by Aristotle essential to tragedy, 101; the drama a conflict (Butcher), 101–102; action and character, 161, 162; of primary importance, 174; must be seen unfolding, 180; should support the dialogue, 181; in Scribe's plays, 182; in Dumas, the elder, 182; in Fédora, 184; of characters, 199, 200, 203; in Shakspere's plays, 202, 215; in the Elizabethan drama, 238; in the poetic drama, 250; in the modern drama, 265; in the *Blot in the 'Scutcheon*, 268; in the passion-play, 291; unity of (See Unity of Action). (See also Human will, Plot, *Scènes à faire*.)

Actors, limitations of, 41–43; eagerness of, for worthy new parts, 258.

Adventure, the tale of, 224.

Adventures of Tom Sawyer, the, quotation from, 12.

Æschylus, 17, 19, 58, 79, 165, 186, 232; *Prometheus Bound*, 58, 146; *Agamemnon*, 106, 165, 186, 247, 280–281; *Persians*, the, 136, 237, 247, 281.

Aldrich, T. B., *Judith*, 262; *Mercedes*, 263.

Alleyne, Edward, 32.

America, 125, 282.

American Indian, the, 133.

Amsterdam, 267.

Analogues, 125–126, 129, 141.

"Apron," the, 61, 62, 63.

Ara Cœli, the, 53.

Arbitrary, the, 121, 194, 195, 197, 201–210, 219, 221, 240, 242, 244.

Archer, William, quoted, 128.

Arena, sports of the Roman, 89–90; stage first cousin to, 103; gladiators in, 103.

Aristophanes, 232; lyrical-burlesque of, 117.

Aristotelian Unities, the, 276.

Aristotle, 20, 21, 88, 101, 102, 141, 152, 176, 208, 257, 274, 275, 276, 277, 279, 280, 281, 282, 283, 285, 286.

Arizona, 13.

Armada, the, 96.

Arnold, Matthew, 233; *Empedocles on Etna*, 253.

Artificial light, 45, 46, 48, 59, 60, 61, 63, 64, 66, 139, 238.

Aside, the, 144–145, 148.

Athenian (See Greek).

Athens, 48, 49, 79, 88, 89, 186, 195, 276, 285.

Atmosphere, in story-writing and in drama, 163.

Attic drama, the (See Greek drama).

Audiences, Elizabethan, 70, 73, 75, 91, 113, 123, 140, 165, 189, 195, 204, 219, 237–245, 256, 257, 270, 287; French- and English-speaking compared, 72, 231; of Terence, 72; of the Italian Renascence, 72; of Lope de Vega, 72–73; of Greece, 73, 74, 193, 195, 209, 239; modern, 74, 76–78, 86, 145, 150–151, 195, 196, 213, 219, 220, 270; sympathy of, 78, 79, 189, 205, 206, 220, 228, 230; characteristics of, 87, 88, 90, 182, 190, 195, 209–210, 218, 269; of Paris, 91; demands of, 98, 105–106, 107–108, 135–136, 139, 178, 180, 191, 192, 198–199, 217–218,

220–223, 224, 269–270; of Molière, 140, 196, 239; of Louis XIV, 145; Italian, 174; of Plautus, 189; not responsible for dramatic failures, 222; and the supernatural, 224–225; and the morality of plays, 226–231; not considered in the closet-drama, 250–253; favorable to poetic dramas, 258, 260, 270; Castelvetro's ideas about, 284; French, 292, 293.

Augier, Émile, 19, 39, 76, 119, 232; *Gendre de M. Poirier*, the, 75–76, 104, 118; *Paul Forestier*, 263.

Augustine, Saint, 90.

Baker, George P., *Development of Shakspere as a Dramatist*, 113.

Ballad-opera, the, 111, 124.

Ballet, the, 103.

Balzac, Honoré de, 155.

Banville, Théodore de, *Gringoire*, 40.

Barrie, J. M., 18, 270; *Peter Pan*, 270.

Bartley, quoted by Planché, 190.

Beaumarchais, 7, 8, 117, 150, 247, 294; *Marriage of Figaro*, the, 95; *Barber of Seville*, the, 247.

Beaumont, Francis, 117, **206, 219.**

Beauval, Mlle., 33.

Béjart, 33.

Béjart, Armande, 33.

Bernhardt, Mme. Sarah-, 35, 37.

Betterton, Thomas, 49.

Blackfriar's Theater, the, 256.

Boileau, 94, 260, 275, 276, 279, 285; quoted, 261 ; *Art of Poetry*, the, 274.

Boissier, Gaston, 52.

Bonaparte, Napoleon, 38.

Booth, Edwin, 139, 167, 168, 216.

Bradley, A. C.; quoted, 68, 150, 214; Hegel's opinions on tragedy, 99–100; *Shaksperean Tragedy*, 149.

Brandes, Georg, 244.

Brotherhood of the Passion, the, 292.

Browning, Robert, 222, 252, 268; *Ring and the Book*, the, 25; *Blot in the 'Scutcheon*, the, 206, 222, 252, 267, 268; *Strafford*, 252; *Pippa Passes*, 269.

Brunetière, Ferdinand, his "law of the drama," 93–108; *Annales du Théâtre*, 93; *Époques du Théâtre Français*, 93; quoted, 132, 250–251.

Burbage, Richard, 30, 49, 160.

Burke, Edmund, quoted, 1, 90.

Butcher, Professor, quoted, 101–102.

Butler, Nicholas Murray, *True and False Democracy*, 82.

Calderon, Pedro, 4, 48, 79, 90, 125, 232, 247; *Alcade of Zalamea*, 247.

Campbell, Thomas, quoted, 24.

Castelvetro, 94, 283–284, 285.

Celler, Ludovic, quoted, 64–65.

Champmeslé, Mlle. de, 34, 43, **160.**

Chance, 201 (See also Accident).

Chapman, George, 236, 256, 257.

Characters, 120, 163, 177, 178, 180, 191–192, 194, 200, 201, 203, 213, 228, 247; as found in farce, tragedy, etc., 121–122; speech of, 136–138, 139, 141, 143, 144; in Greek drama, 146, 159, 164, 165; and the soliloquy, 148, 149, 150–151; vitality of drama resides in, 153, 154, 160, 174; limited means of presenting, 154, 162; must speak for themselves, 155, 156, 158, 201; reality of some famous, 155–156; in French drama, 156, 157, 159, 182, 183, 184–185, 205, 255, 288; relations of, to plot, 156, 160, 161–162, 194, 224; in Turgenieff's novels, 157; in Shakspere, 158, 159, 165, 168–169, 202, 203, 204, 205, 244, 255; in English drama, 167, 226–227, 236; transformation in, 181, 204, 207, 287; artificial use of, 185, 218; in Plautus, 189; in *Secret Service*, 196; isolation of, 198, 199; arbitrary, 202–208, 221; truth necessary in drawing, 204, 219, 222–224; in modern drama, 265; in the poetic drama, 267; Professor Lounsbury on, 267–268.

Chaucer, 261.

Children of Paul's, the, 41.

Chorus, the, 5, 14–15, 17, 49, 50, **51, 57,** 146, 285.

Chronicle-play, the, 17, 97, 102, 111, 112, 113, 238; purpose and character of, 114–115; examples of, 115; of Shakspere, 122.

Cicero, quoted, 83.

Cinthio, Giraldi, 281, 285; *Discourse on Comedy and Tragedy*, 281.

Classification, need of, 110, 114; place and purpose of, 124; as devised by the French, 126.

Closet-drama, the, 26, 80, 111, 266; 276; general discussion, 250–261.

Coleridge, Samuel Taylor, 101, 111, 252; quoted, 99, 278–279; *Remorse*, 252.

Collier, Jeremy, quoted, 272.

Collins, Wilkie, 193.

Colosseum, the (See Arena).

Comédie-Française, the, 52, 81.

Comédie-larmoyante, the, 124.

Comedies, the, of Barrie and Shaw, 18; of Sheridan, 48, 127, 138; of Terence, 52, 72; of Molière, 7, 65, 69–70, 137; English, 41, 78; French, 75; of Plautus, 125; of Augier, 76; of Oscar Wilde, 127; of Shakspere, 119, 122, 124, 130; of Ben Jonson, 119, 289; of Congreve, 138; of Dumas *fils*, 128; of the Greeks and Romans, 144.

Comedy, 100, 103, 113, 115, 117, 118, 120–121, 123, 124, 151, 192, 196, 224; defined, 96; English, 7, 41, 83, 127, 226–227; French, 7, 124, 142; Italian, 142; Greek, 171–172; Latin, 171–172, 259, 283.

Comedy-of-Character, the, 197.

Comedy-of-cloak-and-sword, the, 124.

Comedy-of-humors, the, 111, 119, 125, 126.

Comedy-of-manners, the, 7, 118, 119–120, 121, 197, 221.

Comedy-of-masks, the (See Italian drama).

Communal element in drama, the, 13, 16, 79, 93, 103.

Confidant, the, 146.

Congreve, William, 48, 119, 128, 138, 227; *Way of the World*, the, 118, 127; *Love for Love*, 130.

Content of the drama, the, 217, 222.

Conventions, 199, 220, 284; in Shakspere, 288 (See also Traditions; also chap. vii).

Coquelin, 34, 36–37, 38, 40, 113, 160.

Corneille, 7, 17, 26, 59, 80, 96, 137, 138, 142, 143, 207, 232, 274, 276, 286, 288, 293; *Cid*, the, 91, 93, 94, 116, 136, 143, 293.

Costume-play, the, 261–262, 266.

"Creating a character," 37.

Criterion Theater, the, 77.

Cueva, Juan de la, 285.

Cuvier, Baron, 162.

Cyprus, 286.

D'Annunzio, Gabriele, 67.

D'Arc, Jeanne, 78.

D'Aubignac, Abbé, 94, 276, 285; quoted, 69; *Pratique du Théâtre*, 145; English translation of d'Aubignac, 228.

Dekker, Thomas, 235; *Old Fortunatus*, 235–236; *Shoemaker's Holiday*, the, 236.

Democracy of the drama, the, 24–27, 79–80, 81–82, 85, 89, 91, 282.

Detective-story, the, 112, 191, 224.

Devices, artificial, 185–186; of eavesdropping, 220; of Shakspere, 244; the mansions, a medieval device, 292.

Diagram of interest, the, 212–217, 219; Diagram A, 213; B, 214; C, 214; D, 215; E, 215, 218; F, 216, 218; G, 216, 218; H, 216, 218; I, J, 217, 218.

Dialogue, 92, 105, 114, 122, 127, 128, 129, 180, 236, 251; classification of, 126; condensation of, 135, 136, 139; of Ibsen, 137; of English and French dramatists, 137–138, 184; of Sanskrit drama, 141; as a means of exposition, 181; closet-drama a poem in, 250, 252, 259, 270; in the passion-play, 291.

Dickens, Charles, 126, 175, 193, 273; *Barnaby Rudge*, 193; *Nicholas Nickleby*, 273–274, 294.

Dick Turpin, 150.

Dionysus, theater of, 48, 49–51, 58, 65, 74.

Don Quixote, 155.

Drake, Sir Francis, 241.

Drama, the, origin of, quoted from

Letourneau, 9; from Hirn, 9–10; from Grosse, 10–11; from Jebb, 14; defined, 92–93; its kinship with the "show-business," 103; laws and development of, 125; in the 16th century, 236, 237.

Dramatic-romance, the, 117; of Shakspere, 123, 124, 278.

Drury Lane Theater, 40, 48, 61-62.

Dryden, John, 83, 130, 185; quoted, 68; *Spanish Friar*, the, 186.

Ducange, 18.

Dumas, Alexandre, the elder, 88, 176, 178, 182, 232; *Napoleon*, 115; *Mademoiselle de Belle Isle*, 183.

Dumas, Alexandre, *fils*, 19, 128, 183, 184, 196, 231, 232, 294; *Demi-Monde*, the, 128; *Camille*, 183; *Francillon*, 128, 274, 294; *Femme de Claude*, the, 183-184.

Duse, Eleanora, 35.

Eavesdropping, 220.

Echegaray, 67.

Eckermann, J. P., 80, 253.

Edison, Thomas, 64.

Egypt, the royal tombs of, 134.

Elizabeth, Queen, 41, 70, 233, 237, 238.

Elizabethan audiences (See Audiences).

Elizabethan drama, the, 30, 57, 58, 79, 111, 119, 125, 214, 265, 282 (See also chap. xi).

Elizabethan dramatists, the, 19, 41, 47, 48, 57, 64, 218, 256, 263, 264, 265, 286 (See also chap. xi).

Elizabethan literature, 102, 237.

Elizabethan theater, the, 5, 45, 48, 49, 55-57, 58, 60, 62, 65, 119, 138, 237-238, 239, 265.

Energy of the English race, the, 233, 234.

England, 7, 48, 79, 124, 232, 260, 285, 286, 289, 290, 291, 294

English drama, 258–259, 260, 264 (See also Elizabethan drama).

English, theater, the, 139, 265.

Essential principle of drama, the, 94, 251, 270–271.

Essential quality of drama, the, 21–22, 92–93, 259.

Essential struggle, an, 218.

Eton, 41, 42.

Euripides, 19, 78–79, 181, 232; *Alcestis*, 74, 116; *Medea*, 74, 79, 155, 181; *Iphigenia*, 74.

Europe, 72, 285.

"Exposition," defined, 180; discussed, 181-190; clearness in, necessary, 194–195, 213, 247; in *Othello*, 215.

Fantasy, in Shakspere, 225; in pantomimes and musical-shows, 226; of Musset, 258, 262; in *Peter Pan*, 270.

Farce, 100, 113, 117, 118, 120, 121, 124, 191, 221, 224, 262, 291; defined, 96; in Molière's work, 122; in Shakspere, 122, 123, 124, 161, 188.

Faust, 193.

Fechter, Charles, 168, 216.

Ferrier, M. Paul, *Ilote*, 52.

Fielding, Henry, 191; *Tom Jones*, 191, 193.

Fitch, Clyde, 48, 67; *Barbara Frietchie*, 77–78; *Climbers*, the, 117.

Flaubert, Gustave, 230.

Fletcher, John, 117, 206, 219; *Faithful Shepherdess*, the, 116.

"Focus," the, 61, 139.

Folk-drama, literary drama developed from, 92, 286, 291; despised by Italian critics, 282, 283.

Form of the drama, the, 217, 222.

France, 7, 17, 49, 51, 71, 72, 76, 77, 79, 91, 124, 143, 232, 258, 285, 286, 290, 291, 292, 294.

Francesca da Rimini, 193.

Frederick the Great, 96.

Free will, belief in, favorable to drama, 96; championed by Aristotle, 101; importance to drama explained by Brunetière, 102 (See also Human will).

French Academy, the, 91, 274.

French, characteristics of the, 290–291.

French drama, the, 79-80, 102, 124, 145, 146, 232, 258, 259, 275, 286, 288, 290-294.

French government, the, 84.

French literature, 258.

French painter, the, quoted, 222.

French theater, the, 143; tennis-court of Molière, the, 45, 48, 59–60, 65, 69; Italianate theaters at Paris, 61.

Freytag, Gustave, artificial pyramid of, 213; *Technic of the Drama*, the, 213.

Frobisher, Sir Martin, 241.

Frou-frou (Meilhac and Halévy), 120.

"Function of the crowd," the drama as a, 79, 81, 82, 85.

Garrick, David, 34, 167.

Gautier, Théophile, 85, 234.

German drama, the, 7, 80, 144.

Germany, 7, 80; court-theaters in, 81; subsidized opera-houses in, 81.

Giacommetti, *Marie Antoinette*, 115.

Gillette, William, 196; *Secret Service*, 196.

Globe Theater, the, 58, 143, 153, 238, 242, 256.

Goethe, 80–81, 96, 194; quoted, 186–187, 253; *Faust*, 25, 74; *Wilhelm Meister*, quoted from, 99; *Götz*, 253.

Goldsmith, Oliver, 113; *She Stoops to Conquer*, 113, 120.

Gozzi, Carlo, on the number of situations in drama, 193–194.

Great Britain, 76, 110, 258.

Greece, 79, 110, 142, 232.

Greek actors, 50–51.

Greek drama, the, 57–58, 74, 79, 89, 91, 118, 141, 142, 144, 163–164, 171–172, 232, 237, 265, 279; evolution of, 4–5, 14–15, 17, 145, 285; analyzed by Aristotle, 276–277, 280, 282; the unities in, 277, 279–281, 284–285, 288; the trilogy in, 288 (See also Greek tragedy).

Greek dramatists, the, 73–74, 101, 164–165, 280, 281, 284, 288.

Greeks, the, 277; their good sense in art, 193, 283; their artistic perception, 214; their tragedy cannot be imitated, 254; Sidney's belief regarding, 257.

Greek theater, the, 5, 45, 48, 49–51, 53, 57, 58, 65, 74, 138, 152, 279, 285.

Greek tragedy, 57, 89, 96, 110, 163–165, 213–214, 259, 277; attempted resuscitation of, 253, 254.

Greene, Robert, 119, 246, 247.

Grimstadt, 70.

Groos, Professor, quoted, 103.

Grosse, Professor, quoted, 10–11.

Gummere, F. B., quoted, 14; his treatment of the popular ballad, 110.

Gyp, social satires of, 92.

Haigh, A. E., quoted, 44; *Tragic Drama of the Greeks*, the, 57.

Hamilton, Clayton, quoted, 88.

Hamilton, Sir William, quoted, 109.

Hardy, Alexandre, 17, 293.

Harrigan, Edward, 125.

Harte, Bret, 228.

Hauptmann, Gerhart, 144, 216; *Weavers*, the, 216; *Sunken Bell*, the, 269.

Hawthorne, Nathaniel, *Scarlet Letter*, the, 200, 231, 278.

Hazlitt, William, 187, 246; quoted, 152.

Hegel, 99, 101, 102; quoted on tragedy, 99–100.

Henry IV of France, 96.

Henry VIII of England, 238.

Herkomer, Sir Henry, quoted, 63.

Heroic-comedy, the, 37, 113.

Heroic-play, the, 111, 124.

Heroines of Shakspere, the, 30–31, 158.

Hervieu, Paul, 18.

Heywood, Thomas, 19; *A Woman Killed with Kindness*, 19.

Hibben, John Grier, quoted, 86.

High-comedy, the, 118–119, 120, 121, 223.

Hirn, quoted, 9–10.

History, a type of Shaksperian play, the (See Chronicle-play).

Histrionic temperament, the, 34, 39.

Hogarth, William, 228.

Homer, the poems of, 74; *Iliad*, the, 156.

Hopkins, Miss Priscilla, 41.

Hotel de Bourgogne, 292.

Howard, Bronson, 128; *Banker's Daughter*, the, 76–77.

Hugo, Victor, 146, 199, 207, 215, 232, 234, 257–258, 259, 270, 274, 294; *Cromwell*, 8, 199, 274; *Ruy Blas*, 18, 207, 215–216; preface from, quoted, 88; *Hernani*, 146, 150, 215–216, 258, 294; *Misérables*, the, 150.

Human nature in the drama, 194, 269.

Human will, mainspring of drama, 94, 95, 98, 100–101, 102, 104, 106, 218; Machiavelli's emphasis on, 103; should be spontaneous, 201.

Huxley, Thomas Henry, 255.

Ibsen, 7, 8, 18, 45, 48, 58, 64, 67, 70, 71, 125, 137, 144, 181, 196, 205, 207, 208, 214, 246, 247, 257, 260, 264, 274, 294; *Ghosts*, 7, 116, 181, 214, 247, 274, 294; *Doll's House*, the, 107, 207; *Rosmersholm*, 181; *Hedda Gabler*, 205; *Pillars of Society*, 208; *Love's Comedy*, 264; *When We Dead Awaken*, 264.

Imagination, 110, 191; distinguished from fancy, 111; necessary to character-drawing, 153, 169; in Shakspere, 166; not possessed by the mere playwright, 170; in the Elizabethan poets, 234.

Inevitable, in drama, the, 200.

International formula, an, 67.

Invention, 191; necessary to plot-making, 153; to the mere playwright, 170.

Irving, Sir Henry, 39–40, 138, 168.

Isocrates, 70.

Italian drama, 7; popular, despised by Italian critics, 282–283; comedy-of-masks, the, 47, 59, 117, 142, 172–174, 259, 282, 283.

Italian Renascence, the, art of, 28; scholars of, 72; critics and criticism of, 94, 257, 275, 281, 282–283, 285, 289.

Italy, 142, 260, 282.

James I of England, 233.

James, Henry, 223; quoted, 176.

James, William, quoted, 11.

Jameson, Mrs. Anna, 162; *Girlhood of Shakspere's Heroines*, the, 158.

Japanese theater, the, 140–141.

Jebb, Sir Richard, 23; quoted, 14.

Jefferson, Joseph, quoted, 21.

Jena, 80.

Jenkin, Fleeming, 23.

Jerusalem, the Temple at, 292.

Jewish theater, the, 141.

Johnson, Samuel, 252; quoted, 68, 273, 286; *Irene*, 252.

Jones, Henry Arthur, 67; *Evangelist*, the, 117; *Liars*, the, 118; *Middleman*, the, 144; *Literature and the Modern Drama*, quoted, 261.

Jonson, Ben, 48, 119, 125, 232, 274, 275, 285, 286, 288, 289; *Every Man in his Humor*, 29, 289.

Jordan, Mrs., 167.

Joseph and Potiphar's wife, 72.

Jusserand, Jules, 70, 239; quoted, 240.

Kean, Edmund, 168.

Kemble, John Philip, 32, 41.

King of Rome, the, 38.

Knowles, J. Sheridan, 263; *Virginius*, 261, 264; *Hunchback*, the, 263.

Kotzebue, 44, 170, 260.

Kyd, 165; *Spanish Tragedy*, the, 18.

Labiche, Eugène, 94.

La Harpe, Jean de, 94.

Lamb, Charles, 19, 32, 33, 41, 226–227, 232, 245; quoted, 159, 227; *Mr. H.*, 191; *Specimens*, 245.

Latin comedy, 171–172, 259, 283.

Latin drama, the, 141, 142 (See also Rome, drama of).

Latin dramatists, the, 53.

Latin tragedy, 283.

Lazarillo de Tormes, 113.

Le Bon, Gustave, 86; quoted, 87.

Legouvé, 39, 42; *Memories of Sixty Years*, 38; *Adrienne Lecouvreur*, 38; *Louise de Lignerolles*, 39; *Ladies' Battle*, the, 247.

Lemercier, Népomucène, 94.

Le Sage, *Gil Blas*, 95, 113.

Lessing, 7, 20, 96, 97, 257, 274, 276.

Letourneau, quoted, 9, 89.

Lewes, George Henry, 168.

Line of interest, the, 212, 213 (See also Diagram of interest).

Literary drama, the, developed from the unliterary, 8, 17–18; essential qualities of, 20–23; defined, 92–93; developed from folk-drama, 92, 283, 286, 291.

Literature and drama, 1–3, 20–23; divorced in Elizabeth's time, 237; in the 19th century, 249; closet-drama follows divorce between, 259–260.

London, 72, 76, 77, 91, 186, 236, 238, 289.

London Assurance, 129.

Louis XIV, 45, 69, 139, 144.

Lounsbury, T. R., 267, 290; quoted, 267–268.

Lowell, James Russell, 246; quoted, 251.

Lyly, John, 41.

Lyrical-burlesque, the, of Aristophanes, 117; of the Greeks, 125.

Lytton, Bulwer, 39; *Lady of Lyons*, the, 39; *Richelieu*, 39, 261, 264.

Macaulay, Lord, 227.

Machiavelli, 102–103.

Mackaye, Percy, *Jeanne d'Arc*, 115.

Macready, 39, 252.

Madrid, 73.

Maeterlinck, Maurice, 262; *Intruder*, the, 262, 264; *Pelléas and Mélisande*, 262.

Mahaffy, John P., 78.

"Mansions," 47, 54, 143, 292, 293.

Manzoni, Alessandro, 253.

Marivaux, Pierre de, 294.

Marlowe, Christopher, 17, 32, 48, 79, 232; *Jew of Malta*, the, 32; *Tamburlaine*, 32; *Doctor Faustus*, 247.

Mars, Mlle., 39.

Massinger, Philip, 246, 247, 263; *Roman Actor*, the, 247; *New Way to pay Old Debts*, a, 263.

Medieval drama, the, 15–16, 53–55, 72, 141, 144, 238, 283, 291–292.

Medieval theater, the, 46, 47, 48, 53–57, 142, 143.

Melodrama, 18, 104, 120, 121, 124, 224, 262; in Shakspere, 122; *Hamlet*

developed from, 165–166; *Hamlet* treated by Fechter as, 168; in Chapman's plays, 257; Hugo's plays modelled upon, 257–258, 270.

Menander, 6, 21, 118, 232.

Mermaid, the, 289.

Mimicry in children, 11.

Minturno, 285.

Miracle-play, the, 47, ?38, 259, 282.

Modern drama, the, 67, 114, 141; compared with earlier drama, 125, 265; disappearance of soliloquy from, 144; line of interest in, 213; no excuse for closet-drama in, 260; prose and poetry in, 249–250; chief characteristics of, 265; the Unity of Action in, 277.

Modern dramatists, the, 48, 60, 63, 67, 75, 106, 144, 209, 271; their violation of "rules of the drama," 94; who have handled the comedy-of-manners, 118; their avoidance of the romantic-comedy, 119; discard the soliloquy, 145, 148, 151; their attitude toward the unities, 294; compared with Elizabethan, 246, 265.

Modern theater, the, 48, 63, 67, 70, 119, 138, 139–140, 142, 151, 238, 249, 265, 267.

Molière, 4, 6, 7, 25, 26, 33, 34, 45, 48, 59–60, 65, 66, 69, 71, 80, 83, 90, 96, 122, 125, 130, 131, 137, 140, 141, 142, 148, 149, 155, 156, 157, 159, 161, 163, 166, 186, 187, 195, 196, 230, 232, 247, 255, 271, 283, 293, 294; *Précieuses Ridicules*, the, 4; *Amour Médecin*, the, 4; *Bourgeois Gentilhomme*, the, 33, 163; *Tartuffe*, 33, 82, 107, 112, 121, 147–148, 155, 156, 157, 186, 196, 200, 247, 278; *Misanthrope*, the, 33, 112, 139, 156, 157; *School for Husbands*, the, 60; *School for Wives*, the, 94; *Femmes Savantes*, the, 118; *Scapin*, 126; *Don Juan*, 136, 161, 166, 293; *Miser*, the, 150.

Molière, Mlle. de, 160.

Morality, in the drama, 225–231; in prose-fiction, ?25, 227, 228, 230–231.

Morality-play, the, 17, 30, 111, 119.

Mot, the, 126; *mot d'esprit*, the, 126,

127, 128, 129, 130, 131; *mot de situation*, the, 126, 130, 131; *mot de caractère*, the, 126, 129, 131.

Murray, Gilbert, quoted, 229.

Musical-comedy, the, 124, 125 (See also Musical-shows).

Musical-shows, American, 226.

Musset, Alfred de, 199, 258, 262; Brunetière's lecture on, 93; *On ne badine pas avec l'amour*, 262, 264.

Mystery-play, the, 15–60, 17, 30, 53–55, 72, 97, 111, 114, 143, 238, 282, 292.

Nero, 259, 260.

Netherlands, the, 204.

New York, 72, 76, 77, 88, 125, 141.

Nisard, quoted, 71.

Norway, 71.

Novel, the, and the play, 84, 92, 94, 95, 97, 99, 154, 158, 175, 178, 179–180, 190–191, 197–198, 199, 200–201, 223, 230, 260; and the short-story, 111 ; with-a-purpose, 112; dialogue in, 136; haphazard character of the English, 175; in the 19th century, 236.

Odéon Theater, 93.

Oliphant, Mrs. Margaret, 191–192; *Sheridan*, 191; quoted, from, 192.

O'Neill, Miss, 252.

Opera, the convention of, 134; Tolstoy's attack on, 134; death tolerated in, 195.

Opéra-bouffe, the, 124.

Opéra-comique, the, 124.

Orange, the Roman theater at, 49, 51–53.

Orchestra, the Greek, 49–50, 146, 279, 285; the Roman, 51.

Orestes, 194.

Orientals, have no vital drama, the, 96.

Oriental-tale, the, 112.

Origin of the drama (See Drama).

"Pageants," 54.

Palladio, Andrea, 60.

Pantomime, defined, 2–3; skeleton of a good play always a, 20; the convention of, 134; British pantomimes, 226.

Paris, 38, 70, 72, 76, 77, 88, 91, 142, 186, 292.

Parts, characters composed as, 160, 166–167; in the *School for Scandal*, 167 (See also " Star-parts").

Pascal, Blaise, dictum of, 114.

Passion-play, the, 15, 53–55, 141, 143, 291, 292.

Pastiches, 253.

Pastoral-romance, the, 112.

Perry, Bliss, quoted, 211.

Phillips, Stephen, 265–266; *Ulysses*, 115.

Picaresque-romance, the, 112, 113.

Picture-frame stage, the, 48, 63–65, 151.

Pinero, Sir Arthur, 67, 208, 247; his definition of comedy, 120; *His House in Order*, 208; *Second Mrs. Tanqueray*, the, 247.

Pixérécourt, 18.

Plagiarist, the schoolboy's definition of a, 194.

Planché, James Robinson, quoted, 190.

Plautus, 41, 53, 73, 125, 144, 171, 181, 189; *Amphitryon*, 116; *Captives*, the, 142, 181, 189.

"Play," a, modern definition of tragi-comedy, 117.

Plot, 88, 101, 121, 127, 148, 153, 163, 170, 171, 178, 181, 194, 196, 197, 201, 205, 208, 219; in Shakspere, 147, 165, 187–188, 195, 203, 204, 206, 239, 244, 278; repeated use of old plots, 153, 154, 164, 165, 193–194, 208–209; relation of character and, 156, 160, 161–162, 203; in Molière, 163, 195; in the comedy-of-masks, 174; of the *Weavers*, 216; in Elizabethan drama, 238; in Chapman's plays, 257; Professor Lounsbury on, 267–268; in Greek drama, 280.

Plutarch, 21.

Poe, Edgar Allan, 193.

Poetic-justice, 228.

Poetry, primitive, 14; not a matter of verse, 260–264, 267.

Pompeian pictures, 134.

Portuguese drama, the, 141.

Preparation, the dramatist's art, 183.

Prisoner of Zenda, the, 117, 209.

Probable, necessary in drama, the, 200, 247.

Problem-play, the, 111; of Ibsen, 125.

Prodigal Son, the, 3.

Prologue, the, 181; in *Fédora*, 184; in the *Captives*, 190.

Prose-Fiction (See the Novel).

Psychology of the crowd, the, 86–88.

Punch and Judy, 226.

" Quarrel of the Cid," the, 274.

Rachel, 38.

Racine, 21, 34, 43, 74, 80, 137, 232, 247, 288, 293, 294; *Phèdre*, 146, 247.

Red Bull Theater, the, 256.

Regnier, 39.

Rehearsal, the, 130.

Rembrandt, 267.

Restoration, the, comedy of, 7, 226; theater of, 46, 48–49, 61–62, 63, 65, 238.

Reynolds, Sir Joshua, quoted, 1.

Richelieu, Cardinal, 91, 96, 274; theater of, 60.

Rip Van Winkle, 150.

Robortello, 94, 281; quoted, 281.

Roman sculptures, 135.

Roman theater, the, 49, 51–53.

Romance, 110, 111.

Romance-of-chivalry, the, 112.

Romantic-comedies, of Shakspere, the, 119, 123, 124, 278.

Rome, drama of, 89, 91, 129, 144, 259, 260 (See also Latin drama).

Roscius, 34.

Rostand, Edmund, 37, 58, 67, 113, 258, 259; *Cyrano de Bergerac*, 35, 37, 113; *Aiglon*, the, 38.

Rowe, Nicholas, 62.

" Rules of the drama," 73, 91; declared invalid by Brunetière, 93; compared with " law of the drama," 96–97 (See also chap. xiii).

Ruskin, John, 235.

Saint-Gaudens, Augustus, quoted, 175.

Salamis, 96.

Salvini, Tommaso, 168.

Sand, George, quoted, 230.

Sandeau, Jules, 119; *Gendre de M. Poirier*, the, 75–76, 104, 118.

Sanskrit drama, the, 141.

Sarcey, Francisque, 20, 105, 106, 107, 209, 276; his principle of the *scènes à faire*, 105–108, 219; quoted, 231.

Sardou, Victorien, 35, 184, 185, 186, 204; *Fédora*, 35, 184; *Oncle Sam*, 84; *Nos Intimes*, 184; *Famille Benoiton*, the, 184; *Théodora*, 184; *Gismonda*, 184; *Patrie*, 204–205.

Satires of Sheridan and Beaumarchais, 117.

Scaliger, 274, 283, 285.

Scenery, 5, 45, 46, 47, 49, 50, 51, 55, 56, 57, 58, 59, 60, 62, 63, 65, 66, 138, 139, 142, 238, 265, 285, 293.

Scènes à faire, the, 105–108, 219.

Schelling, Felix E., 114.

Schiller, 80, 96, 194, 207; *Robbers*, the, 207.

Schlegel, quoted, 99.

Scott, Sir Walter, 175; *Woodstock*, 175–176; *Heart of Midlothian*, the, 200 ; *Waverley Novels*, the, 260.

Scribe, Eugène, 19, 20, 21, 40, 42, 44, 76, 170, 182, 184, 186, 246, 247, 260, Brunetière's lecture on, 93 ; *Adrienne Lecouvreur*, 182; *Ladies' Battle*, the, 247.

Sea-tale, the, 112.

Semi-medieval drama, 238, 239, 295; the theater, 48, 119, 244, 256, 257, 265 ; playwrights, 240, 246; audiences, 242 (See also Elizabethan drama).

Seneca, 102, 259.

Sense-of-humor, the, 110; of Sheridan, 128.

Sentimental-comedy, the, 111, 124.

Serious drama, the, defined, 95; tragedy, as a type of, 117, 118, 121; as distinguished from melodrama, 124, 224; truth necessary in, 223; of the French, 294.

Sévigné, Mme. de, 43.

Shakspere, 4, 5, 8, 19, 26, 29, 30–33, 34,

44, 46, 48, 49, 57, 58, 60, 62, 65, 66, 69, 70, 73, 74, 78, 79, 90, 91, 96, 112, 113, 114, 115, 119, 122, 123, 124, 130, 131, 137, 138, 140, 141, 142, 143, 147, 148, 149, 157, 158, 159, 165, 166, 168, 169, 173, 181, 186, 187, 188, 189, 195, 201, 202, 204, 206, 213, 230, 232, 233, 237, 238–239, 242, 243–244, 247, 248, 255, 257, 258, 260, 263, 264, 266, 268, 269, 271, 274, 275, 278, 281, 287, 288, 289, 290; *Hamlet*, 18, 20, 29, 30, 32, 82, 104–105, 112, 124, 136, 139, 152, 155, 159, 165–166, 168, 169, 205, 215, 225, 270, 278, 288; *As You Like It*, 29, 30, 31, 105, 128, 140, 157, 168–169, 194, 203, 204, 263, 270; *Measure for Measure*, 30, 123, 195, 264; *All 's Well that Ends Well*, 30, 123, 264; *Twelfth Night*, 30, 266; *Merchant of Venice*, the, 30, 119, 138, 153, 244, 268, 278; *Much Ado about Nothing*, 30, 119, 203, 204, 244, 278; *Titus Andronicus*, 31, 122; *Romeo and Juliet*, 73, 136, 150, 173, 174, 187, 201, 244, 266, 278; *Macbeth*, 107, 113, 122, 159, 188, 200, 225, 239, 263, 278, 288; *Othello*, 107, 121, 122, 147, 155, 157, 159, 167–168, 169, 181, 187, 188, 191, 193, 205–206, 215, 231, 239, 243, 244, 247, 278, 281, 286; *Winter's Tale*, the, 117, 123, 153, 154, 188, 204, 278; *Comedy of Errors*, the, 122, 126, 187, 188–189, 209; *Merry Wives of Windsor*, the, 122, 161; *Taming of the Shrew*, the, 122; *Troilus and Cressida*, 122, 124; *Cymbeline*, 122, 188, 243, 244 ; *Tempest*, the, 123, 159, 289, 290; *Midsummer Night's Dream*, 123, 224–225; *Falstaff*, 131; *Henry V*, 136; *Julius Cæsar*, 136, 137, 263, 287; *Richard III*, 143; *Henry IV*, 161; *Two Gentlemen of Verona*, 204; *King Lear*, 244.

Shaw, G. B., 18.

Shelley, Percy Bysshe, 252; *Cenci*, the, 252; quoted, 229.

Sheridan, R. B., 7, 8, 40–41, 48, 61–62, 65, 66, 117, 119, 127, 128, 130, 138, 167, 186; *School for Scandal*, the, 40–41, 61–62, 107, 118, 121, 127, 131, 155, 167, 191–192, 193; *Rivals*, the, 128; *Critic*, the, 128, 130, 146, 186.

Short-story, the, 109, 112; a type by itself, 111.

Sidney, Sir Philip, 46, 116, 257, 274, 282, 285; *Defense of Poesy*, the, 91, 274, 289.

Situations in the drama, number of, 193–194.

Smith, 41.

Social-drama, the, 104; of Ibsen, 7, 18, 71, 137, 196, 207; of Hauptmann, 216.

Soliloquy, the, 64, 143–151, 181, 186, 187.

Sophocles, 7, 8, 15, 19, 26, 29, 33, 34, 44, 48, 57, 58, 65, 69, 70, 79, 90, 101, 146, 159, 160, 165, 208, 209, 214, 232, 247, 257; *Œdipus the King*, 7, 52, 101, 121, 155, 160, 161, 165, 200, 208–209, 214, 231, 247, 278; *Antigone*, 74, 160, 161.

Spain, 7, 48, 79, 204, 232, 245, 285, 286, 290, 294.

Spanish drama, the, 79, 96, 124, 125, 138, 232, 245, 286.

Spanish theater, the, 48.

Sparta, 79.

Spectators, the (See Audiences).

Spencer, Herbert, Economy of Attention, 178, 223.

Spingarn, 281, 283.

Standardizing of the playhouse, 66.

" Star-parts," examples of, in plays, 29–30, 32–43 (See also Parts).

" Stations," 54, 143, 291, 292.

Stendhal, quoted, 253.

Stephen, Sir Leslie, quoted, 256.

Stevenson, R. L., 23; quoted, 92, 99, 106, 229; his methods of story-writing, 163.

Stock-figures, of the theater, 171; of Latin comedy, 171-172; of Greek comedy, 171–172; of the comedy-of-masks, 172–174.

Stoker, Bram, 39.

Subject of a drama, the, importance of to success, 176; Aristotle's dictum on, 176; in the poetic drama, 267.

Sudermann, Hermann, 247; *Heimat* (Magda), 75, 247; *Honor*, 144.

Supernatural, the, in Shakspere's

plays, 75, 159, 224-225; audiences will accept, 224.

Swinburne, Algernon, 235, 245, 257, 258; *Atalanta in Calydon*, 253, 254; *Marino Faliero*, 256.

Taine, H., 25; quoted, 232.

Technic, significance of, 5-6; compared with that of the novel, 175-176; Goethe, on Molière's, 187; necessary to the dramatist, 217-218; not mastered by Tennyson, 252; studied by real dramatic poets, 260.

Tennis-court theater, the (See French theater).

Tennyson, Lord Alfred, 40, 46, 252; *Becket*, 39-40, 115, 252; *Queen Mary*, 115.

Terence, 52, 72, 73, 150, 171.

Thackeray, W. M., 154, 155, 191, 228, 230; *Vanity Fair*, 155, 228, 278; *Henry Esmond*, 191, 193.

Thebes, 79.

Theobald, Lewis, 62.

Theocritus, idyls of, 92.

Thespis, 17.

Thomas, Augustus, 67.

Thorndike, Ashley H., 117; *Tragedy*, 110; quoted, 249.

Tokio, 140.

Tolstoy, 134; *Anna Karénina*, 200, 231, 278.

Traditions, 47, 54, 55, 220, 265; in Greek tragedy, 164-165, 193; in Shakspere, 288 (See also Conventions; also chap. vii).

Tragédie-bourgeoise, the, 124.

Tragedies, Greek, 5, 51, 52, 74, 118, 144; of Corneille, 7, 137; of Sophocles, 65, 165; of Seneca, 102; of Shakspere, 113, 122, 124, 130, 137; of Racine, 137; of Æschylus, 165; of the Romans, 144.

Tragedy, 97, 104, 111, 115, 116, 117, 120, 121, 201, 207, 221, 222, 282, 283; defined, 95; Schlegel, Coleridge, and Hegel on, 99-100; Aristotle on, 101; Butcher on, 102; development of English, 102; Roman, 129; classicist French, 146; *Secret Service* as, 196;

in Ibsen, 207; Bradley on, 214; the unities in, 275 (See also Greek tragedy).

Tragedy-of-blood, the, 18, 32, 102, 111, 112, 115, 122, 123, 124, 241; *Hamlet* developed from, 165-166.

Tragi-comedy, 111, 124; discussed, 115-117.

Trilogy, the (See Greek drama).

Trissino, 281.

Troy, fall of, 186, 280.

Tudors, drama under the, 46, 55.

Turgenieff, Ivan, his method of writing a novel, 157; *Smoke*, 200, 278.

Twain, Mark, *Huckleberry Finn*, 113-114.

Udall, Nicholas, 42; *Ralph Roister Doister*, 41-42.

United States, 76, 258.

Unity, in dramatic development, 46-47; necessity of, 198; of impression, in the *Weavers*, 216; of theme, necessary, 247; in Shakspere's tragedies, 278.

Unity of Action, the, 275, 277, 279, 283, 284, 288, 290, 294.

Unity of Place, the, 59, 275, 283, 284, 289, 290, 291, 293, 294.

Unity of Time, the, 275, 279, 281, 283, 284, 287, 288, 290, 294.

Unliterary drama, basis of the literary, the, 8, 16, 17-19, 291.

Valenciennes, mystery-play at, 54.

Vega, Lope de, 4, 48, 66, 72, 73, 79, 232, 274, 285, 286, 287, 290; *New Art of Making Plays*, the, 73, 147, 287.

Verga, Giovanni, 67; *Cavalleria Rusticana*, 35.

Vergil, *Æneid*, the, 156.

Versailles, 139.

Vicenza, theater at, 60.

Visualizing a play, 22-23, 211, 212.

Voltaire, 60, 99, 176, 286, 294; *Sémiramis*, 61.

Wagner, Richard, 3; music-dramas, 51; *Tristan und Isolde*, 134.

Waterbury, Conn., 139.

Weber and Fields, Messrs., 125.
Webster, John, 236.
Weimar, court-theater at, 80.
West Point, N. Y., 138.
When Knighthood was in Flower, 117.
Whistler, James McNeill, quoted, 267.

Wilde, Oscar, 127; *Lady Windermere's Fan*, 118, 126, 127, 130.
Will (See Human will).
Wordsworth, William, quoted, 85.
Wycherley, William, 227.

Zola, Émile, *Germinal*, 84.